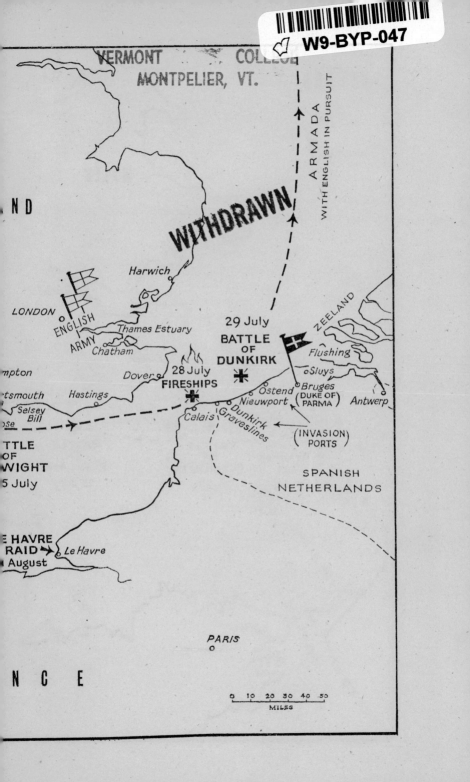

ARMADA
WITH ENGLISH IN PURSUIT

WITHDRAWN

ND

Harwich

LONDON
ENGLISH
ARMY
Thames Estuary
Chatham

ZEELAND

29 July
BATTLE
OF
DUNKIRK

Flushing

Sluys

mpton

Dover
28 July
FIRESHIPS

Ostend
Nieuwport

Bruges
(DUKE OF
PARMA)

Antwerp

rtsmouth
Hastings

Selsey
Bill
ose

Calais
Dunkirk
Graveslines

(INVASION)
PORTS

TTLE
OF
WIGHT
5 July

SPANISH
NETHERLANDS

E HAVRE
RAID
August

Le Havre

PARIS
o

N C E

0 10 20 30 40 50
MILES

From Merciless Invaders

Alexander McKee

FROM MERCILESS INVADERS

An Eye-witness
Account of the
Spanish Armada

SOUVENIR PRESS

London

First published 1963 by Souvenir Press
Ltd., 34 Bloomsbury St., London, W.C.1,
and simultaneously in Canada by the
Ryerson Press, Toronto, 2, Canada

*Set in 10 pt. Baskerville 2 pt. leaded, and printed
in Great Britain at The Central Press, Aberdeen*

Contents

CONTENTS

Illustrations

1*

ILLUSTRATIONS

*Acknowledgment is made to the National Maritime
Museum for permission to reproduce the painting
" The Battle of Gravelines " by P. J. de
Lotherbourg on the jacket*

Foreword

There cannot be fewer than 150 ships of all Sorts; and several of them
called Galleons and Galleasses, are of a size never seene before in our
seas, and appear on the surface of the water like floating Castles. But
at Sun-set we had the Pleasure of seeing this invincible Armada fill all
their sails to get away from us.

Report in the *English Mercurie*, 23 July, 1588

THE LONDON journalist who thus wrote up the story of the first
sighting of the Armada was working for a newspaper "published
by Authoritie for the prevention of false reportes"; but the slight
sensationalism with which his tale was tinged started many hares
in the pages of later writers. The first historian to approach the
subject, Petruccio Ubaldino, had the inestimable advantage of
being able to interview some of the chief witnesses on both sides,
including Lord Howard, Drake, and Don Pedro de Valdes; but
the necessity for tact, and possibly security considerations also,
prevented his work from being as informative as it might have
been. It was not until the 1890s that the existing mass of
documentary evidence, both English and Spanish, was collected,
edited, and published; affording a field day to naval historians
whose interests were largely technical and critical.

When I came to study the documents, in 1954, as the basis
of a feature programme for the B.B.C., what impressed above all
was the quality of the eye-witness narratives. Never, in the long
history of England's wars, can a set of combat reports have been
written to equal these. The red-hot phrases shower from the battle
like sparks from a grinder. One ceases to marvel so much at
Shakespeare.

Therefore, I have chosen to present this story of the Armada
Campaign strictly as a narrative of adventure told by more than
a hundred eye-witnesses, drawn impartially from both sides. In
them, the atmosphere of the age is almost perfectly preserved; and
such errors, exaggerations, or evasions as there may be, are
genuinely Elizabethan.

But as essays in interpretation cannot quite be avoided, I
would claim for the method of close reconstruction from contemporary narratives, that it forces the author to consult at every

9

step the statements of participants; hinders the too easy formulation of delusive theories; and arms the reader against any errors into which the author, nevertheless, may fall.

Some areas of dispute will most probably always remain. Although arguments on technicalities, such as that concerning Armada guns, might even now be resolved by undersea exploration, a field of research much neglected by students of maritime affairs, only Sir Francis Drake in person could settle authoritatively those discussions which concern tactics; Ubaldino had the chance, but neglected to take it, losing us the opportunity forever. I must, however, acknowledge my personal debt to him; for when I came a few years ago to write the history of that campaign, the Battle of Britain, which is a real parallel to the story of the Armada, I took a leaf out of his book, disdained the documents, and sought out the witnesses instead.

ALEXANDER McKEE

Hayling Island, Hampshire.
March, 1963.

The Witnesses

THE STORY is told in extracts from the orders, reports, letters, diaries, pleas, narratives, interrogations, and reported speech of the following:—

IN THE ENGLISH AND DUTCH FLEETS

Lord Charles Howard, Lord Admiral of England:
H.M.S. *Ark Royal*

Sir Francis Drake, Vice-Admiral of England: H.M.S. *Revenge*
Sir John Hawkyns, Admiral under Howard: H.M.S. *Victory*
Sir Martin Frobisher, Admiral under Howard: H.M.S. *Triumph*
Lord Henry Seymour, Admiral in the Narrow Seas:
H.M.S. *Rainbow*

Sir William Wynter, Admiral under Seymour: H.M.S. *Vanguard*
Thomas Fenner, Captain: H.M.S. *Nonpareil*
Henry Whyte, Captain: of fire-ship: Bark *Talbot*
             Transferred as Volunteer: H.M.S. *Mary Rose*
William Monson, Lieutenant of pinnace: H.M.S. *Charles*
Richard Thomson, Lieutenant of London ship:
Margaret and John

Thomas Cely (late of *Estrella* galley), Captain of pinnace:
Elizabeth Drake

Mathew Starke, Officer: H.M.S. *Revenge*
Nic Oseley, Merchant, Spy, Intelligence Officer: H.M.S. *Revenge*
Edward Wynter, Officer
Sir Horatio Palavicino, Genoese Banker, Volunteer with the
    English Fleet
William Borlas, Liaison Officer, with Fleet of Sir P. van der Does
Giles Napper, Mariner; escaped slave from Turkish & Spanish
    galleys
Patrick Catnihavil (?), Catholic Irish Student; served unwillingly
    & by accident: H.M.S. *Ark Royal*
Simons of Exeter; Master of a Bark of Mousehole; Fisherman of
    a Bark of 'Hampton, etc., etc.

IN ENGLAND

The Council   London
Sir Francis Walsyngham, Principal Secretary of State: London

11

Lord Burghley, Lord High Treasurer of England: London
Sir Thomas Heneage, Vice-Chamberlain of the Household:
                                                   London
Earl of Leicester, Army Commander: near London
Marmaduke Darell, Victualling Agent for the Navy
Sir Francis Godolphin, M.P. for: Cornwall
John Popham, Attorney-General & Spymaster: Wellington
Sir Walter Raleigh, Governor: Plymouth
William Hawkyns, Mayor of: Plymouth
Richard Pitt, Mayor of: Weymouth
John Jones, Mayor of: Lymne Regis
John Gilberte ⎫ Deputy   *Rosario*, Torbay & Dartmouth
              ⎬ Lieutenants
George Cary   ⎭ of Devon: *San Pedro el Mayor*, near Salcombe
Sir Anthony Ashley, Official, Devon: *San Pedro el Mayor*,
                                                   Salcombe

George Trenchard ⎫ Justices of the
                 ⎬   *San Salvador*, Weymouth
Francis Hawley   ⎭ Peace for Dorset
John Thoms, Dockyard Clerk: *San Salvador*, Portsmouth
Earl of Sussex, Garrison Commander: Portsmouth
Sir George Carey, Garrison Commander: Isle of Wight
Rychard Barrey, Governor: Dover Castle
Petruccio Ubaldino, Florentine Historian
Dorothy Cely, Wife of Captain Thomas Cely

IN IRELAND

Sir Wylliam Fytzwylliam, Lord Deputy of Ireland: Dublin
Sir Richard Bingham, Governor of Connaught: Athlone
Sir John Popham, English Official:
Mr. Secretary Fenton, English Official
Lady Denny, Wife of Governor of: Tralee
James Trant, Official: Dingle
Auncyent Dallawaye, Official: Ulster
Sir Henry Bagnall, Soldier: Ulster
Eustace Harte, Merchant: France & Ireland
David Gwynn, Interpreter: Drogheda
Sir George Carew, Master of the Ordnance,   Dingle
                & Salvage Operator: and Dunluce

MISCELLANEOUS

The States of Zeeland: Report on *San Felipe, San Mateo, San Antonio de Padua*

Prince Maurice of Nassau: Report on the interrogation of prisoners from above

IN THE ARMADA

Don Alvaro de Bazan, Marquis of Santa Cruz

Don Alonso Perez de Guzman, Duke of Medina Sidonia:
San Martin

Don Jorge Manrique, Inspector-General of the Armada:
San Martin

Captain Marolin de Juan, Navigator-General of the Armada:
San Martin and galleass *Zuniga*

Prince of Ascoli, natural son of King Philip II:
San Martin and a pinnace

Don Luis de Miranda, Staff Officer: *San Martin*

Captain Vanegas, Staff Officer: *San Martin*

Juan Martinez de Recalde, Vice-Admiral of the Armada:
San Juan of Oporto

Emanuel Fremoso, Portuguese Mariner (POW):
San Juan of Oporto

Emanuel Francisco, Portuguese Mariner (POW):
San Juan of Oporto

John de Licornio, Biscay Mariner (POW): *San Juan* of Oporto

Pier o Carr (?), Flemish Mariner (POW): *San Juan* of Oporto

Miguel de Oquendo, Admiral of the Guipuzcoa Squadron:
Santa Ana

Don Pedro de Valdes, Admiral of the Andalusia Squadron:
N.S. del Rosario
and POW in H.M.S. *Revenge*

Vicente Alvarez (POW), Captain of: *N.S. del Rosario*

Gregorio de Sotomayor (POW), Portuguese Gentleman:
N.S. del Rosario

Fray Bernado de Gongora, a Friar: *N.S. del Rosario*
transferred *San Martin*

Pedro Coco Calderon, Auditor-General of the Armada:
vice-flag hulk *San Salvador*

Log of: vice-flag hulk *San Salvador*
Marcos de Aramburu, Purser of the Castille Squadron:
                                                San Juan Bautesta
Pedro Iqueldo, Purser of the Biscay Squadron: *Santa Ana*
Francisco Cuellar, Captain of: galleon *San Pedro*
                  & placed under open arrest in Levanter *Lavia*
Don Alonso de Luzon, Camp Master, tercio of Naples (POW):
                                           La Trinidad Valencera
Master of: *La Trinidad Valencera*
Juan de Nova, Servant to Don Juan de Idiaquez:
                                           La Trinidad Valencera
Francisco de Borja: *La Trinidad Valencera*
Don Diego de Pimental, Camp Master, tercio of Sicily (POW):
                                                 San Mateo
Six prisoners from: *San Mateo*
Pedro Estrade, Reinforcement Officer: *San Marcos*
A Gentleman of Salamanca (POW):   flag galleass *San Lorenzo*
Witness of Capture (crew member?)   flag galleass *San Lorenzo*
Juan de Saavedra, Captain, tercio of Naples: galleass *Zuniga*
Summarised Diaries of the Crew of: galleass *Zuniga*
Italian Mariner   galleass *Girona*
David Gywnn, Welsh galley slave: galley *Diana*
James Machary of the Cross, Pressed Man: *Duquesa Santa Ana*
Antonio Maneses (or Monana), Son of the Pilot of:

                                                S.M. de la Rosa
Ensign Esquival, commanding: Pinnace
Master of: Seville Ship
Don Juan de Monsalve, Captain of: hulk *San Pedro el Menor*
Gonzalo Gonzales (POW):   hospital hulk *San Pedro el Mayor*
Statement of the captured Crew of:

                            hospital hulk *San Pedro el Mayor*
Log of: hulk *Palomar Blanca*
Don Balthasar de Zuniga
Padre Geronimo de la Torre
Antonio de Taso Aquereis, Infantry Officer
Hassan, the Marquis of Santa Cruz' freed slave
Two Dutch Mariners (deserters); 14 Dutch Mariners (deserters);
   etc., etc.

14

IN EUROPE

Philip II, King of Spain
Alexander Farnese, Duke of Parma: Bruges
Don Bernadino de Mendoza, Spanish Ambassador: Paris
Don Diego Guzman de Silva, Spanish Ambassador: London
Count de Olivares, Spanish Ambassador: Rome
Giovanni Gritti, Venetian Ambassador: Rome
Father Robert Parsons, emigré leader: Rome
Captain Luis Cabreta, Naval Adviser
Garcia de Villego, Naval Official
Marco Antonio Messia, Genoese, Spanish Agent   London
Antonio de Vega, Spanish Agent: London
Miscellaneous Spies and Couriers in and from: England
Miscellaneous Agents: Bruges, Dunkirk, Antwerp, Rouen, etc.

CHAPTER ONE

The Enterprise of England

From merciless invaders,
   From wicked men's device,
O God! arise and help us
   To quell our enemies!

Strike deep their potent navies,
   Their strength and courage break,
O God! arise and arm us,
   For Jesus Christ his sake.

Though cruel Spain and Parma
   With heathen legions come,
O God! arise and arm us,
   We'll die for our home!

John Still (1542-1607)

THE SUMMER of 1588 was miserable with rain and sudden, gusty storms. The sound of the sea breaking on the shores of the island was more often a roar than a murmur. In this year of decision the very elements themselves seemed to favour England, presenting to the invader an impassable barrier of sullen, gale-white water. The bonfires ready on hill and headland were soaked by the driving rain or torn by the winds that howled about them. Somewhere beyond those grey leagues of tossing sea was the mighty, long-awaited Armada of Spain, storm-bound and seasick. Surely it would not come now?

In the western entrance to the Channel, the watchful English pinnaces pitched and rolled, too few to guard that stretch of water a hundred miles and more across; but the English western fleet, under Howard and Drake, had put back to Plymouth, their victuals exhausted. With this south-westerly wind, they would find it hard to get out again.

Out at sea, a few sails moved upon the waters, those of merchant ships, to whose owners and captains time was money. Among them was a nameless bark from Mousehole in Cornwall. All that we know of her master is, that he was a resolute man, determined to pass across the Channel to France, collect a cargo of salt, and return. On his way, he was hailed by a French flyboat, also on patrol, in this uneasy time which was neither peace nor war. The Frenchman closed him, and, finding that this was an English ship, shouted from deck to deck across the heaving water a friendly warning: " In any wise, as you love your life, do not proceed, for the Spanish fleet is on the coast! "

But the Cornish ship stood on for France, that 19th of June, 1588. And, hours later, her master saw, rising slowly up over the horizon, a forest of masts. He could have fled from them, but he did not. He altered course to intercept, steering into history with empty holds, but prudently aiming for the windward position. If it was the Armada, the salt would keep. By the time his men were starting to count the numbers of the strange ships, it was clear that they had seen him. Two flags fluttered briefly at the mastheads of the leading vessels, a sighting report for their flagship, no doubt of that. It was strange to know that, if these were Spaniards, then, even now, across the heaving waves, the guns were being run out, the matches being got ready. An enemy would want information. Well, that was what he wanted, too.

As the distance rapidly closed, the mass of ships grew in size, became a squadron. They were large ships, some very large, towing boats or pinnaces behind them. The oddest thing was the markings on their sails. Each vessel had a great red cross, not unlike the English Cross of Saint George worn by the Queen's ships, emblazoned on her foresails. Rapidly, the silhouettes of three of the strange ships began to alter, as they turned out of line towards the inquisitive Cornishman. It was time to go; time to take back the news to England.

" Being bound for France to lade salt," he reported to Sir Francis Godolphin, " I encountered with nine sail of great ships between Scilly and Ushant, bearing in North-East with the coast of England. Coming near unto them, and doubting not they were Spaniards, I kept the wind of them. They, perceiving it, began to give me chase. So in the end, three of them followed me so near that I doubted hardly to escape them."

We can almost hear Sir Francis' impatient interruption of the man's proud narrative, which brought the Cornishman to the point.

" Yes, they were all great ships, and, as I might judge, the least of them from 200 tons to five and 800 tons. Their sails were all crossed over with a red cross."

Sir Francis, who was M.P. for Cornwall, soon had further news to send post haste to the Lord Admiral of England at Plymouth. Two more strange squadrons, one of six sail, the other of 15 sail, were reported in the western entrance to the Channel by yet another Cornish merchant ship. Hot with the excitement of battle, her master poured out his story. He had run in so close, to test their intentions, that when they had opened fire, his ship had been hit. All these vessels, too, had been marked on their sails with a great red cross. There was no doubt about it. This was the Armada, brazenly sailing in colours almost a copy of the insignia of England. That was just the sort of insulting arrogance one might expect from Spaniards. Did they think they had conquered the island already?

* * *

" Your Majesty is now master of the Portuguese Empire. I am prepared, if you will allow it, to add England to your Dominions. Everything is favourable. The troops are ready, the fleet in high condition. The cost may be great, but the cost of the English raids is greater. If one looks at difficulties, nothing will be done. I beg your Majesty to take courage and undertake this campaign, and I hope in God to come successfully out of it, as I have out of everything else."

There had been many Spanish proposals for the crushing of England, but none with the authority of this, written as it was in August, 1583, after a victorious campaign, by the victor, the formidable Don Alvaro de Barzan, Marquis of Santa Cruz. But politically, the moment was not favourable, in the judgement of the cautious Philip II, King of Spain, Portugal, Naples, Sicily, Milan, Franche-Comté, the Netherlands, America, Brazil, the Atlantic Islands, Guinea, Angola, Mozambique, Macao, and the Philippines. He thanked Santa Cruz for his suggestion, but regretted that there could be no firm decision yet. Some initial preparations might be made; nothing more.

England and Spain, although not openly at war, had been opposing each other for years. They were engaged in a struggle for positions of initial advantage, military and diplomatic. When these were resolved in the definite favour of one side or the other, then there might be war; but not before. The scales had first to tilt. And the peace—which would follow the war—would have to be carefully considered. There was no point in expending great resources in a conflict which would be of more benefit to outsiders than to the victor. But if there was no war, there was no peace, either. Spanish troops aided the rebel Irish against their English conquerors; English soldiers fought against Spanish in the Low Countries, helping the Dutch rebels. There was the continual tension of an underground struggle waged by diverse means—embargo, espionage, excommunication, execution, sedition, assassination. And if Spain was militarily dominant in Europe, England had the power to strike hard at the King's dominions overseas.

In 1585, two years after Portugal had been overwhelmed by Spanish arms, twenty-five of the Queen's ships, commanded by Drake, took, sacked and burned some of the most important Spanish colonial towns in the New World. In one of those fallen towns, the prisoners were herded into the ornate Government House, with jeers and insults. " By some of our company it was told them," reported one of Drake's captains, " that if the Queen of England would resolutely prosecute the wars against the King of Spain, he should be forced to lay aside that proud and unreasonable reaching vein of his; for he should find more than enough to do to keep that which he had already, as by the example of their lost town they might for a beginning perceive well enough."

The fury of the Spanish reaction gave to the often-discussed " Enterprise of England ", its first tangible form. Philip asked Santa Cruz to prepare detailed estimates for a projected invasion of England. The great admiral replied: " It will be necessary to mobilise, and to concentrate in the English Channel, the whole naval power of Your Majesty's dominions; together with large land forces." And he listed the requirements at length : 596 ships, manned by 17,000 seamen; carrying an invasion army of 55,000 soldiers, equipped with 130 field guns, 1,600 horses, 1,400 mules, a siege train, quartermaster stores, and a field hospital. To take the assault troops ashore, 200 special landing craft would have to be constructed, and carried on deck by the store ships. This was more, far more, than a fighting fleet. It was an enormous amphibious task force, completely self-contained—an armada.

Nowhere did such a force exist. It would have to be assembled—by construction, by conversion, by conscription. Santa Cruz pointed out how it could be done, by the dockyards, by the requisitioning of merchant ships, by the withdrawal of forty war galleys from the Mediterranean, and so on. The loss of 10,000 men, by the wastage of battle, sickness, and desertion, would have to be allowed for. The stores of food, drink, powder, shot, etc., would have to be calculated on the basis of a campaign likely to last eight months. Santa Cruz went on to consider how many sandals must be held in the storerooms, and how many pikes, and how much medicine, and how much it would all cost. And the cost was appalling.

" The plan I think extremely good," wrote the King, " but very costly. I must consider it."

Santa Cruz may have been employing the standard method of military demand, by which everyone indents for far more than is actually required in the certain knowledge that half of it will be disallowed anyway. Certainly, this was what happened. The King approved the plan in principle, subject to one vital amendment. He reduced by two-thirds, the number of soldiers who would sail in the Armada from Spain, thereby making at one stroke an immense saving in trained manpower, in warlike and other stores, in draught animals, and in the staggering amount of water and fodder which the latter consume; and at the same time, the tonnage of merchant shipping required to transport the army could be brought down to something like manageable proportions, without much affecting the power of the fleet in a sea battle. Indeed, by reducing the number of slow and semi-armed transports and store ships, the fighting fleet would be better able to fight. And he planned to achieve all this without any great weakening of the military force which would actually invade England.

The reason was, that he already had a great army in the Low Countries, commanded by the best general in Europe, Alexander Farnese, Duke of Parma. All that kept them from England was thirty miles of sea and the English fleet. Parma could be ordered to provide his own transport for the brief crossing, by building and requisitioning flat-bottomed boats and barges seaworthy enough just for that; the Armada would join him and drive off the English fleet; and then, together, Santa Cruz and Alexander Farnese would enter England with 50,000 men. Soon, the Queen of England would be suing for peace. The King set the date of the Enterprise for the summer of 1587—a year ahead.

But Santa Cruz, now that his dream was about to come true, lost all drive and enthusiasm. Perhaps because he was an old man, and had not long to live; perhaps also because he saw that there was a fatal weakness in the King's version of his own ambitious scheme. The Armada would no longer be a self-contained assault force, capable of invading England without support; it had been turned into a weaker hybrid, dependent for success on many doubtful factors—smooth liaison with Parma, perfect timing, the sea-worthiness of the Dutch barges, the Armada's ability to protect them as they emerged from many small harbours into the open sea. This vast assembly of shipping, much of it terribly vulnerable, would be at the mercy of the wind; indeed, relied solely on the wind for motive power. It would be difficult enough as an exercise, with only an imaginary enemy barring the way; as an operation, it could end in dire calamity.

Parma himself, when told the details, was equally lacking in enthusiasm; he suggested a postponement, until such time as he had captured, not merely another poky Channel haven, but a great harbour large enough for the entire Armada, where it could ride in safety until the weather was favourable, and where his men could embark in real ships instead of cockleshells.

War, however, is a game for two; and before the Armada finally sailed, two further amendments to the plan had been forced by English action. The Spanish fleet did not sail, as intended, in the summer of 1587; because the English fleet did. Armed with the Queen's commission, Drake struck at the Armada while it was still mobilising and fitting out, and then blockaded the coast, disrupting the flow of materials and stores to the ports. This was war in its most economic and efficient form, fighting far away from England on the enemy's frontier; striking crippling blows to which the enemy had no reply. In its tactical implications, it was equally serious.

The Spanish harbours were defended by the standard type of Mediterranean warship, the galley. These were long, light, race-horse craft, powered by oars; they could enter shallow water; and they could manoeuvre, as no sailing ship could, with the instant precision of a drill squad. They were the backbone of the Spanish navy, and no less than forty were earmarked for the Enterprise of England. At this stage of planning, there were to be only about ten sailing warships in the Armada, the galleons of Portugal, stiffened by some thirty converted merchantmen of various types. Half the fighting power of the Armada was in its galley component.

Santa Cruz had helped win the great victory of Lepanto in 1571, fought between galley fleets; and he believed in galleys. Other Spanish officers were less tradition-minded, and Captain Luis Cabreta had already warned the King: " It is all very well to say that Your Majesty has a hundred galleys. They may be of some little use in the Mediterranean but they are of small importance elsewhere, especially on the high seas." This was theory. After Drake's raid on Cadiz in 1587, it was fact. Drake wrote afterwards to his brother captain, Thomas Fenner: " I assure your honour there is no account to be made of his galleys. Twelve of her Majesty's ships will make account of all his galleys in Spain, Portugal and all his dominions within the Straits, although they are 150 in number. If it be to their advantage in a calm, we have made such trial of their fights that we perfectly see into the depth thereof."

Spain would have to maintain a two-ocean navy; galleys inside the Straits of Gibraltar, sailing ships outside. An enormous drain on resources. Reluctantly, the number of galleys earmarked for England was reduced to four. Why they were sent at all is not clear, but probably because they could go into shallow water and manoeuvre there with precision, which would enable them to cover the emergence of Parma's vulnerable host of landing craft from the tiny havens which served as invasion ports. At that point, and in their passage between the sandbanks for many miles out to sea, the landing craft would be wide open to attack by the host of small armed sailing ships owned by the English and the rebel States of Zeeland. None of the larger ships on either side could interfere; the water was far too shallow. Without such protection, or a surprise move, Parma's army was due for a bloodbath in the surf.

That autumn, by the capture of Sluys, Parma gained yet another small haven in which to assemble his invasion craft; and the King decided to make a move which would stagger his enemies with its unexpectedness. He ordered Santa Cruz to sail for England as soon as he possibly could, regardless of the hazards of winter. To him, the fall of Sluys appeared to be " the door that God has opened for us in Flanders, whence the passage to England is short and secure. It is clear," he wrote to Santa Cruz, " that great risks are involved in the moving of a mighty Armada in winter, particularly in the Channel with no port secured; but the other reasons which have induced His Majesty to take this resolution are even weightier." Among them was an unfounded belief that Elizabeth's army would be reinforced by foreign troops next year, and that the Turkish galleys would make a diversion for her in the Mediterranean. But above all, he reasoned, surprise; no one would expect a great invasion at that season. " Our forces, if skilfully united, would assure us of victory, if we do not delay to use them, in view of the enemy's present unpreparedness, and the fact that the expedients he is devising for next year, cannot serve him in this, and would utterly collapse if we should win the first move. The roadstead of Margate is excellent, but without defences; the river of London is also undefended."

He wrote to Parma in similar terms. " The Marquis of Santa Cruz will anchor at Margate Point, having first sent notice to you at Dunkirk, Nieuport, or the Sluys, of his approach. When you see the passage assured by the arrival of the fleet at Margate, or at the mouth of the Thames, you will, if the weather permits, instantly cross with the whole army in the boats which you will have ready. Until then, the Marquis is not to allow himself to be diverted from assuring your safe passage, keeping at bay any force of the enemy which may come out to prevent it. But you will see the danger of any delay, the Armada being there and you behindhand. Until your passage is effected it will have no harbour for shelter, whereas when you have crossed over it will have the safe and spacious River Thames. Otherwise it will be at the mercy of the weather. You must not forget that the forces collected and the vast money responsibility incurred, make it extremely difficult for such an expedition again to be got together if they escape us this time, while the obstacles and divisions which may arise (and certainly will do so) next summer, force us to undertake the enterprise this year or else fail altogether."

What may have been intended as a crack of the whip for his commanders, proved to be an accurate prophecy. Neither the Armada gathering at Lisbon under Santa Cruz nor the fleet of landing craft being collected by Parma in all the creeks of the Low Countries, were even remotely ready; and nothing was done in 1587. And then, in January of the new year, 1588, the Marquis of Santa Cruz died. The greatest Spanish commander, the master mind behind the enterprise, was gone. There were many possible successors, but no one man was pre-eminent, as Santa Cruz had been. To succeed him, the King appointed neither an admiral nor a general but a military unknown, the Duke of Medina Sidonia; and, for history, if not for Spain, this was most fortunate. The King had had no need to tell Santa Cruz the aims and objects of the campaign, and to advise him on naval and military tactics would have been impertinent. But Medina Sidonia knew nothing, and had to be told everything.

CHAPTER TWO

The King's Force is Marvellous Great

The Duke Receives His Operation Orders—1588

" DEAR DUKE and Cousin," Philip wrote to Medina Sidonia, " I have decided to confer on you the office of my Captain General of the Ocean. Your first action will be to take charge of the Armada which I have ordered to assemble in Lisbon. And as speed is particularly important, if within eight or ten days you find that you are able to set out with the galleons provided with their full complement of sailors and soldiers, I charge you to embark and proceed straight to the mouth of the river of Lisbon without loss of time. The general opinion here lately has been that it would be as well to spread abroad the report that the galleons are bound for the Indies, so as the more easily to recruit personnel, particularly seamen. Now, however it may be that recruits will respond more readily to the call of the Armada, than to that of the Indies. Yet, as far as the sailors are concerned, I feel it would be well that they should believe the report of the Indies." Perhaps the sailors knew better than the soldiers, what sort of a reception they might expect in the English Channel.

But the most unwilling recruit His Majesty's Armada ever had was its commander-in-chief Medina Sidonia, the newly-appointed " Captain General of the Ocean."

He replied at once. " My health is always bad, and from my small experience of the water I know that I am always sea-sick. The expedition is on such a scale and the object is of such high importance that the person at the head of it ought to understand navigation and sea-fighting, and I know nothing of either. I have not one of the essential qualifications. Were I competent otherwise, I should have to act in the dark by the opinion of others. If you send me, depend upon it, I shall have a bad account to render of my trust."

Two prophecies now. The King's, that an attempt in 1588 would " fail altogether "; and the Duke's, that he would have

a " bad account to render ". Both to be fulfilled. It will be seen
why Philip continued with the enterprise, in spite of his own
prediction; but the position in which he put his unfortunate
cousin was appalling.

Not one word of Medina Sidonia's pathetic letter was
exaggerated. The Duke, although the senior nobleman of Spain,
had always lived the quiet life of a country gentleman who
enjoys looking after his estates. He had no experience of command, high or low; no experience of war. He was therefore
entirely without ideas on the subject. Possibly it was this which
was his real recommendation. The King had been extremely
worried about that junction of Santa Cruz with Parma, and not
on technical grounds only. Here were two equally eminent
men of war, with more than their fair share of brains and
character; if they differed as to ways and means, their
dissensions could rend the enterprise. It had been impossible
to appoint one over the head of the other, and Philip had been
forced to stress in his letters that they should always " co-operate
closely with each other," adding that " there will be fame enough
to spare for all." It is clear, however, from the hints to Santa
Cruz, that in his opinion the land element should take precedence over the sea element, which was merely a means of
transport and of temporary defence.

Santa Cruz might well have gone off, fighting sea battles
on his own account; whereas Medina Sidonia would obey his
orders to the letter, under expert advice on the spot, and
then hand over without regret to Parma, who would take the
burden off his hands and command the actual invasion. If
the Armada could merely parade up-Channel, the appointment
was doubtless a good one; but if it had to fight, swift and
accurate decisions would be required of its commander. Medina
Sidonia would have no time to learn, he was to be pitch-forked
off to the English Channel at a few weeks' notice, and might
well be engaged in the sea-fight of the century the moment he
got there. There was no escaping his destiny, for the King was
determined on the appointment. "All of what you say I
attribute to your excess of modesty," he told the Duke,
charmingly. " In this belief, I have permitted my decision to
be made public here, and written to Portugal and Flanders."

There could be no drawing back now. Medina Sidonia left his estates at San Lucar and went to join the Armada concentration at Lisbon, in Portugal, with the determination at any rate not to fail from want of zeal or application. He discovered that great risks had been taken to assemble the force; the guard ships which normally escorted the annual treasure fleet from the Indies had been withdrawn for service against England, and this year the treasure was to cross the Atlantic, alive with loot-seeking English raiders, in light craft which could hope only that their speed would be sufficient for escape. Even so, the Armada was neither ready nor particularly formidable. There was a hard core of warships; but the bulk consisted of sadly under-gunned merchantmen, and a desperate search was going on for ordnance to put in them. That it cannot have been very successful is shown by the English inventories of a captured Spanish flagship; some of the armament being of iron, and so old that even the light-fingered English sea captains did not bother to "liberate" it. From other scraps of evidence which exist, some of the weaker ships had only 10, 15, or 18 pieces of ordnance, mostly light weapons—not the heavy, short-range cannon or the long-barrelled high-velocity culverins, the latter being the favourite armament of the English ships, according to the partial evidence available. Listed in the Gun States rendered to the Duke, were 1,497 bronze guns of various calibres, including cannons, half-culverins, and pedrero cannons, the latter firing stone-shot, a primitive form of shrapnel; and 934 cast iron guns. This was the sum total, including the very light weapons used for repelling boarders. Whether it also included the weapons intended for land use, and possibly stored in the holds, is not known. But the powder stores were very large, being intended to last out a land campaign, plus 123,790 cannon-balls—enough for weeks of fighting at the old rate, enough for about four days by the size of the demands Drake was making in England.

The undoubted strength of the force lay in its infantry, as the King had said. With a paper strength of about 19,000 men, it included some 10,000 seasoned soldiers, by reputation the terror of Europe; the rest were half-trained conscripts, 2,000 of them Portuguese; shepherds, vineyard workers, and so on. Medina Sidonia found that many of the ships, the converted merchantmen, had insufficient protection for these men, and had the carpenters set to work building up fighting bulwarks and castles for them, musket-proof at least, which made the ships tower menacingly high. Even the hulks of the transport squadron, armed with iron guns, at least appeared formidable after that, although such modifications still further reduced their sailing qualities. As almost every noble family in Spain, and many in Portugal and Italy, had at least one volunteer present with the fleet, there was much petty quarrelling as to precedence and quarters; indeed, some of the more insolent types had boarded up part of the gun decks, in order to make private cabins for themselves, thus lowering still further the fighting efficiency of the ships already over-crammed with men. As the premier nobleman of Spain, the Duke could come down hard on that sort of thing, and did so, as soon as he got to know about it. Women were supposedly forbidden on board, but we know of one at least who sailed as far as the Channel; however, she may have been privileged, the wife of a foreign master gunner, a highly important man. It was more difficult to prevent the contractors from making high profits by supplying inferior stores; and the problem of arranging sufficient water and fodder in the transport ships for the hundreds of horses and mules of the army's artillery train, was a nightmare. The Duke was soon caught up in the interminable tasks of organisation which are the greater part of war.

Not the least of his problems was the bewildering international mixture of the force. Captive Portugal was supplying a squadron of galleons and four galleys. Italy had sent a squadron of armed merchantmen and four Neapolitan galleasses (hybrid warships, half sail, half oar). A great many Dutch mariners were serving throughout the fleet as well as German artillerymen, and Frenchmen. There were Scotsmen, whose country was neutral, Irishmen, whose country was captive to England, and many English renegades who would help to govern any English territory which was captured. Almost any nationality might be found among the galley slaves labouring at the great sweeps of the galleys and galleasses; there were Spanish convicts, Frenchmen, and at least one Welshman amongst them. All told, the Duke was responsible for 30,000 men in

130 ships, the total being made up by a mass of fast, light craft for scouting and despatch-carrying duties—Zabras (Biscay smacks) and Pataches, or pinnaces.

The death of the all-round man of war, Don Alvaro de Bazan, Marquis of Santa Cruz, had led to a hasty shuffling and re-shuffling of the command system. Medina Sidonia was nominally in charge; but as he said himself, he knew nothing about it. Nothing about ships, nothing about soldiers, nothing about war in any shape or form, let alone at its most complicated— an amphibious operation involving all arms. His flagship, the *San Martin*, was nominally the Armada *capitana*, or fleet flagship. But, to advise him on naval matters, Diego Flores de Valdes quitted his own squadron *capitana* to go aboard the *San Martin*, leaving Gregorio de las Alas as the new admiral of the Armada of Castille. To advise him on military tactics, not on land, but at sea, the Duke asked for the Marquis de Penafiel who was commanding the Portuguese galleon *San Marcos*. But Penafiel preferred to go to war in good company, with his old comrades, and refused the honour of holding Medina Sidonia's hand. In his place was appointed an experienced regimental commander, Camp Master Don Francisco de Bobadilla, as military expert. There was no distinction then made between war at sea and war on land, as the principles were the same in any case; but it was recognised that, ideally, a war commander who fought at sea part of the time should know as much about handling ships as he did about soldiers. But as Santa Cruz was dead, this compromise, this committee of three sailing in the *San Martin*, was adopted.

No ideal solution, it was made more confused by two other, virtually rival, appointments. The senior sailor in the Armada, the man with a far greater reputation than Diego Flores, could hardly be left out. This was Admiral Juan Martinez de Recalde, nominally commander of the Armada of Biscay, "a man of service," as one of his men told the English, accurately enough. He shifted his flag from the *Santa Ana*, the flagship, or *capitana*, of the Biscay Squadron, to the great *San Juan* of Oporto, which thereby became the vice-flagship, or *almiranta*, of the whole fleet. His official appointment was now Admiral-in-Chief, Medina Sidonia being described, quaintly enough, as the "General."

At the same time, there was a soldier with talents and fame in his own field equal to that of Recalde. This was Don Alonso de Leyva, who was in effect Land Forces Commander, using as his headquarters ship the equally imposing *Rata Encoronada*, nominally a private, or non-flagship of Martin de Bertendona's Armada of the Levant. In the opinion of many, either Recalde or de Leyva should have had Medina Sidonia's job. Both men fought brilliantly and bravely throughout the campaign, until death overtook them; and afterwards, many Spaniards were sick at heart with all the useless " might-have-beens." But the King made the fatal appointment, in full knowledge of the facts, over Medina Sidonia's own protests. He did not realise the magnitude of the task he had entrusted to the self-effacing Duke. After all, the Armada was immensely strong, defensively; if it held formation, the English could not break it. All the Duke had to do was to sail to the Straits of Dover, and hand over his responsibilities to Parma, the most brilliant general of the age. At best, Parma might not even have to fight.

Parma reported that he was ready, but so were the English; he could not move until the Armada arrived. And by April, the Duke had received his operation orders. They were in three parts. A General Instruction, which told him what Santa Cruz had already known, but Medina Sidonia needed to know, about the invasion plan, the latest sea fighting tactics, and the probable dispositions of the English. A Secret Instruction, which told the Duke what to do in the event of failure. And a Sealed Despatch, which instructed Parma what peace terms to offer, in the event of a severely limited success.

The first part of the General Instruction concerned the public image of the Armada which Philip was anxious to establish, that of a European Catholic crusade. " In the first place," he wrote, " victories are God's to give, and His to take away, as He sees fit. But the cause you are defending is so peculiarly His as to give us hope of His help and favour if it is not made unworthy by our sinfulness. For this reason you must take particular care in the Armada against sin of any kind, but especially the sin of blasphemy, by providing heavy penalties, to be rigorously carried out. . . ." Cynics professed to believe that the Armada represented the King of Spain playing at

2

power politics; and as the chief cynic was the Pope himself, it was essential to disclaim all earthly considerations. Besides, there were many Catholics in England who, it was confidently expected, might help the invaders if these came as religious liberators rather than as foreign conquerors.

The next part of the Instruction directed the Duke to proceed to Margate Cape along the English coast, avoiding the French side of the Channel because of the shoals and banks, a very great hazard to clumsy wind-propelled ships. As the Duke already knew, the Armada was very fully supplied with the necessary charts and there were many expert pilots available, particularly among the squadron of armed merchantmen commanded by Miguel de Oquendo. As he also knew, a master navigator had been appointed, to take that part of the burden off his shoulders. Where the Duke needed guidance was in the strategy of the campaign—when and when not to fight; and in tactics—how to fight, if he had to.

" The success of this enterprise depends on your going to the heart of the matter," wrote the King. " Even if Drake should have sailed for these waters with a fleet, to create a diversion, you will not turn back. If, however, he should pursue and overtake you, you may attack him. You should also attack if you meet Drake with his fleet at the entrance to the Channel, because if the enemy's forces are so divided, it would be well to defeat him by stages." Philip's intelligence was accurate. The English fleet was divided into Drake's powerful western squadron, based on Plymouth, and a smaller squadron in the Narrow Seas between Dover and Calais. The King gave Medina Sidonia leave to attack whatever he found in the Narrows; a squadron only, or the English fleet united. But he did not stress that it had to be destroyed, before Parma could cross.

The King had very accurate information, too, as to the new English tactics which they would certainly employ. " You should take special note," he warned the Duke, " that the enemy's aim will be to fight from a distance, since he has the advantage of superior artillery and of the large number of fireworks with which he will come provided." To counter this, he wrote, " Our aim must be to attack, and come to grips with the enemy at close quarters; and to succeed in doing this you will need to exert every effort. That you might be forewarned, you will receive a detailed report of the way in which the enemy arranges his artillery so as to be able to aim his broadsides low in the hull and so sink his opponents' ships."

Philip stressed the importance of rigid formation-keeping. "God granting victory, as a prudent commander you should see that your squadrons do not break their battle formation and that their commanders, moved by greed, do not give pursuit to the enemy and take prizes. I therefore charge you particularly to take every precaution against the occurrence of disorder producing grievous results. I have ordered instructions to be sent to you concerning the order of precedence it is desired to maintain in the distribution of prizes and booty, and you must see that it is scrupulously adhered to."

The King asked Medina Sidonia to co-operate fully with Parma, and to pay great attention to the quality and quantity of the food served in the ships, concluding, " these are all the instructions which for the time being it occurs to me to give you." There seemed to be quite a lot left out; in particular, the King had not really indicated what he thought the Armada ought to do about the English fleet. Having given the Duke permission to fight it in the Narrows, he inserted a contradictory sentence in the summing up: " It is understood that you will fight only if you cannot otherwise make secure the passage across to England of the Duke of Parma. . . . It will be well to keep our forces intact."

If Medina Sidonia was puzzled to understand his master's meaning, his doubts may have been resolved when he opened the second document, the Secret Instructions. In effect, these were his instructions in the event of failure. " If God gives you the success which is desired," they ran, " you are to follow strictly the order of my public instructions to you. If, however, through our sins it should fall out otherwise, and the Duke of Parma should not be able to cross to England, nor you for that reason meet him, then, after communicating with him, you will see whether you are able to capture the Isle of Wight, which is not so strongly defended as to appear able to resist you. Once captured, however, it can be defended, and you will have a secure port in which the Armada may take shelter

and which, being a place of importance, would open the way
for further action by you. You should take care to use the
Eastern entrance, which is wider and longer than the Western."

With the Secret Instructions was a Sealed Document addressed
to Parma. Medina Sidonia was to give it to him "either after
he has landed in England, or in the event of his doubting the
possibility of landing there." In any other event, it was to be
returned, un-read, to the King. It was vitally important because
it contained the peace terms to be offered to England. In effect,
it showed exactly what he expected to gain by the Armada;
or, rather, the most probable result of the enterprise.

"If the result be not so prosperous that our arms shall be
able to settle matters, nor, on the other hand, so contrary that
the enemy shall be relieved of anxiety on our account, and
affairs so counter-balanced that peace may not be altogether
undesirable, you will endeavour to avail yourself as much as
possible of the prestige of the Armada, bearing in mind there
are three principal points upon which you must fix your
attention.

> "1. That in England the free use and exercise of our holy
> Catholic faith shall be permitted to all Catholics, native
> and foreign, and that the exiles may return;
>
> "2. That all places in my Netherlands which the English
> hold shall be restored to me;
>
> "3. That the English shall recompense me for the injury they
> have done to me, my dominions, and my subjects; which
> will amount to an exceedingly great sum. (This third
> point may be dropped; you may use it as a lever to
> obtain the other two.)"

In short, Philip seemed to have accepted the logic of his
own reasoning, that the enterprise must fail to conquer England
if carried out in 1588 instead of 1587; he was therefore fully
prepared to use the massive threat of invasion as a bargaining
counter. To do that, the Armada had to be kept in being,
not bled in battle with the English. Anchored at Spithead,
inside the Isle of Wight, it might be the real lever to gain him
his two main points. And these points, if granted, might in
time lead to the overthrow of Elizabeth. Point 1 would tend

to revive his influence inside England; Point 2 would give him the bases by which the pressure from outside could be sharply increased.

The King had another, and excellent, reason for putting his soldiers ashore on the Isle of Wight, even if they advanced no further; he had been promised a substantial subsidy by the Pope on the day that his troops actually landed in England. Throughout the campaign, the King's ambassador to the Vatican, Count de Olivares, was trying to get the money in advance, by proclaiming that the matter was as good as over. Olivares was to complain bitterly to Philip: "The answer he gives *me* is that the terms of the agreement have not yet been fulfilled. His excuse to *others* for not paying the money is that the Armada business is nothing but a trick, and that Your Majesty has not raised the fleet for the English enterprise at all, but for brag, and to frighten the Queen of England into making peace. He shows reports he has received to this effect. However unlikely a report may be, it matters not to His Holiness if it serves his purpose."

Giovanni Gritti, the Venetian Ambassador in Rome, reported in much the same terms to his own masters, the Doge and Senate. He quoted the Pope as saying: " The King goes trifling with this Armada of his, but the Queen acts in earnest. We are sorry to say, but we have a poor opinion of this Spanish Armada, and fear some disaster."

Meanwhile, Medina Sidonia in Lisbon was issuing his sailing orders. "From the highest to the lowest," he wrote, "you are to understand the object of our expedition, which is to recover countries to the Church now oppressed by the enemies of the true faith. I charge you, one and all, to abstain from profane oaths. All personal quarrels are to be suspended. Each morning at sunrise the ship boys shall sing *Good Morrow* at the foot of the mainmast, and at sunset the *Ave Maria*." In a speech to the captains and men of the Armada, he said: " By God's help, the war in Flanders will be ended, and we shall be saved the drain of blood and substance which it draws from Spain; it will be profitable also because of the plunder and endless riches we shall gather in England, and with which, by the favour of God, we shall return, gloriously and victoriously, to our homes."

Nearly 60,000 tons of shipping, more than 30,000 men, were assembled at Lisbon. The tension and rising excitement of a great expedition infected them all. An infantry officer, Antonio de Taso Aquereis, captain of 200 men, wrote home to Andalusia. "Do you pray to God that in England he doth give me a house of some very rich merchant where I may place my ensigne. But I do fear that seeing us they will presently* yield and agree unto all that the King will demand of them, for that the King's force is marvellous great as well by sea as by land. It is impossible to signify unto you the people that are therein, as well soldiers, gentlemen, as of noblemen; only I can say that every day is given twenty-two thousand rations of meat, and this only to Spaniards, besides strangers. All things are now embarked even to the mules that must draw the artillery; and commanded here, upon pain of death, no man to go ashore; only do we tarry for a fair wind to go to sea."

* The word has since changed its meaning. Then, "presently" meant "instantly."

CHAPTER THREE

Stop Him Now and Stop Him Ever

THE GREAT Armada took weeks to come down from Lisbon
to the mouth of the Tagus. There was no secret about its
composition. On 29 April, Medina Sidonia had sent a full list to
the King of the ships, guns, and men actually assembled for the
Enterprise. An almost identical list, not quite so detailed and
with some confusion over the Spanish names, was in the hands
of the English Government by 1 May. Reports from agents
in Spain, and from escaped prisoners, also reached England, and
these, almost invariably, were greatly exaggerated. That would
have pleased Philip had he known, for it added to the intimidating aura of invincible power which shone on Spanish arms.

The visible aspect of that power lay in numbers of soldiers
and not in numbers of ships. The combined sea power of
Spain, Portugal, and Italy available for the Enterprise had produced a fleet of 130 sail. The Queen of England was to mobilise
for the campaign 197 ships, of which about 140 were actually
used against the Armada. On paper, the two fleets were almost
equal. But in design, they were not; and each side had its
strengths and weaknesses. The King had launched his campaign at a time of revolutionary change; in consequence, his
Armada consisted of an amazing collection of the modern, the
new-fangled, the obsolescent, and the obsolete.

At one end of the scale were the four war galleys of Portugal,
commanded by Diego Medrano. In one of them, the *Diana*, some
of Elizabeth's subjects laboured at the rowing benches, including
a talkative fellow named David Gywnn. The war galley had
a documented history reaching back to the fourteenth century
B.C.; and the Spaniards had been loath to abandon them
entirely. In their most perfect form, they had been Greek,
beautiful as butterflies; the Romans had built a heavier, slower
ship, with a formidable ram, had crowded them with armoured
soldiers, and fitted catapults in the bow. The introduction of
gunpowder altered them little. The fore castle of the Roman

37

galley, virtually a pillbox, became a gun platform, mounting light cannon firing forward. No broadside guns could be fitted, the banks of rowers prevented it. Sails were invariably used for cruising, when the wind served; but the galley was a Mediterranean ship, designed for high speed in a smooth and smiling sea. Like the racing shells of present-day oarsmen, scaled up, it was light, long, narrow, extremely fast and manoeuvrable. It did not perform so well in the cruel and broken water of the Atlantic; it was excessively vulnerable not only to cannon fire but to small arms as well; and its once formidable ram was useless against the stout, bolted hull of a sturdy sailing ship.

At the other end of the scale was the galleon, the new type of sailing warship. There were ten of these in the Armada of Portugal, including the Duke's own flagship *San Martin*; and ten of Spanish design in the Armada of Castille, originally commanded by Diego Flores. The latter squadron also had four "great ships," a convenient term much used at the time to denote any large ship, such as a nao or carrack, which had the high build and tubby lines typical of merchant ships and the old-fashioned type of warship. Its finer lines distinguished the galleon as a modern warship; a vessel in which cargo capacity had been sacrificed for speed, handiness, and room to emplace and serve the guns. From sea level, the difference would not immediately be apparent; the merchant ship converted to war purposes would appear as formidable as a galleon.

The Swedish galleon *Vasa*, based on a French design, and completed in 1628, forty years after the time of the Armada, is the nearest we can get to an idea of the proportions of the hull.* The low, cramped gun-decks, like a smaller and more primitive edition of Nelson's *Victory*, show what living conditions must have been like in normal circumstances, and what

---

* We may in time learn more of what an actual Spanish galleon was like, not from documents but from undersea exploration. The present author has seen such a ship in the Tyrrhenian Sea, her upper deck covered by an inch or so of sand, at the foot of precipitous underwater cliffs, in that strange world at 140 feet where colour has been filtered out and the fish look like grey ghosts. One can lie down on her deck and sift the sand for musket balls, or pick up ironwork which has been so long in the sea that it has dissolved into the concretions and left only a mould. No real excavation has yet been attempted, the discovery being so recent and the depth so prohibitive.

a hell at sea such a ship would become when, in addition, two
or three hundred soldiers, complete with weapons and field kit,
were crowded into this small and stifling space. In the English
warships there were few soldiers; the decks were clear for the
men to serve the guns. For it was with guns and not with
soldiers that the English intended to fight, as the King had
warned.

But the Mediterranean people could not at first reconcile
themselves to the loss of oared propulsion, and the battle manoeuvrability it gave. By going ahead with the oars on one side,
and backing on the other, a galley could spin round 360 degrees
on her own axis, without changing position; until the introduction of the twin-screw steamship, nothing at sea could match
them for perfect control. Consequently, while the English were
pursuing the opposite line of research, towards the perfection
of the galleon, so that in speed and handiness it might approach
the galley, the Latin races clung to the old idea. They attempted
to design a compromise between the galley and the galleon, which
they called a galleass.

Basically, the galleass was a lightly-constructed galleon, with
the lower tier of broadside guns taken out and replaced by
oars and the rowers' benches. The hull had to be somewhat frail,
otherwise it would be too heavy for the oars to move it effectively;
but the design did give broadside fire, manoeuvrability, and fairly
high speed in calm water. It was a real warship, of an experimental type, of which great things were expected. Four Neapolitan galleasses went with the Armada, commanded by Don Hugo
de Moncada in the *San Lorenzo*.

Besides the galleys, galleons, and galleasses, there were four
squadrons of " great ships," mostly merchantmen converted into
warships by the fitting of a few more guns and the building of
high castles at bow and stern. In effect, they were second-class
battleships. They were organised on a territorial basis as the
Armada of Biscay—10 great ships nominally under Juan Martinez
de Recalde; the Armada of Andalusia—nine great ships and one
" hulk " under Don Pedro de Valdes; the Armada of Guipuzcoa—
nine great ships and one " hulk " under Miguel de Oquendo;
and the Armada of the Levant—10 great ships under Martin de
Bertendona, one of which carried Don Alonso de Leyva, the

2*

General of the army contingent earmarked for the invasion role.

The largest single squadron consisted entirely of "hulks," or store-ships, 23 of them in all, under Juan Gomez de Medina. They carried the horses, the mules, the wagons, all the miscellaneous impedimenta of an army; as well as many of the soldiers. Two of them were hospital ships.

Most of the squadrons had light craft specifically attached to them for scouting and communications duties; and there was in addition a self-contained squadron of these craft under Don Antonio Hurtado de Mendoza, whose flagship, of 300 tons, was somewhat larger than the rest of his force. The two main distinctions made by the Spaniards among these light craft differentiate between the *zabra*, a Biscay smack, and the *patache*, which the English referred to as a " pinnace."

The Great Armada was, therefore, not a battle fleet in the ordinary sense. For thousands of years, a war fleet had been a galley fleet; and, since the Punic Wars, the main offensive weapon had been soldiers. Battles were fought, first, by military manoeuvring for a position of advantage, and then by pouring overwhelming numbers of armed men onto the enemy's decks. Later, a battle fleet was to consist entirely of heavily-gunned sailing ships, which would use their guns to beat down resistance first of all, and then capture by boarding.

Neither the English fleet nor the Armada fitted exactly into one pattern or the other. The English fleet relied entirely on gunfire from better ships, the Spaniards largely, but not entirely, on boarding. This was the consequence, not so much of design, but of the facts as they were. Spain had a large, highly-trained professional army; England had not. It would be quite wrong even to consider the Armada as a battle fleet, for it was no such thing; it was an amphibious task force, and the task was the invasion of England.

Defensively, it was enormously strong; the numbers of soldiers carried necessarily made it so. In any case, the attacker who boarded at sea was at a terrible disadvantage. His men had to get out from behind the bulwarks, raked by fire, and try to cross the swaying gap between the two hulls; inevitably, the attackers arrived in penny packets, and were cut down. Even if they did get inboard in numbers, the only practical place of entry was into the low waist of the enemy ship, where they would be caught by murderous fire from the twin castles at bow and stern. In effect these were light pillboxes, built to keep out small-arms fire only, and fitted with the equivalent of modern automatic weapons sited to sweep the decks between them. Indeed, one of the most popular of these weapons was in fact dubbed the " Murderer "; it was a big, breech-loading shot-gun on a swivel, which produced the required " watering can " effect. It could be re-loaded very rapidly, by means of trays holding musket balls (or old nails and scrap-iron, if necessary), and could fire, therefore, in really devastating bursts at short intervals.

Ships so equipped could be taken only by greatly superior numbers of men, at the cost of very heavy losses. The English, therefore, could not expect to take a single Spanish ship; but the Spaniards had enough trained manpower to overwhelm an English ship. Further, the newer types of English ship had almost dispensed with the bow castle, and were weaker in this respect than most of their enemy's vessels. Also, these new types were smaller than their Spanish equivalents, and held fewer men. The older type of English " great ship " would be harder to take; but even so, in any hand-to-hand fight on the decks, the overwhelming advantage lay with Spain.

The obvious counter to the system of light defensive castles at bow and stern was to blow them to splinters with gunfire, kill or stun their occupants; rake and smash the waiting assault infantry on the main deck, momentarily reducing the survivors to shocked, shaking cowards. Then an assault by boarding might succeed, if the attackers had enough assault troops; but the English had not. They would have to fight by gunfire alone. This would be a severe test of the new English weapons and methods. Of the 15,000 men in the English fleet, only about 1,500 were soldiers; their ships were designed as fast, floating gun platforms, and their chosen weapon was mainly the culverin. This was a long-barrelled, high-velocity gun firing medium size shot a long way, as opposed to cannon, which fired heavier shot a much shorter distance. The two types had developed in land warfare: the cannon as a castle-cracking implement, the culverin as a counter-battery gun firing from the castle, to harass and smash the cannon before they could be emplaced.

Under normal circumstances, the English could expect to stay just out of effective range, and blow their enemy into surrender or immobility; but the infantry complement of the Armada was so large that it posed a special problem. Even a badly damaged Spanish ship would probably have enough soldiers left to put up an effective defence against boarding by the small numbers the English could muster. Actually to sink a Spanish ship was unlikely, except after prolonged bombardment. But, even so, this was only half the problem confronting the English, for the Great Armada represented only half the Spanish effort.

If possible, the Armada was not to fight; it was to join Parma's Flanders army, prior to making a joint descent on the coast of England. That army amounted to 60,000 men, counting the fortress troops of Antwerp, Ghent, and Charlemont, but excluding the detachments of occupation scattered throughout the Spanish Netherlands. This, like the Great Armada, was an international force and consisted of highly-trained professional soldiers. On 19 April, Parma reported the latest muster as: 8,718 Spanish infantry; 5,339 Italian infantry; 3,278 Burgundian, Irish, and Scots infantry; 17,825 Walloon infantry; 11,309 High German infantry; 8,616 Low German infantry; 3,650 Italian and Spanish light horse. Half of this force, or about 30,000 men, were earmarked for the Enterprise of England; although, in the event, sickness and other wastage reduced the figure.

The threat which faced England was that of invasion; and she was ill prepared to meet it. One small country, alone, was defying attack by forces drawn from Spain, Portugal, Italy, Holland, Germany, France, Scotland, and Ireland. The odds were overwhelming. It was impossible to be strong enough everywhere. And the lessons of history, up to that time, provided only depressing precedents. As the Jesuit exile, Father Parsons, pointed out to King Philip and the Pope: "Sixteen times England has been invaded. Twice only the native race have repelled the attacking force. They have been defeated on every other occasion, and with a cause so holy and just as ours we need not fear to fail. Two-thirds at least are Catholic at heart, though many conceal their convictions in fear of the Queen. The Puritans have none of them ever seen a camp. They have not a man who can command in the field. In the whole realm there are but two fortresses which could stand a three days' siege. The people are enervated by a long peace, and, except for a few who have served with the heretics in Flanders, cannot bear their arms."

On 27 November, 1587, six months before the Armada sailed for its rendezvous with Parma's Army of Flanders, Queen Elizabeth had held a Council of War to decide on counter-measures. Among those present were Drake and Raleigh. In the opinion of the Council, the most probable invasion areas were Milford in South Wales, Helford and Falmouth in Cornwall, Plymouth and Torbay in Devon, Portland in Dorset, Portsmouth in Hampshire, and the Isle of Wight, south of Portsmouth, which had known French troops within living memory. It was therefore no coincidence that the English fleet was later to give battle off Plymouth, Portland, and the Isle of Wight, for these were especially vital areas among the possible invasion objectives; no coincidence either that they did not go into action when off unlikely areas not included in this list. Clearly, the strategy had been decided on long before.

If the fleet failed, and the Spanish troops did come ashore, the soldiers present advised: "That at his landing he may be impeached, if conveniently it may be done." In short, the debatable forward strategy of "fight them on the beaches and the landing grounds" instead of "drawing them to a head" and smashing them later with a concentration. The debate was exactly the same as that among the German High Command in Normandy in 1944. But there was no disagreement about what was to be done if the enemy established his beachhead and broke out; the defenders were to employ "scorched earth" tactics. "If he march forward, we advise that the country be driven so as no victuals remain to them but such as they shall carry on their backs, which will be small." There was to be a measure also of guerilla warfare, "that he may be kept waking with perpetual alarms." The policy of "defend the landing" was later qualified by the injunction: "but in no case should any battle be adventured until such time as divers lieutenants be assembled to make a gross army, except upon a special advantage." But how much chance was there of that?

Sir Walter Raleigh later put his thoughts on paper, summing up the problem: "Great difference I know there is, between such a country as France is, strengthened with many fortified places; and this of ours, where our ramparts are but the bodies of men. I say this, that an army transported over the sea, and the landing place left to the choice of the invader, cannot be resisted on the coast of England, without a fleet to impeach it; except that every creek, port, or sandy bay, had a powerful army in each of them, to make opposition. I hope that this question shall never come to trial; Her Majesty's many movable forts will forbid the experience. I take it to be the wisest way, to employ good ships on the sea, and not trust to any intrenchment upon the shore."

Drake went much further than that. He wrote to Walsyngham, the Secretary of State: "I assure your honour the like preparation was never heard of or known, as the King of Spain hath and daily maketh to invade England. Prepare in England strongly and most by sea. Stop him now and stop him ever." He did not wish to wait until the Armada was in the Channel, arrayed in battle order; he believed in striking when and where the enemy was weakest—on his own coast, while he was still assembling. In spite of his success at Cadiz, this was still regarded in some quarters as reckless and revolutionary thinking. But Drake knew that if you waited until you were fully prepared, the enemy was likely to be ready, too. As late as May, 1588, he was urging in vain: "The advantage of time and place in all martial actions is half a victory; which being lost is irrecoverable."

This indeed was the general opinion of the English seamen, whose knowledge of their enemy was necessarily greater than that of the land men. One of them had already advised a raid on the Spanish fishing fleets at the Newfoundland banks. " Give me five vessels," he had written to the Queen, " and I will go out and sink them all, and the galleons shall rot in Cadiz harbour for want of hands to sail them. But decide, Madam, and decide quickly. Time flies, and will not return. The wings of man's life are plumed with the feathers of death."

On 21 December, 1587, four weeks after the Council of War, and shortly before the death of Santa Cruz, Elizabeth appointed her own commander-in-chief at sea. " Know ye that we, reposing special trust and confidence in the fidelity, prudence, zeal, experience, circumspection, industry and diligence of our belowed Councillor, Charles, Lord Howard, Baron of Effingham, knight of our illustrious order of the Garter, High Admiral of England, Ireland, Wales, and of the dominions and islands thereof . . . ran the flattering preamble to Howard's commission, at least as flowery as Philip's appointing Medina Sidonia " Captain General of the Ocean." Both men were appointed to the supreme command for the same reason; they were noblemen of such seniority that they would be unquestioningly obeyed and could therefore impose a unity upon their forces. Otherwise the more bold and skilful seamen, of whom there were many on both sides, would tend to jealous professional quarrels. Howard, however, had this much advantage over the Duke of Medina Sidonia, that the position of Lord Admiral of England was his by right of birth; he was the ninth member of his family to hold the appointment. He had grown up with the right background, could understand the technical issues, and was not incapable of giving swift and sound decisions.

But, like Medina Sidonia, who was to find his ships plagued with artificial partitions and unofficial beds, he began the campaign on a mundane level. He issued a fleet order concerning lighted candles. Reporting a small fire in the galleon *Elizabeth Bonaventure*, he wrote: " There were two poor knaves that came from Chester, that strived for a place to hang up their netting for to lie in, and the one of them had a piece of candle in his hand, and in striving, the candle fell down where there lay some oakum. It might have bred some mischief, but it was quickly put out."

The next mishap was more serious; one man was killed at Portsmouth and others wounded, when a gun in one of Drake's ships burst during target practice. Howard had to be very tactful with his great subordinate and second-in-command; no one in Spain had ever heard of Howard, whereas the name of Drake was a legend. Indeed, Spaniards spoke of " Drake " when they meant the English fleet, so awe-inspiring was his reputation.

Howard, therefore, asked Walsyngham, the Secretary of State: "If you would write a word or two unto him to spare his powder, it would do well." Still new to his command, he had in fact touched on one of the two major deficiencies of the fleet, which had been worrying the professionals. But by 1 February, 1588, they had "put him in the picture," and he was writing to Walsyngham from his temporary flagship, the *White Bear*: "I do warrant you our state is well enough known to them in Flanders, and as we were a terror to them at first coming out, so do they now make but little reckoning of us; for they know we are like bears tied to stakes. . . . I have a good company here with me, so that if the Queen's Majesty will not spare her purse, they will not spare their lives."

On the same day, Drake's old partner, John Hawkyns, also fired on Walsyngham: "If we stand at this point, in a mammering and at a stay, we consume, and our Commonwealth doth utterly decay."

The ships were being rationed for so limited a period that they could hardly put to sea, let alone sail down to the enemy coasts and smash the Armada at source, as Drake and Hawkyns wanted to do, and as they soon convinced Howard he must do. Nor was there anything like enough powder and shot for the gun battles that Drake intended to fight, for the full implications of his methods were not yet understood in London. And rumour after rumour came into the country, from travellers and spies, that the Spaniards were about to sail.

On 10 March, Howard wrote: "Yesternight there came one to me of purpose from Dunkirk, who doth assure me that the Spanish forces by sea are for certain to part from Lisbon the 20th of this month with the light moon. I pray to God her Majesty do not repent this slack dealings. All that cometh out of Spain must concur to lie, or else we shall be stirred very shortly with heave and ho. As for her Majesty's four great ships, I am out of hope to see them aboard; they shall be to keep Chatham Church when they should serve the turn abroad." And as, in spite of all the Spanish preparations, peace talks were still going on, he added: "Sir, I pray you to let me hear from you how the peace is like to go on; for if I may hear in any time

46

that it is not like to come to pass, I will make some provision for the choking of Dunkirk haven."

By 30 March, Drake was urging to be gone. "With fifty sail of shipping we shall do more good upon their own coast, than a great many more will do here at home." And he stressed the need for a great effort to improve munition supplies. "The proportion in powder and shot for our great ordnance in her Majesty's ships is but for one day and a half's service, if it be begun and continued as the service may require; the powder for 24 of the merchant ships will be scant sufficient for one day's service." He could hardly break off a battle far out at sea, he hinted, in order to return to the Tower of London for more powder and shot.

Equally serious was the food situation. On 8 April, Howard wrote to Burghley, the Lord High Treasurer of England, in terms that no one has since dared to use to the Treasury. "We shall be now victualled, beginning the 20th of this April, unto the 18th of May, at which time the last month's victual doth end; and by the advertisements that giveth the largest time for the coming out of the Spanish forces, is the midst of May, being the 15th. Then (i.e., on that day) we have three days victual. If it be fit to be so, it passeth my reason." The "advertisements," or intelligence reports, were accurate enough, surprisingly so, when the delays peculiar to sailing ships are considered, and Howard, unlike some Elizabethan apologists since, was taking no excuses from the Treasury. "I think since ever there were ships in this realm it was never heard of but a month's victual was prepared. King Harry, her Majesty's father, never made a lesser proportion of supply than 6 weeks."

Here was the point of giving Howard the chief command; no mariner, no matter how brilliant, could talk to the Government like that. Howard could, because he was one of them. The Queen even began to consider the possibility of a spoiling attack, and asked Drake how he would propose to do it. But his answer was apparently so reckless—sail at once, with the ships he had and the food he had, and have reinforcements and supplies sent after him—that the Government hesitated.

On 28 May, Giles Napper, an escaped slave from the Spanish galleys, arrived at Portsmouth. He had an extraordinary story

47

to tell, of capture from a ship of Sir Thomas Leighton's by the Turks, of two-and-a-half years slaving at a Turkish oar; and then capture by the Spaniards, and one-and-a-half years servitude in a Spanish galley, after which the Spaniards had tried to sign him on as a mariner on a voluntary basis. He had got away from Spain in a French ship on 26 April, and could report that the departure of the Great Armada was imminent, if it had not already sailed. The talk among the " common people " in the Spanish ships was, " that if they set their foot on land, they hope to find some friends, and look for help from the Scots; but that they think the Englishmen will be hard for them at sea."

On the day that Giles Napper got home, Howard was still forced to plague Burghley about the rationing situation. "Your Lordship shall understand that we have scarcely three weeks victuals left. My good Lord, there is here the gallentest company of captains, soldiers, and mariners that I think ever was seen in England. It were a pity they should lack meat, when they are so desirous to spend their lives in her Majesty's service. God send us the happiness to meet with the Spaniards before our men on the land discover them, for I fear me a little sight of the enemy will fear the land men much."

The letter was dated from Plymouth, 28 May. The Armada had already been nine days at sea.

CHAPTER FOUR

The Most Fortunate Armada

The Armada Sails—May-June, 1588

THE FIRST three weeks of May were a happy time for Don Alonso Perez de Gusman el Bueno, Marquis of San Lucar de Barramada, Count of Niebla, Duke of Medina Sidonia, Captain General of the Ocean, and commander-in-chief of *La Felicissima Armada*—the " Fortunate," or " Most Happy " invasion force of Spain, as it was styled officially. No one claimed authoritatively that it was " Invincible," but the Duke was beginning to feel that, after all, it might be. Two months hard toil had turned a motley collection of shipping and men, drawn from all over the Latin world, into a united, disciplined force. From the 1st to the 18th May (the 11th to the 28th by Spanish reckoning),* the ships were casting off from Lisbon quaysides and passing down the river in groups, as the wind and their degree of readiness allowed, to the mouth of the Tagus. The war galleys were proving most useful—as tugs and hufflers. They could push the clumsy sailing ships with their bows; point them in the right direction, or get them out of trouble, if the wind shifted. On the 18th, the Duke wrote: " The weather is not good, and a N.N.W. wind is blowing, but I have sent some ships down the river, and some more went down today with a great deal of trouble. They are at anchor on the bar. If a land wind blows tomorrow morning I will go down with the rest of the fleet. Not an hour has been, or shall be, lost."

He was feeling easier in his mind about the fighting, too. The experienced Admirals under his command had been feeding him with ideas, and in place of an unwelcome blank, he thought he knew now what to expect, and exactly how to deal with it.

*There was 10 days' difference between the " Old Style " calendar still used by the English and the " New Style " employed by the Spaniards, which is identical to our present-day calendar. All dates given here are in " Old Style." For conversion, add 10 days.

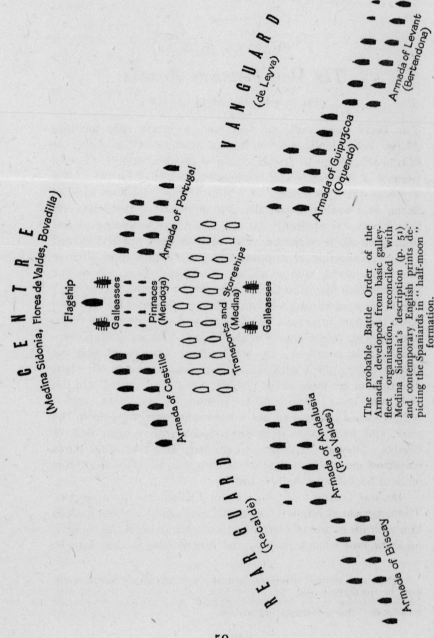

VANGUARD
(de Leyva)

Armada of Guipuzcoa
(Oquendo)

Armada of Levant
(Bertendona)

CENTRE
(Medina Sidonia, Flores de Valdes, Bovadilla)

Flagship

Galleasses

Armada of Portugal

Pinnaces
(Mendoza)

Armada of Castille

Transports and Storeships
(Medina)

Galleasses

REAR GUARD
(Recalde)

Armada of Andalusia
(P. de Valdes)

Armada of Biscay

The probable Battle Order of the Armada, developed from basic galley-fleet organisation, reconciled with Medina Sidonia's description (p. 51) and contemporary English prints depicting the Spaniards in "half-moon" formation.

A constant stream of reports from agents in England showed that the enemy fleet was in three separate sections: Drake's formidable force at Plymouth, a smaller force in the Straits of Dover, and a mass of ships fitting out in the Thames as reinforcements. Men were being pressed into them from the streets, those to become soldiers being given red coats, those to be sailors blue coats. The enemy would be burdened by raw recruits, too. Drake would be a fool to fight when he first saw the Armada; it was much more likely that he would merely follow the Spaniards up-Channel, until in sight of the Dover force, and then both English forces would combine in an attack on the Armada from front and rear simultaneously. The Spanish Admirals had explained how, by adopting a fleet formation closely based on that used by galley forces, this combined attack could be met. " I have taken every precaution," wrote the Duke. " Either of the two horns of our formation, with their supports, and two of the galleasses which accompany the first four ships, would be able to cope with one of the enemy's fleets; whilst I with the rest of our vessels leading, could deal with the fleet in front of us, my centre being supported by the vessels I have appointed for the purpose, and the other two galleasses which are attached to my flagship."

The English would suffer severely in any close combat, being over-topped by the higher Spanish ships, and vastly out-numbered in soldiers. For the preliminary horror, just before boarders were let loose into them, a rain of stones would be hurled down from the high Spanish decks, poops, and fighting tops. In his Fleet Orders, the Duke had already ordained that "each ship will carry two shallop loads of casting stones, to be made use of during a fight."

In his mind flickered pictures of English ships, broken, disabled, captured, floating on the still waters as Spanish prizes, while the mighty Armada swept on to its junction with Parma; which would decide everything. Now, he was as confident as the most exacting ruler could wish. " The opinions of those whom I have consulted here is that the best course would be to break up the enemy's sea force first. When this is done, as

I hope it will be, if the enemy will meet me, the rest will be safe and easy. I will redouble my care, that if the enemy will face us he will meet the fate he always has done when he has encountered Your Majesty's forces." When the Armada finally sailed on 19 May, the Duke noted that "all the men are in good health and spirits, ready for the fight if the enemy will face us." The enormous force of shipping, the tens of thousands of bright-armed men, the bugles, the trumpets, the ritual, the deference to himself, the commander of it all, had not been without effect even on so self-effacing a man as Medina Sidonia. He had now, for a moment, reached the mental state of that infantry officer who had written from Lisbon: "I do fear that seeing us they will instantly yield and agree to all that the King will demand of them, for that the King's force is marvellous great as well by sea as by land."

There was a flash and a cloud of smoke from the fleet flagship, Medina Sidonia's galleon *San Martin*, followed seconds later by the sound of the explosion rolling across the sea. In all the ships, crisp orders were barked; men ran to be ready at the anchor cables and at the rigging. Soldiers came up from below, where they had been making themselves as snug as possible on the troop decks, cumbering them with bedding, trunks, and boxes, with much argument as to seniority and its privileges. There could be no fatal quarrels because the Duke, foreseeing strife in so mixed a force, had forbidden them to wear their daggers. It was a moving moment for everyone, this final departure into the unknown. Behind and to starboard lay the known, the coast of Portugal; now, they were sailing into the future. How many would come back? How rich would be the plunder? How great the fame?

A bugle shrilled out from the flagship, sad and lonely across the tossing wastes of water, echoing one part of their mood.

The capstans ground, hauling in the dripping anchor cables, wet and slimy from the deep. The flagship shook out her sails. The rest followed suit and began to form up, each ship in its allotted space. The white wakes tumbled astern, as the vessels heeled, under the wind, came alive and began to move forward —to England.

The wind was light, and the Duke was still a man of iron. As evening fell, the ships one by one came to leeward of the plunging galleon *San Martin*, to ask for orders and the watchword for the night; from the great ships, bugles sounded the salute and every man, at attention, cheered twice on the word of command. From the lesser ships, which had no bugles, the twittering of fifes preceded the disciplined cheering. As the sun sank into the Atlantic, and last light dulled the waves, the masthead lookouts began to count sails. If they counted 130, all was well. If there were more, it might be the great Drake closing in on them. The captains had memorised the signals. Dip the main topsail twice and fire a gun, to give the alarm. When it became possible to count the unknown sails, there were two signals. For four ships or less: take in maintopsail, hoist flag over its yard, fire one gun. For more than four: take in maintopsail, hoist flag to mainmast head, fire two guns in succession. The lookouts strained their eyes to count strange sail; but there was none. So they settled down to watch the flagship's stern lantern. If a second light appeared there, and a gun was fired, that meant she was altering course. If no gun was fired, but two fresh lights appeared, one half way up the rigging, that meant that she was shortening sail, and that they must conform also. The captain of any ship which got ahead of the flagship could expect to be severely disciplined.

The Duke's orders for bad weather were inflexible. " No ship belonging to or accompanying the Armada, shall separate from it without my permission. If any should be forced out of the course by tempest, before arriving off Cape Finisterre, they will make direct for that point, or for Corunna. Any infraction of this order shall be punished by death and forfeiture. On leaving Cape Finisterre the course will be to the Scilly Isles, and ships must try to sight the islands from the south, taking great care with their soundings. If on this voyage any ships should get separated, they are not to return to Spain on any account, the punishment for disobedience being forfeiture and death with disgrace; but are to continue on the course. If on their arrival at the Scillies the Armada be behind them, they will cruise off the place; or if it has passed them, they will make for Mounts Bay, between Cape Longnose (Land's End) and the Lizard." With such splendid panoply, and with such inflexible determination, did Medina Sidonia undertake his unwanted task.

The orders, however, had been drafted on shipboard in the Tagus, comfortably moored to the quay. The quiet lapping of the waves against the hull was almost soothing, even when the wind blew strongly, as it did in the first week of May, causing Medina Sidonia at the time to write: "God ordains all things, and He has not seen fit to send us weather for the sailing of the Armada; it is as boisterous and bad as if it were December."

The same wind at sea was a different matter. The bows rolled and plunged, lifting bursts of white spray back across the deck; the masts swept back and forth across the horizon, the wind roaring through the loose, flying rigging; nothing in the high-perched, tottering stern cabins stayed still for a moment, unless it was lashed down, and to walk a man had to balance carefully, or hold on to something firm. In the low troop decks, the situation was indescribable. The soldiers, seeing to their own comfort, had brought masses of kit aboard; many of them had embarked truckle beds, instead of hammocks; and all this gear was loose, slithering backwards and forwards on the heaving, vomit-slimy decks, colliding with the guns run in behind closed ports, smashing into the piles of ready-use ammunition and powder bags, bringing down rows of stacked pikes and other weapons. Of course, to the sailors it was nothing. But to the land men—and to the commander of the entire enterprise—it was hell without end. It would not cease, could not cease, until the whole expedition was over and the Armada safe at anchor in the land-locked Thames. The men longed for England in a way they had not done before. If Drake came and drowned them all, it would not matter. Nothing mattered, if only the world would be still for once.

During this period, while the men were still getting their sea-legs, there were few entries in the "relations" and diaries of the soldiers. One officer, Pedro Estrade, sailing in the *San Marcos*, a galleon of the Armada of Portugal, summed it up later. "We were with foul weather until 4 June, that we saw Cape Finisterre, whereas we were turning up and down till Sunday the nineth of the same. Then entered the flagship *San Martin* and some other of our ships into the Groyne, and the rest kept along the coast." Medina Sidonia had had enough. He had written to the King on 31 May: "Provisions are bad and short, the hulks slow, the weather contrary, and a long voyage may be anticipated. The victuals are so rotten and stinking that many have been thrown overboard to save the men from pestilence. I beg of you to send fresh supplies after us." After a week, he is telling the King that the pilots advise him to put into Corunna or Ferrol, but he wants to avoid this, to prevent the soldiers and sailors deserting, "as usual." Next day, 9 June, his letter to the King is actually date-lined Corunna, and he gives the dismal news that he is there with a few ships only. The rest of the Armada is still at sea; but he expects them to enter port in the morning. The next news he has to give, is that those outside were caught in a storm during the night, and scattered into various ports all over the three provinces of Biscay, Asturias, and Galicia. That some are wrecked or damaged, and others lost or missing. By 14 June, an awful thought had occurred to the Duke. Some of the missing ships may have obeyed his own inflexible Fleet Order to go on the Scillies, or even Mount's Bay, on pain of "death with disgrace," there to rendezvous with their inflexible commander. They might not suspect that the flagship had been the first to give up.

An even more horrible thought presented itself. The English, or even the French, would soon hear what had happened, and might sally out to make short work of the stray Spanish ships. He immediately sent out "two very swift oar pataches, well armed, with an experienced ensign in each, to order any ships that may be there, at the Scillies, to return hither." Then he began to compose a long and lamentable letter to the King, who should have sacked him on the spot, the moment he received it. "The weather, though it is June, is as wild as in December. No one remembers such a season. It is the more

55

strange since we are on the business of the Lord, and some reason there must be for what has befallen us. I obeyed your orders, and now I am here in Corunna with the ships dispersed and the force remaining to me inferior to the enemy. The crews are sick, and grow daily worse from bad food and water. Most of our provisions have perished, and we have not enough for more than two months' consumption. The men are out of spirit. We are no longer strong. Do not deceive yourself into thinking that we are equal to the work before us. We are now going against a powerful kingdom with only the weak force of the Prince of Parma and myself." That was the gist of it; the actual letter just goes on and on, page after page. It was the second letter he had written to the King that day; the first having concluded with a paragraph describing the company of infantry which he had paraded on the Corunna quayside to prevent his force deserting.

The King must have received, much at the same time, a letter written on 12 June by the Duke of Parma, who referred to optimistic letters received by him from Medina Sidonia. " He (Medina Sidonia) seems to have persuaded himself that I may be able to go out and meet him with these boats. These things cannot be, and in the interest of Your Majesty's service I should be very anxious if I thought the Duke were depending on them." He then went on to hint, most politely, that the King's operational orders were not always as clear as they might be. " There must be no mistake about my having the 6,000 Spaniards from the Armada. With regard to my going out to join him, he will plainly see that with these little, low, flat boats, built for these rivers and not for the sea, I cannot diverge from the short direct passage across which has been agreed on. Otherwise the armed English or rebel ships could destroy us with the greatest of ease. This was one of the principal reasons which moved Your Majesty to lay down the precise and prudent orders you did, that your Spanish fleet should assure us the passage across. . . ." It was a smooth but determined letter, for Parma did not intend to allow either the King's woolly strategy or the well-meaning bungling of Medina Sidonia to put paid to his fine army in half an hour, which would certainly be its fate if it ventured out unprotected. The English Admiral, Sir William Wynter, who was waiting outside for Parma in his flagship *Vanguard* was of exactly the same opinion, for, on 20 June, eight days after the date of Parma's letter, he wrote to Walsyngham: " I should live until I were young again ere the Prince (Parma) would venture to set his ships forth; his forces dare not come to the seas." In fact, he said more than plainly that the Dutch ships alone, or the English ships alone, could keep Parma penned in harbour. In short, that he was wasting his time; his ships might better be employed elsewhere.

The snarl almost leapt out of the paper, as he jeered at the Queen's peace negotiations with Parma, then in progress, and suggested instead: " If we did make a sharp war out of hand (entertaining Scotland as our friend) and to spare the pride of our backs and some of our glutton's fare I do not doubt (by God's grace) we should then make Her Majesty's enemies come to reason shortly." He was speaking for virtually everyone in the Queen's navy, and indeed, every Englishman at sea. They were raging to be away for the Spanish coast, even though they had rations for less than a week. Had the Queen neglected her diplomacy to let them go, at this time, there must have been a Spanish disaster of some magnitude.

For the Armada's transports and storeships—the hulks or *urcas*—were parading up and down between Scilly and Cornwall, looking for their Captain General of the Ocean, who was not there, as he said he would be, but sitting in Corunna dealing out severe punishments to common deserters. The slow, weakly armed hulks were essential to the whole enterprise, for they carried the heavier gear of the army, as well as the reserve stores, which included 8,000 leather bottles, 5,000 pairs of shoes, 11,000 pairs of sandals, 20 gun-carriages for the land batteries, plus 3,500 cannon balls, 40 artillery mules, 7,000 harquebusses, 10,000 pikes, the army's transport requirements of waggons, limbers, harness, and so on.

It must have been either on the 18th or 19th of June that the bark from Mousehole in Cornwall had speech with the French flyboat which warned him that the Spanish fleet was on the coast. The Frenchman, to substantiate his story, added the detail that, not only had he spoken to the Spaniards, but to some Englishmen who were aboard them. They had told him they had been kept in Spain for two years, after their ships had been seized. Not believing this tall tale, the Cornish captain had kept on for France until he had " encountered with nine sail of great ships between Scilly and Ushant, bearing in North-East with the coast of England."

His arithmetic was probably right, for one of the two pinnaces that Medina Sidonia had sent to Scilly, to issue the recall, and got back half-swamped, reported seeing nine Spanish ships near there. The two flags the Cornishman saw spread were, in fact, the Armada code for "Strange sail in sight"; but he reported them larger than they were, and did not, of course, know that they were store ships and hospital ships. But the total number of Spaniards in the area was much greater, for the separated portion of the Armada had become separated among themselves, and they were mostly beating about near the first rendezvous south of Scilly. And, of course, there were the two oared pinnaces sent after them.

The largest Spanish group consisted of a dozen *urcas* and some other ships, led by the *almiranta* of the hulks, the vice-flagship of the transport squadron, the *San Salvador*, 650 Spanish tons. More like 500 by the English reckoning. According to her log, this group lost sight of the seasick Duke and the warships on 6 June. Undeterred either by rough weather or the thought of Drake's Western fleet of 60 sail which might come up over the horizon at any moment, they plugged on slowly for England until the morning of 18 June, when they saw sails near Ushant. They gave chase until well within sight of the French coast; then, towards nightfall, turned north for the Scillies, pursued by six ships, presumably French, which came out after them and fired on the rearmost Spaniard, the 500-ton *San Pedro el Menor*. France was then in a ferment of civil strife, and no one, English or Spaniard, could know on whose side a French ship might be. Apart from that, there were always privateers, who were on no one's side but their own.

For the next three days, there was the sporadic rumble of gunfire out to sea. On 20 June, one of Howard's fleet of pinnaces which were patrolling between Scilly and Ushant reported two additional groups of Spaniards, of six and 15 sail respectively, the latter obviously that led by the *San Salvador*. According to Howard's report, " one Simons of Exeter gave advertisement that he was chased with a fleet of great ships, having some of his men hurt with shot from them; escaping their hands, landing in Cornwall, and came post to Plymouth unto the Lord Admiral." He added, in a letter to the Queen, " Seven of the ships they met withal were of 800 and 900 tons. The others were Biscayans of 300. It is very likely that this stormy weather hath parted the fleet." And he chose the moment to ram home again the futility of defending England on the English coast with sailing ships dependent on the wind; the wind which brought Spaniards into the Channel would take him down to the Isle of Wight. In any case, he could not move; the new rations had only just arrived, and although " no man shall sleep nor eat " until they were aboard, he would not be able to sail until the following day.

On 20 June, the same day that Simon of Exeter's pinnace had closely reconnoitred the various groups of Spaniards, a Spanish pinnace was making a reconnaissance of the English coast. It was a fast, oared patache, commanded by Ensign Esquivel; one of the two sent to recall the missing ships. Leaving Corunna on 17 June, it had come up with several Spanish units near the Scillies, given them the Duke's order to return, and then carried on towards the furthest rendezvous he had appointed so optimistically—the distinctive St. Michael's Mount. "At daybreak," reported Esquivel, " we sighted St. Michael's Bay and Cape Longnose, five or six leagues distant. We took in all sail and rowed inland some four leagues. We then stood by for night to come on, and a sail passed to leeward of us at two leagues distance. I wished to chase her, but the pilots opposed it, as it was late, and we were uncertain of catching her. The general opinion was that, being so near the land, we should hardly fail to catch a fisher-boat during the night. The wind then rose in the S.W., with heavy squalls of rain, and such a violent gale that during the night we had winds from every quarter of the compass. We did our best by constant tacking to keep off the land."

At dawn, the wind firmly settled in the north, and the patache was forced to run before it, the rising gale raising waves which poured water into the frail craft. A pipe of wine and two butts of drinking water were thrown overboard, to lighten her, but at four o'clock in the afternoon still higher waves culminated in a monster comber which swept the pinnace from end to end. " We were flush with the water, and almost lost," wrote Esquivel, " but by great effort of all hands the water was baled out, and everything thrown overboard. We lowered the mainmast on to the deck, and so we lived through the night under a closely reefed foresail." They fled to the security of Corunna harbour and the Duke of Medina Sidonia in his port-bound flagship.

On this same day, 21 June, the log of the *San Salvador* recorded that a " violent N.N.E. wind had sprung up "; but, although they rolled terribly, the bulky transports were not in danger. Indeed, they were ready to fight, when they saw sails coming from the direction of the Irish Sea. "At daybreak we sighted two ships which were emerging from St. George's Channel between Cape Longnose and the seven stones." As they came up and began to pass the Spaniards, two of the hulks bore down on them. The 400-ton *Gato*, with 22 sailors and 40 soldiers aboard, drove alongside one with a grinding of bulwarks, and the Spanish boarders poured down into her. For a moment there was a desperate melee on deck, before the crew surrendered, with two of their number dead and another mortally wounded. The merchant ship had been so shattered by the shock from the heavier vessel, that she heeled over and began to sink. She disappeared under the white-capped waves, with the wounded man still aboard.

Meanwhile, the 250-ton *Paloma Blanca*, with 20 sailors and 56 soldiers, had grappled the second merchantman less violently, but breaking her main-yardarm and starting her planks, so that although she was taken in tow she was in a sinking condition by nightfall and had to be cast off, according to the Spanish version of the affair. Out of this ship came four prisoners, but at the cost of two broken ribs to the Spanish Admiral, who found re-boarding his own ship in those wild seas a difficult matter. When the prisoners were questioned, it was found that the ships were not English at all.

Both had come from Dublin, with a dozen men aboard each. One ship was Irish, bound for Biscay in Spain with a cargo of wheat and tanned hides. The other was Scots, bound for France with a cargo of coal and two refugee friars, a Bernardin and a Franciscan, who were fleeing from the English troops in Ulster, " where two important monasteries had been burnt in the last six weeks; the friars being burnt as well. These two had fled to the woods. They said they were escaping from terrible cruelties," recorded the writer of the log of the *San Salvador*. " Only to meet others on the high seas," he might have added, but didn't. In any event, it was a Spanish victory at sea, the only one the Armada was to have. And it was won by the mule-ships and spare footwear transports of the store fleet.

Next day, on 22 June, the English fleet saw its first action of the Armada campaign. Admiral Lord Henry Seymour who, with Sir William Wynter, was conducting the blockade of Dunkirk from his flagship the *Rainbow*, saw two small vessels slip out of Parma's invasion port and crowd on all sail for Gravelines. The big *Rainbow*, with her 250 men, could not close that shallow coast, with its treacherous banks; but the light ships could. " Two of our pinnaces chased them, with the discharging of some saker shot, and yet they would not strike, till at last one of our shot struck down the mainmast of one of their vessels, being a French bottom belonging to Calais, and had Monsieur Gourdan's hand for his pass." Gourdan was Governor of Calais. Here was another case of mistaken identity! But Seymour was furious.

" I demanded what he meant, not to strike his sails and come to the Queen's ships, knowing us so well. He answered that he took us for the King of Navarre's fleet, making himself ignorant of what to do. I replied that if the Duke of Parma, or the Duke of Guise, should do the like, I would sink them, or they should distress me; adding further that my Sovereign Lady was able to defend her country against the Holy League, besides able to master any civil discord; and so dismissed them, with some little choler."

The other ship, whatever she was, was no luckier. " He ran himself hard aground right over against Gravelines, and they voided themselves out of their vessel, wading through the water, and cut their sails from the masts, taking them also away. My boat, which I manned with some shot (musketeers), came upon their skirts, but a little too late; yet came there very near a hundred men, horse and foot, but durst not approach us. By which time our men had some little leisure to cut down their masts, and would have fired her, but that suddenly the wind arose at North and by East, enforcing us to weigh for Blackness, where we anchored, with marvellous foul weather, some thirty hours."

Seymour added a postscript, to explain that he had dictated the letter, because " I have strained my hand with hauling of a rope "; yet another casualty of flag rank. The two sea skirmishes, the Spanish battle by boarding, and the English gun action, were, as it happened, exactly representative of the different tactics which the two main opposed fleets hoped to employ in the great Channel conflict to come. They explain it better than any learned treatise could. The rapid and violent fate of the two ships which tried to get out of Dunkirk, make very clear the reason for Parma's reluctance to emerge with his clumsy, flat-bottomed barges before the Armada was firmly in control of the crossing. According to Seymour, whose business it was to know what Parma had, " His own private strength (without the assistance of Spain or France) doth not exceed 40 sails of flyboats and 220 bylanders." A " bylander " was a Dutch river boat, virtually a landing barge. "A time must be to land them and a time to back them," he adds. "All I fear is they will never offer themselves. We have twice showed ourselves at Gravelines, desiring nothing more than to suffer them come out, rather than to stop them in by sinking vessels with stones or timber, which will be recovered again upon every ebb, and will serve them for their strength and better fortification."

Seymour knew it, Wynter knew it, Parma knew it; the King of Spain, it seems, did not; the Duke of Medina Sidonia definitely did not. He did not allow himself to. He was now trying to convince himself that all he had to do, really, was get as far as Nieuport and Dunkirk, where Parma would take the whole burden off his shoulders. And the King, instead of dismissing

DRAKE'S COMMISSION TO RAID CADIZ

The Royal Letters Patent, bearing the Queen's Great Seal, giving to Drake the command of the fleet fitted out in 1587 "For the honour and safetie of our Realmes and Domynions". More than thirty Spanish ships were burned or sunk, and the sailing of the Great Armada delayed by a full year

Map of the Isle of Wight, drawn by Baptista Boazia in 1591, showing English galleons and a galley. The shaded area by the compass points represents the Owers bank, the submerged part of the Selsey peninsula, as it was at the time of the Armada.

him with a convenient excuse, such as illness, of which Medina Sidonia had complained, instead sent him an eminently reasonable and, for once, burningly eloquent letter designed to spur him onwards to the Channel. The unwilling sailor had to go to sea once more.

CHAPTER FIVE

The Blood of his Beheaded Mother

The Armada Sails Again—July, 1588

THE KING began by saying, " His Majesty continues firm in his
resolution to carry forward the task." Then he repeated the
public line he was taking: that the enterprise was "least of all
influenced by motives of personal interest "; the " chief consideration being to defend God's cause." If the affair was abandoned
now, what capital the Protestants would make out of it! " The
enemies of the Catholic religion would interpret the damage
inflicted by the storm as authority for their heresies, twisting
in their favour God's tolerance." This was shrewd, for the
Protestants did in the end actually strike a medal, to com-
memorate the scattering of the Armada by the winds of God.

" Of the enemy's ships, some are old; others small, and
inferior to ours in strength and general excellence; do not forget
the numerical superiority of our crews, and the long experience
enjoyed by many of them. The enemy's crews, on the other hand,
consist of novices, drawn from the common people—a tumultuous
crowd, lacking military discipline." There was a grain of truth
here, but, awfully, it was not the whole truth. That would not
be known until the two fleets engaged in battle, for fleets such
as this had never clashed before; there was little experience to go
on. And what evidence there was, drawn from Santa Cruz's
victory at the Azores, supported the King's expressed views.

Having, as perhaps he thought, heartened the Duke in what
was essentially a difficult and disputable technical matter, Philip
went on to show that, at this juncture, England stood entirely
alone, stripped of all allies. " Had aid come from France, it
might have been formidable; but they are in no condition there
to send help owing to their internal feuds. The rebels in
Holland and Zeeland care more for their own interests. The
German protestants are at most only able to create some slight

64

diversion which cannot avert the blows which the Armada will deliver. The Danish king, the enemy's most powerful supporter, who could have reinforced the English fleet, is dead, and that news has caused hope to fade in England of receiving help from that quarter. As for the King of Scotland, no help can be looked for from him, for the blood of his beheaded mother is not yet congealed. One might rather expect that the Scottish forces would themselves move to attack the English from their side. Thus there appears no possibility of considerable reinforcements or help reaching the enemy from any source whatever."

"From its present anchorage," he added pointedly, "the Armada can, with six days of fair weather, reach the appointed place. If it were now to remain in Corunna, this would be construed as a proof of our weakness, and, far from enhancing our prestige at the treaty negotiations (if, indeed, we were working to conclude a treaty), would provide the enemy with an opportunity to rise to greater heights of insolence."

The letter reached Medina Sidonia the next day, when it found the King's Captain General of the Ocean in more happy mood. Most of the ships had made port that day, some with severe gale damage, but the major catastrophe had been avoided; none had been snapped up by the English as a result of the Duke's desertion of them. The narrow escape from such a disaster made him almost gay. He replied: "Those who go down to the sea in ships are exposed to these vicissitudes." Almost, he was playing the veteran seaman. He even managed to forget the rather depressing reports of the Council of War he had held on 17 June.

Don Jorge Manrique, the Inspector-General, had stated: "Although it was asserted that 27,884 men had been shipped in the Armada, he found that only 22,500 were effectives, after deducting general and field officers, staff, cabin, and ship's boys, gentlemen adventurers, officers of justice, hospital staff, artillery officers and ministers of religion, as well as the oarsmen of the galleys and galleasses."

Don Pedro de Valdes, commander of the Armada of Andalusia, had reported: "He had gone round his own squadron, and although he found they had a store of biscuit for three months, part of it was in bad condition. There was more than enough wine for three months, but the bacon, cheese, fish, sardines, and vegetables were all rotten and of very little use."

All those present had concurred; they "wished to mention the great complaints which both soldiers and sailors were making about the food. With the exception of the bread (and that is very bad), the wine, rice, and some of the pulse, the victuals were of no use whatever, for the men would not eat them."

The King responded with commendable vigour to that report, sending his Secretary, Andrés de Alba, "post-haste to the city of Corunna," with sweeping powers to investigate the obvious corruption, not merely of the food, but of the contractors who supplied it; to punish; and to put right. The English, fighting from home bases, might be able to make do with rations for a short period; but the Armada could not, and this was a serious matter.

Morale, also, was not good. On 21 June, Medina Sidonia reported to the King: " The closest possible watch is being kept on our soldiers and sailors, guards being posted all along the shore, and in the roads and passages by which they might escape." On 1 July, Admiral Juan Martinez de Recalde, commanding the Biscay squadron, and Vice-Admiral of the Great Armada, wrote to the King: "I hear great complaints about the command of those companies which are conferred upon quite young fellows because they are gentlemen. Very few of them, therefore, are soldiers, or know what to do, and their officers the same. This is greatly to the prejudice of Your Majesty's treasury, as there are companies with very few men in them."

Medina Sidonia reported that reinforcements reaching the Armada were of a poor standard: " The 400 Galician soldiers sent by the Count de Lemos, and some that came from Monterey, are so useless that they are no good, even for pioneers. Besides this they are nearly all married and have large families; and are, indeed, absolutely unserviceable old men. Their wives have been coming in with their troubles and lamentations to such an extent that it goes against my conscience to ship the men. The captains themselves have refused to have anything to do with them, as it is evident that all the use they would be is to die on board the ships and take up space. Not a soul of them knows what a harquebuss is, or any other weapon, and already they are more dead than alive; some of them have not eaten anything for two days. Under the circumstances, therefore, I have thought it best to send them all away and they have gone to their homes."

On 1 July, most of the storeships returned safely from their dangerous visit to the Scillies, " smelling of England," as Recalde put it. This seemed a good omen, that the slowest and weakest ships of the fleet had dared the English in their own waters with impunity. Only two of them, the *Casa de Paz Chico* and the *Paloma Blanca*, had not put into Corunna; they were still sheltering from the weather in the bay of Muxia. The *Paloma Blanca* had been in action again. After taking part in the "battle" with the Scots and Irish ships, she had been chased by an English ship, which took her for a merchantman, not realising that she had a company of infantry aboard. " The hulk allowed the Englishman to come up with her and then discharged a volley of artillery and musketry which made the enemy retire," reported Medina Sidonia. " The hulk would have chased her, but for an accident that happened. One of the soldier's powder-flasks caught fire and fell on some cartridges, which might have resulted in the burning of the whole ship. It was thought best to set all hands to avert this danger rather than follow up the Englishman." Incidents of this sort, similar to the case of the raw recruits with the lighted candle in the *Elizabeth Bonaventure*, were an ever-present hazard in highly-combustible wooden ships, particularly in the chaos of battle, when naked flame and gunpowder were in close proximity.

A number of ships had been badly damaged by the storm. The *Trinidad de Scala*, which put into Gijon the same day, was in such a state that in places " her planks had gaped four inches apart." On the other hand, those which had made port earlier were nearly ready again. The *Santa Maria de la Rosa*, an important unit of Admiral Oquendo's squadron, had been fitted with a new mast the previous day. Twenty-six coopers were at work, repairing the wine and water butts, which had been badly knocked about with the rolling of the ships. On 5 July, Medina Sidonia reported: " I have been round some of the ships to see to the execution of the order for demolition and throwing overboard of all the cabins, partitions, bunks, bedsteads, etc." He had ordered this to be done several times already, but the officers and men were very tenacious of their comfort. The Duke was discovering every day that it was one thing to give an order; quite another to ensure that it was carried out. "With God's help, I hope to have everything ready for sailing by tomorrow, or the day after, weather permitting. I have already had the squadrons of Diego Flores, Valdes, Oquendo, and Ojeda towed out of the harbour, and the rest will go outside tomorrow. We can then take advantage of the first fair wind to get clear away. At present a north wind is blowing, which is contrary for us. The men are in excellent spirits, and eager for an opportunity to serve Your Majesty."

A wind which kept the Spaniards in port could bring the English out; and vice versa. But if the English sailed down to the Spanish coast, to snap up the few stragglers and storm-battered hulks still trying to get back into Corunna, it was war. And the Queen's ambassadors were then in the Low Countries, talking peace to Parma; Elizabeth still hoped to avoid an all-out clash. She preferred the alarms and excursions of "cold war" to the wealth-devouring trial of strength involved in a "hot war," which might become "total," but could never be really decisive in the sense of the complete overthrow of one side or the other. Philip's advisers knew that, too. A "Report on the Expedition against England," written in 1587, which summed up the various moves available to Spain, concluded: "Even if the expedition succeeds, it will be extremely difficult to hold the Island, and the loss will be greater than the gain." The writer of the report recommended, as a course of action, that the King make peace on terms so good as to ensure the evacuation of English troops from their Dutch bases; protect his overseas possessions by building up the sailing fleet of powerful galleons; then make war later, on any pretext, however slight, from a much more advantageous position.

But the cautious Philip and the cautious Elizabeth, careful of the ultimate good of their countries, had set in motion forces which acquired their own momentum. They had set the world ringing with threats and defiances, allowed into the arena powerful armed forces straining to be off the leash. Once these were set free, the rulers had lost close control; the sequence of events would be decided by the unpredictable hazards of war. Philip, representing the power with the greatest resources, was less reluctant than the Queen to risk a clash; but even so, he thought he had curbed the dangers by instructing Medina Sidonia not to give battle in the Channel, but to proceed direct to his junction with Parma. Once this vast force was assembled in sight of the English peace commissioners, it would give point to his proposals, that the English withdraw their army from the continent.

Meanwhile the English Admirals, on short rations, were cruising up and down in the " Sleeve," the wide western entrance to the Channel, afraid that the Armada might slip past them unseen. On 6 July, the day after Medina Sidonia had reported to Philip that his squadrons were being towed out of harbour, Howard summarised for Walsyngham's benefit the events of the previous few days. " The discovery of certain of the Spanish fleet not far off from Scilly, made me to make as much haste out to sea as I could; for upon Sunday our victuals came to us, and having the wind at North-East, I would not stay for the taking in of them all; but taking in some part of them, I appointed the rest to follow with me, and so bare to Scilly, thinking to have cut off those Spanish ships from the rest of their fleet. But the wind continued not 16 hours, but turned South-South-West, that we were fain to lay it off and on in the Sleeve, and could get no further." He sent a force under Drake down to Brest, to look into the " Trade ", the inshore route along the French coast by which the Armada might come. And Drake, with his ten English fighting ships screened by three or four pinnaces, came upon the trail of the hulk *Paloma Blanca*.

The English were not relying on God to give them warning of the coming of the Spaniards. Small, fast merchant vessels were sent out on patrol, pretending to be traders sailing on their lawful occasions. Off Ushant, before reaching the " Trade," Drake came up with one of these spy ships which had been beating up and down for 10 days. Her master had not seen the Spanish fleet, but he had hailed " an Irish bark which had been with the great ships of the Spanish fleet west of Scilly.

The Spaniards had taken out of the said bark five of her most principal men, and left in her but three men and a boy. One of the greatest Spanish ships towed her at the stern by a cable, which in the night time, the wind blowing somewhat stiff, brake, and so she escaped in the storm."

This throws a revealing light on Spanish veracity and Armada seamanship, for this Irish bark was the one, bound for Biscay with wheat and hides, which had been captured by the *Paloma Blanca* and taken in tow. Her loss was reported in the log of the flagship: "During this time the sea was running immensely high from the N.E., and at nightfall the *Paloma Blanca*, seeing that the ship that had been captured was going down, was ordered by the Admiral to cast her off, which she did." That was on 21 June. But the bark, with her three men and boy, and not much worried by the "immense" seas, was still very much afloat when hailed by the English patrol boat—a "ghost ship" indeed. Nor had she been "cast off"; the tow rope had broken, that was all, they said. This was not the last time that an official Spanish report was to contain glossy deceits of this nature; the Duke's own narrative shows many examples.

In addition to his screen of disguised "listening posts," Howard was employing other stratagems for reconnaissance right up to the Spanish coast and into their harbours. "Sir, I sent a fine Spanish caravel an eight days agone to the Groyne (Corunna) to learn intelligence, such a one as would not have been mistrusted; but when she was fifty leagues on her way, this southerly wind forced her back again to us. I have divided myself here into three parts, and yet we lie within sight one of another, so as, if any of us do discover the Spanish fleet, we give notice thereof presently the one to the other, and thereupon repair and assemble together. I myself do lie in the middle of the Channel, with the greatest force. Sir Francis Drake hath 20 ships and four or five pinnaces, which lie towards Ushant; and Mr. Hawkyns, with as many more, lieth towards Scilly. Thus are we fain to do, else with this wind they might pass by and we none the wiser. Whatsoever hath been made of the Sleeve, it is another manner of thing than it was taken for; we find it by experience and daily observation to be an hundred miles over; a large room for men to look unto."

In Howard's next letter dated, significantly, 13 July, he explained to the uncomprehending landsmen in London the variety of the reconnaissance precautions, being particularly proud of the trick of using fast, Spanish-built vessels. "Both before my coming, by Sir Francis Drake, and since my coming, there hath been no day but there hath been pinnaces, Spanish caravels, flyboats, and of all sorts, sent out to discover there. The winds hath been so southerly and such foul weather as that they could not recover the coast of Spain so near as to take any of their fisher boats. My own pinnace hath been well beaten and hath had 18 great shot, which hath torn her hull and sails. We have at this time four pinnaces on the coast of Spain, and I am sending out two pinnaces more."

What he neglected to mention was that between the dates of the two letters, 6th and 13th July, he had himself been on the coast of Spain with the English fleet. On 11 July, reported Pablo de Arambur, captain of the galleon *San Juan Bautesta*, "we saw at three in the afternoon sixty or more English sails, and among them ten very large. They might have been 40 shore-leagues due North of Llanes and their course N.N.E." The course for England. One of the ships the Spaniard was looking at was the *Elizabeth Drake*, commanded by Captain Thomas Cely, still smarting from prison experiences under the Inquisition and in the Spanish galleys, and very loath to give up. "My Lord was in a good way, if God had not sent a contrary wind," he grumbled. "If the wind had holden two days and two nights longer, we had them in the Groyne."

The English now knew that they had missed catching the Spanish store ships off the Scillies by one day, having had to put back to port because the rations were expended. They had got to within two days of Corunna harbour, and the whole Armada, and again had to put back because of shortage of food, as soon as the wind changed. They had just enough to make Corunna and back; but no reserve to allow of any delays due to contrary winds. They returned, altogether out of temper, to continue the battle with the civil servants in London; with the kingdom in hazard and no victuals for the ships, all the Government could do was to plague Howard with impractical schemes for sending fishing boats to Spain to get news. Howard

71

had passed that one to Drake, and Drake's reply, suitably watered down, was enclosed with Howard's letter of 13 July: "As for fisherboats, they are neither meet nor can they endure the seas." And Howard added, pointedly, " I know not what weather you have had there, but there was never any such summer seen here on the sea. Well, Sir, I would her Majesty did know of the care and pains that is taken here of all men for her service. We must now man ourselves again, for we have cast many overboard, and a number in great extremity which we discharged. I have sent with all expedition a prest for more men." With that grim picture, of the dead men being committed to the sea, Howard ended his letter to Walsyngham, a harsh blast from the Channel.

The previous day Admiral Seymour, guarding the Narrow Seas between Dover and Calais, had written from the new galleon *Rainbow*: " Such summer season saw I never the like; what for storms and variable unsettled winds . . . with southerly winds . . . with westerly great gales. . . ." And in a sharp postscript, he warned: " The Duke (of Parma) levelleth at many marks, yet shooteth but at one, I mean Zealand; which, once obtained, his attempts for England will be far easier." Seymour could not have been more right, if he had been rummaging through Philip's files at the Escurial. The desperate fear of the seamen, that the Government would let them down, that Elizabeth would be too clever by half, once too often, pervades all the correspondence of this period. Seymour's letter was short; his point was made by a list enclosed with it, of ships which had left his fleet for various reasons. The *Daniel*, *Galleon Hutchin*, *Bark Lamb*, and *Fancy*, all of Newcastle, had sailed as escort with the cloth fleet convoy to Stade, on the Elbe. But the *Griffin*, *Little Hare*, and *Handmaid*, all of Hull, had been discharged on 17 June. Reason: " want of victuals." The *Marigold*, of Aldborough, had been discharged on 13 June. Reason: " want of victuals." Two pinnaces had also been discharged, " for want of victuals."

On the same day that Seymour penned his letter in the *Rainbow*, at anchor in the Downs, Medina Sidonia sat down in the fleet flagship *San Martin*, and made the first entry in the

War Diary: "On the 22nd of July (12th July by English reckoning) the Duke and all the Armada departed from the Groyne with a south-west wind, which they held for some days, and thereby made good progress." The wind which had driven Howard back to Plymouth had brought the Spaniards out.

CHAPTER SIX

In Sight of Cape Lizard

Corunna to the Lizard—12-19 July

> Good my Lord, have patience with you in reading, for that it is ill written. Consider where I am, in a miserable prison. They have condemned me to the galleys for four years, notwithstanding my three years in close prison, and thirty-two sundry torments in the Inquisition with the apretatos—you term them in English rackings. I have lost little less than two thousand ducats, besides my cruel torments, and wife and children undone forever.
>
> *Captain Thomas Cely, of Bristol, 1579*

No PROTESTANT heretic disliked the Pope quite so much as the Spanish Ambassador to the Vatican, Count de Olivares. Had his correspondence with the King of Spain been published, it would have rent the Enterprise. He wrote from Rome on 9 August: "When I received Your Majesty's advice of 17 July, that the Armada had sailed, I was so hopeless of obtaining any money of the Pope until the terms of the arrangement were fulfilled, that I sent the news by my secretary, and avoided saying anything about the money. When that subject is broached, the only effect is that, the moment my back is turned, he babbles the most ridiculous nonsense, such as would not be said by a baby of two years old. He possesses no sort of charity, kindliness, or consideration, and his behaviour is attributed by everyone to the repulsion and chagrin that he feels as the hour approaches for him to drag this money from his heart. His excuse to others for not paying the money is that the Armada business is nothing but a trick, and that Your Majesty has not raised the fleet for the English enterprise at all, but for brag, and to frighten the Queen of England into making peace, which Your Majesty would make in any case. He shows reports he has received to this effect. However unlikely a report may be, it matters not to His Holiness if it serves his purpose."

The Pope probably was not far wrong in his judgement, and it was a prudent precaution, as matters turned out, to insist on a Spanish landing in England before handing over his subsidy towards the costs of the Enterprise. But in the minds of the English, the King of Spain and the Pope were one; and the sea-faring population of England had for years dealt with Spaniards as if they personally represented the Holy Office. The enmity was of long standing, dating from the time of Henry VIII. Trading with Spain had become dangerous; for any dock-side brawl could develop into arraignment on the deadly charge of heresy, the moment tongues became unguarded. And men could easily be goaded by insults to their religion, or their Queen, or their country. Captain Cely, for instance, admitted: "Truth is, I did strike their secretary as I was before the Inquisidores, they sitting in judgement. I had great reason to do it." He was imprisoned, tortured, and sentenced to the galleys. His wife, however, far from being "undone forever," bombarded the Queen with demands, not for help, but for permission for Cely's friends to raid Spain and treat Spanish subjects in the same fashion, "so that all may know that her Majesty cannot and will not longer endure the spoils and torments of her subjects, and that the Spaniards shall not think this noble realm dares not seek revenge of such importable wrongs."

The stories of stake and rack were true enough; and so were the tales of savage and indiscriminate revenge. Sir William Monson, who served against the Armada, afterwards observed: "It is strange what misery such men will choose to endure in small ships of reprisal, though they be hopeless of gain, rather than serve her Majesty, where their pay is certain, their diet plentiful, and their labour not so great. Their owners are men of as base condition as themselves, making no more reckoning what outrages their ships commit at sea than the men themselves that commit them." All this long-pent-up hatred on both sides, religious, personal, and national, was now to have its release. But as the Armada ploughed slowly on towards its appointment in the Channel, not even the simplest ship's boy could be unaware of the fact that, for merciless invaders, there would be no mercy. Anyone who tried to surrender, and lived to tell of it, could think himself lucky.

The Armada had cleared Corunna harbour on 12 July, and had then been becalmed while still only a few miles out to sea. But a brisk south-east wind next day enabled them to clear the headland of Cape Ortegal, and a course was laid direct for England. When, on 15 July, the Duke sent a staff officer in a fast pinnace to warn Parma that the Enterprise had begun, the Armada had had three days of favourable winds. " No better weather could have been desired," he wrote. " Really, if three or four of our ships had cared to clap on sail, even though they were not very swift, they might have arrived at the mouth of the Channel by now. But I, in this galleon, could only sail as fast as the scurviest ship in the fleet, as I have to wait for the slowest of them—verily some of them are dreadfully slow— so I was obliged, anxious as I was to get forward, thus to tarry on the way."

But next day, 16 July, the Armada was becalmed once more, the ships drifting, scattered in a dense fog that lay on the quiet sea. That afternoon, the fog was blown away by a rising wind from the north; violent squalls splattered the waves with sudden rain; and the wind continued to increase, veering west. Soon, foaming white horses flecked the wave crests, and the ships began to roll and plunge violently. The scattered fleet tacked first east, then west, zig-zagging across the Bay of Biscay, but making little progress now towards England. Already the galleass *Zuniga* had had trouble with her rudder, damaged soon after leaving harbour; now the galleys were seen to be in difficulties. Their long, low hulls were almost hidden from sight by the Atlantic rollers; occasionally, the ram bow of one of them would rear skyward on a wave, the white water pouring from her sides and seeming to engulf her amidships. Then she would rise under the lift of the wave and stagger forward again, heeling dangerously under her lateen sail.

Leading the four war galleys was the *Diana*, in which the Welshman, David Gywnn, was fettered to a rowing bench. He was less favoured than Cely, who during his time in the galleys, in the typical fashion of Englishmen, had " got his feet under the table " and even struck up a friendship with the Alexandrian *amiga*, or sweetheart, of a Spanish captain of infantry. " This woman doth talk with me very often, and I make fair weather of her," he had reported. " She doth what she can for me." But poor Gywnn stayed chained at the oar, and, unlike Cely, did not obtain important information to send back to England. When his time of release came, he simply invented it.

That time was now not very far off, for it was speedily becoming apparent to Admiral Medrano, commander of the galley squadron, that his warships were unlikely to see England. He sent a pinnace to tell the Duke that Pantoja, the *Diana's* captain, had decided to turn back to Spain, and to ask permission for his three remaining galleys to run for shelter on the French coast. "I begged him to make every effort to continue with the fleet," wrote the Duke. "I sent two pataches to stand by the galleys in case they should require assistance, and all that day the three galleys were in sight. But after nightfall, when the weather became thick, with very heavy rain, they were lost sight of and we have seen them no more."

In fact, the King had news of them before Medina Sidonia. "Of the four galleys that sailed from Corunna," he wrote to his Paris Ambassador, "one arrived two days afterwards at Vivero on the coast of Galicia and two of the others, after having reached Ushant, were so clumsy, that instead of entering one of the Breton ports they came to the ancient channel near Bayonne, where one was wrecked and the other ran ashore, the crews escaping and deserting from both of them. I pray that the King of France will order the governor of Bayonne to deliver the two galleys, or what may remain of them. . . ." The wretched galley slaves, Gywnn among them, begged their way to Rochelle, destitute; and there Gywnn, in rags and starving, approached some English merchants with tales of how much he knew about the Spanish fleet and about the English traitors in high places who, he said, were only waiting for the right moment to make a prisoner of the Queen.

Meanwhile, the Armada was bucking a July gale. "Not only did the waves mount to the skies," reported Medina Sidonia, "but some seas broke clean over the ships, and the whole of the stern gallery of Diego Flores' flagship was carried away. It was the most cruel night ever seen. The next day (18 July) was clear and bright, with less sea, although it was still very rough. On counting the ships of the Armada, forty were found to be missing, namely, Don Pedro de Valdes's ships, the hulks, and some of the pataches." The Duke sent off pinnaces to look for them. On Friday, 19 July, he noted: "The pinnace which had been to the Lizard returned with news that the missing ships were in front, under the charge of Don Pedro de Valdes, who had collected them and was staying for the Armada." Now, only the four galleys and the *Santa Ana*, flagship of the Biscay squadron, were missing; and they would never rejoin.

Recalde had been wise to transfer from her to the *San Juan* of Oporto, but apparently the King had not been informed, for when he received the news that a *maestre de campo*, a regimental commander, was in command, thought the report must be false. In other respects, however, she was a normal flagship, carrying the bulk of the money for her squadron, and a purser to account for it. The Chief Accountant, Pedro Coco Calderon, serving in the vice-flagship of the hulks, duly noted: "The captain of the *Santa Ana* was Juan Perez de Mucio, and she carried 98 sailors, the Camp Master, Nicolas Isla, with 284 soldiers, the Purser Pedro de Iqueldo, and, it is said, 50,000 ducats in gold belonging to the King." Putting first into a Brittany port for shelter, she crept eastward as far as Le Havre, apparently out of the action, missing the glory.

For on Friday, 19 July, at four o'clock in the afternoon, the coast of England rose out of the sea beyond the bows of the Armada's flagship. The thunder of a three-gun salute poured from the sides of the *San Martin*, and a standard was hoisted to her maintop; hoisted also were a crucifix and a representation of the Virgin. Prayers were said, and Medina Sidonia penned an immediate letter to the King, which would go back to Spain in a fast pinnace. "God Almighty grant that the rest of our voyage may be performed as we and all Christendom hope it will be," he wrote, concluding proudly, "Written in sight of Cape Lizard, on board the galleon *San Martin*."

The Great Armada had arrived, short of four galleys and one great ship missing in the storm, and two pinnaces sent away with messages. But it was still a formidable force, and this was a proud moment; England in sight, and not a sign of an English ship, let alone the great Drake. They were daring the English fleet in its own waters, and defying the common prediction that "the English would be hard for them at sea." As recently as April, the Venetian Ambassador in Madrid had reported on public opinion in the Spanish capital in pessimistic terms. " It is generally held," he wrote, " that the King of Spain will not undertake so vast an enterprise, and although His Majesty is justly provoked, it is thought he will not, for the sake of revenge, hazard upon a doubtful and uncertain battle the peace and liberty of his many states and kingdoms. For he knows well how high he must rate a fleet like the enemy's, seeing the number of its vessels, and that the Englishmen are of a different quality from the Spaniards, bearing a name above all the West for being expert and enterprising in all maritime affairs, and the finest fighters upon the sea. A battle will in any case be very bloody; for the English never yield; and although they be put to flight and broken, they ever return, athirst for revenge, to renew the attack, as long as they have breath of life."

As the great fleet surged slowly on past Cornwall, smoke began to rise from a headland, and then from the next, and the next. " Many fires were made on the land as a signal that they had seen us," wrote Bernado de Gongora, a friar serving in the *Nuestra Senora del Rosario*, flagship of Don Pedro de Valdes. Now, they were in enemy territory, and at any moment might have to fight for their lives.

CHAPTER SEVEN

Fires and Smokes

Waiting for the Armada—July, 1588

THE RECENT and revolutionary changes in ship design had gone further in England than anywhere else, but were less immediately apparent; indeed, even at the highest planning levels, the Spaniards were much misled by superficial appearances. On the other hand, their own Armada, with its galleys, galleasses, great ships, and galleons, was almost a floating illustration of naval history and its technical progress. Its best modern equivalent would perhaps be an aerial parade of pure-jets, prop-jets, piston-planes, and airships. The latter, like the galleys, would hardly stand the test of service. The English, however, had only one galley in their whole fleet; and they used her as a guardship in the Thames, to supplement the boom they were throwing across the river. They also used her as a suitable depositary for an elderly senior official of the regular navy, who had fallen out with Sir Francis Drake, and got the worst of it. He could potter up and down in sheltered waters, in a state of minor importance, pretending that he was guarding the capital and the Queen. As the English had no belief in the future of the oared warship, they had not ventured up the blind alley of development which had led the Latins to produce the heavily-gunned galleasses, regarded at the time as an innovation of impressive potential.

They had been busy turning out a new type of sailing ship, handy, hardy, practical vessels; and were immensely pleased with them. They were to stand the test, not only of the Armada campaign, but of the sea-fighting which raged in many oceans thereafter. Looking back on his sea experiences years later, when the developments were in perspective, Admiral Sir William Monson, who had served against the Armada as lieutenant of the pinnace *Charles*, wrote down some observations: " The marvel I speak of is, that notwithstanding the apparent dangers and casualties of the sea aforesaid, yet not one of her Majesty's ships ever miscarried, but only the *Revenge*, which, in her voyage of 1591, was taken by the Spaniards by the unadvised negligence and wilful obstinacy of her captain, Sir Richard Greynville." Unaware that he was taking the gilt off the gingerbread of romantic poets not yet born, Sir William roundly condemned Grenville's tactics in the famous action off the Azores, as gross misuse of a fine vessel, which was Drake's flagship against the Armada. Only a damned fool like Sir Richard would employ methods for which the new-type galleons were never intended. Then Monson returned to his main thesis.

" If we compare these fortunes of the Queen's with those of her father's, who next to her had the greatest employment for his ships at sea, you will find great differences betwixt them, although we cannot properly call them voyages in King Henry VIII's time. For his ships were never so far from home but they might return again with a good wind in twenty-four hours' sail; as the others never expected to see the English shore, under four, five, or six months, and many times more."

Monson went on to list some of the disasters which had occurred to King Henry's ships, the most famous of which was the capsizing of the *Mary Rose* at Spithead, on 20 July, 1545, during a battle with a French force threatening the Isle of Wight. Contemporary illustrations of such ships show great, heavy " carracks," with towering castles at bow and stern, which look as if they would never float, but merely lie down on their sides and die, if put in the water. Even allowing for the imprecise impressions of artists unfamiliar with ships, this is a valid criticism of the older type of sailing warship. They were slow, immobile, unweatherly.

The new-type galleons were rather smaller, but quite different in design. A number of pictures have survived, some not very helpful, but there is one set of plans from a naval architect's drawing board which shows precisely what an Elizabethan galleon was like. It is dated 1586, and depicts a smart, yacht-like vessel; painted in Tudor green and white, the impression of rakish agility and speed would be even more pronounced. Elegant is the only word to describe her lines, which sweep down in a free-flowing curve from a high stern to amidships, where there is a well-deck, which sweeps up again into a neat and comparatively low forecastle. To an old-fashioned sailor, accustomed to ships which were little more than drifting forts, she might seem too light and unmilitary for battle; in fact, it was her mobility, combined with the hitting power of her guns, which made her deadly.

To an outside observer she would certainly appear to be overtopped by the more formidable-seeming "carrack" type, which was well represented in the Armada, and this no doubt partly explains the persistent legend of the small English ships attacking the mighty Spaniards. In the same way, an airship looms much more impressively than an aeroplane, and in the early days of aviation, they were more feared.

Sir Walter Raleigh outlined the essential handling differences between the two types of ship, and showed how greater mobility could be used to make a given gun-power even more devastating. "We find by experience that the greatest ships are the least serviceable, go very deep to water, and of marvellous charge and cumber, our channels decaying every year. Besides, they are less nimble, less mainable, and very seldom employed. *Grande navio grande fatiga*, saith the Spaniard. A ship of 600 tons will carry as good ordnance as a ship of 1,200 tons; and though the greater have double her number, the lesser will turn her broadsides twice before the greater can wind once. The high charging of ships it is that brings them ill qualities, makes them extreme leeward, makes them sink deep in the water, makes them labour and makes them overset. Men of better sort and better breeding would be glad to find more steadiness and less tottering cage-work."

It was the "tottering" bow and stern castles of the "high-charged" ship which were the main trouble; they caught the wind, like sails which could not be furled, or set at a variable angle. Nevertheless, they were only obsolescent, not yet obsolete. Monson summed up their advantages as: "Majesty and terror to the enemy; more commodious for the harbouring of men; carry more artillery; of greater strength inboard and make the better defence; will over-top a lower and snug ship; the men cannot be so well discerned." The coming battle in the Channel was to be a conflict, not only of Englishman with Spaniard, but of ship design and tactics.

The English fleet was organised in quite a different way to that of the Spaniards; in fact, it was less organised. The Armada was arrayed in precise squadrons in such a manner as to delight the heart of the military purist; in this lay its great strength, and its weakness, too. The two lists, that of Lisbon and Corunna, signed by Medina Sidonia, both show it. The English list, on the other hand, certified correct by Roger Langford, reveals how the ships were raised locally, and states how they were paid.

Thirty-four were " Queen's Ships "; that is, proper warships, part of the English navy. Thirteen were large, eight " middling," 12 small. Next in importance came the " Merchant Ships appointed to serve Westwards under the charge of Sir Francis Drake," of which 14 were middling and 14 small. There were 30 small to middling ships " Set forth and paid upon the charge of the City of London "; 33 small to middling " Merchant ships serving under the charge of the Lord Admiral, and paid by Her Majesty "; 20 small to middling " Coasters under the charge of the Lord Admiral, and paid by Her Majesty "; 23 small " Coasters appointed under the Lord Henry Seymour, whereof some were paid by Her Majesty, but the greatest part by the Port Towns "; and 23 small to middling " Voluntary Ships that came into the Fleet after the coming of the Spanish Forces, and paid by Her Majesty for the time they served."

The glittering, martial look of the Spanish lists, with their "Armadas" of Portugal, of Biscay, of Castille, of Andalusia, of Guipuzcoa, and of the Levant, is quite absent from the apparently prosaic record kept by the English. But what that record showed was an immense, and largely voluntary effort, by a sea-faring island people to defend their homeland; for they equipped and armed 197 ships, outnumbering the Spaniards by about three to two. The Armada, drawn not merely from Spain alone, but from Portugal and Italy as well, numbered only some 130 ships, of which about 124 actually arrived in the Channel. Where it outclassed the English was in numbers of men—roughly 30,000 to 15,000. Odds of two to one. And in terms of fighting men, the Spanish superiority was crushing. Nearly 19,000 soldiers had been gathered at Lisbon, of whom 2,000 were Portuguese conscripts. Rather more than half this force were veterans. Numbers varied greatly from time to time, owing to sickness and casualties, but they probably had a ten to one superiority of force over the English, in terms of assault infantry; and, as far as the veterans were concerned, a very real advantage in quality.

On the other hand, the Armada's 130 ships were manned by only 8,000 mariners; the English had far more sailors than the Spaniards, which meant that the English ships would be far better handled. And the Armada carried only 167 gunners—that is, officers capable of supervision and fire-control. Indeed, the gunners were out-numbered by the priests and friars, of whom there were 180.

Although, on the face of it, the coming clash in the Channel was to be, and was for long to be regarded as, the first true sailing ship battle, clearly, it was no such thing. It was a special conflict; there had never been anything like it before, and there was never to be anything like it again. In that way, it closely resembled the Battle of Britain.

The legend of the tiny English ships is seen not to be so false after all, for, out of the 197 only some 24 were real fighting warships, matching roughly the same number of warships on the Spanish side; and a further three dozen or so were merchantmen large enough to go into the thick of the fight, matching a more or less equal number of armed merchantmen on the Spanish side. In fact, in numbers of heavy units, the two fleets were well matched. Many of the English armed merchantmen, however, were very well armed indeed, being accustomed to privateering (and sometimes piracy); they often fought for profit, now they were to fight for their country.

Many of them had homely names or no names at all, and were simply called after their owners. Whereas some of the Spanish ships had liquid-sounding names, almost poetry; for instance, the *Nuestra Senora de la Rosa*, vice-flagship of Oquendo's squadron. Something like half of them had been named after saints, or had religious significance, and there was even a small pinnace called *La Concepcion de Francisco de Latero*.

The names of the English great ships had a hard bright ring about them, like glittering golden coins—*Ark Royal, Bonaven-*

ture, *Golden Lion*, *White Bear*, *Revenge*, *Victory*, *Dreadnought*, *Antelope*, *Triumph*, *Swiftsure*, *Swallow*, *Nonpareil*. Howard had moved out of the *White Bear*, owned by a relative, and was now at Plymouth, flying his flag in the *Ark*. Originally owned by Raleigh, she had formerly been known as the *Ark Raleigh*; now that she was a Queen's ship, she was called the *Ark Royal*. The great *Triumph* was Frobisher's flagship, the largest ship at sea during the Armada campaign; she was high-charged, on the old style, of great " majesty and terror to the enemy," but still far more modern in design than many of the Spaniards which she superficially resembled. Drake's *Revenge*, half her size, was the first of the new class of warships; she was that and nothing else; whereas the older types could carry cargo, or a load of soldiers, if required. She, and the others of her class, were specialised fighting ships, the most modern afloat.

Among the big armed merchantmen were names like the *Galleon Leicester* (Leicester's galleon), *Merchant Royal*, *Roebuck*, *Golden Noble*, *Griffin*, and *Minion*. The smaller ships had names ranging from the poetic to the homely—the *Galleon Dudley*, *The Virgin*, *God Save Her*, the *Bark Bond* and the *Bark Buggins*, the *Diamond of Dartmouth* and the *Rat of Wight*, the *Heartsease*, *Speedwell*, *Bear Yonge*, *Chance*, *Delight*, and *Nightingale*. The *Bear Yonge* was the *Bear*, owned by Captain Yonge, so-called to distinguish her from similarly named ships, such as the great *White Bear*. The English ships are therefore very easy to identify in the many contemporary narratives of the fighting; not so the Spanish, where as many as a dozen different ships had the same name—*San Juan*, for instance, or *San Juan de Bautesta* (St. John, or St. John the Baptist); or, less frequently, *San Pedro* (St. Peter).

The strength of this fleet was, that it was entirely English; the land forces also were composed only of Englishmen. The force was all of one nationality, one language, and one purpose. The Queen had not, as the King Philip had feared, reinforced her troops with Germans or other foreigners; nor were the English at sea relying on the Dutch rebel warships to keep Parma locked up in Nieuport, although these were perfectly capable of doing so; they were relying entirely on themselves. Indeed, in this crisis, there was a dislike of all foreigners, friendly or otherwise, openly and contemptuously expressed; so much so that the authorities tried to suppress it on the grounds that it might lead to public disorder. Petruccio Ubaldino, the Florentine historian, himself a foreigner, noted with care the precautions taken against the mass of aliens, many of them refugees from religious oppression, who had flocked to England in recent years.

"Because of the common danger, watch had to be kept on the great crowd of foreigners from the Low Countries, France, and other places, who lived in London on their earnings as craftsmen." There was no proof against them, but all were suspect. "No more was known of some of them except that they had come on account of their religion; but the city was full of such as might be faithful or not under the cloak of the same religion. And not being so very sure of them as could be wished, amid such cares and dangers, they needed watching." They were not arrested and interned, merely watched, but " every day these foreigners received insulting words from the prentices and the lower classes, people who are naturally the enemies of foreigners, which fact disturbed the careful magistrates. For that reason all the principal cross roads were guarded day and night for the keeping of the peace."

The precautions were not baseless. There were Spanish spies in London; their reports, unsigned, are in the Spanish archives. They operated under code names, such as "David." One at least was an Englishman. He reported, on 16 July: "People here do not fear the Spaniard any more, as they are convinced that he has returned to Spain. All the principal Catholics have been sent to the Isle of Ely in the custody of Lord North." This was perfectly true; a limited number of the leading English Catholics had been interned in Wisbech Castle, but not as suspected traitors. Elizabeth was far too wise, far-seeing, and politic for that. It is hard to read a man's soul. It was merely suspected that some might be tempted to turn traitor, if the Spaniards landed in force. That, in the absence of any proof, was not justification enough to brand them all, publicly, as traitors to their Queen and country. Therefore, she did not do so. She publicly proclaimed that their internment was not for the safety of her realm, but for their own safety, because, in case

of a Spanish landing, the more riotous elements of the population, already insulting all foreigners, might well attack them.
Considering that there had been a number of Catholic plots to
assassinate her, this showed an iron nerve on Elizabeth's part.
Many of her high-born subjects were more sanguine. The assassination of their Dutch ally, William the Silent, in 1584, had
filled them with cold rage and a determination that Philip of
Spain should not get his way, assassination or no assassination.
They formed a secret society, the Bond of Association, the
members of which pledged themselves to lynch anyone who, as
a result of a successful attempt on Elizabeth's life, should succeed
to the throne. In short, the death of Elizabeth would also be
the death warrant of Philip's claimant; and there would be no
legal niceties about it.

No doubt this shocked Philip; it shocked the whole Catholic
world when, in 1586, they went grimly further and cleared the
ground in advance by forcing Elizabeth to execute the Queen of
Scots. That was serving notice with a vengeance. It was in face
of pressure from these fiercely determined men, utterly decided
to take no chances, that Elizabeth held to her coolly balanced
policy of internment without shame. In Ubaldino's view, she
was absolutely right. These Catholics could hardly avoid wishing
to see a return of the old religion—but at the price of Spanish
invasion and conquest? That was a different matter indeed.
" The change of religion threatened by the Spaniards did not so
much encourage their rebellion as anger them, when they heard
that the Spaniards had determined to conquer the kingdom,"
commented Ubaldino. He added, feelingly, " It being easier to
find flocks of white crows than one Englishman (and let him
believe what he will about religion) who loves a foreigner, either
as a master or companion in his own home, even if a benefactor."

To gather in the waverers, and buttress the determination of
the loyal, a different policy was used. " In those days news was
spread (and perhaps not by chance in London, for preachers in
several churches discussed the matter extensively), which served
to incite even further the feelings of the English people," noted
Ubaldino. " These preachers, in public sermons, stated that the
Spaniards were carrying in their fleet a large number of women
of every kind, and together with this report was spread the

rumour that in the Spanish ships were many instruments of torture with which to afflict the English people. These things being easily believed, the whole of the lowest and most credulous part of the people were moved to a mortal and dangerous hatred of all foreigners living there."

A report from another Spanish agent in England, this time a Genoese, contains the details of these stories: " Being in great alarm, they made the people believe that the Spaniards were bringing a shipload of halters in the Armada to hang all the Englishmen, and another shipload of scourges to whip women, with 3,000 or 4,000 wet nurses to suckle the infants. It was said that all children between the ages of 7 and 12 would be branded in the face, so that they might always be known. These and other things of the same sort greatly irritated the people. During the time the Armada was in the Channel all foreigners in London were forbidden to leave their houses, and the shops were to remain closed."

The English precautions were undeniably efficient. The flow of letters from agents died to a trickle and then stopped, while the actual fighting was taking place in the Channel. In effect, the English sealed off their coasts; and little got through, even from privileged diplomatic sources. For more than a month the King of Spain had to wait, anxiously, for news of what had happened to his Armada. And all he got were baseless rumours. The precautions were not technically so complete as those enforced in 1940, when the entire south coast of England was declared a prohibited area and road blocks set up to prevent all unauthorised entry; nor so complete as in 1944, when the expected invasion was in the other direction. But the sparsity of population and slowness of communications, in the time of Elizabeth, rendered them just as effective. The Spanish spy network was hamstrung, and if indeed there was a fifth column, it had been rendered harmless with a minimum of effort and fuss. There was no Chief of the Imperial General Staff charging round, spreading baseless stories of traitors in high places. That role was left to David Gywnn, the imaginative ex-galley slave. There was no fifth column scare; Elizabeth did not allow it.

In the fleet papers there is only one reference to a single case of suspected treason; and that was in February, in the *White*

Bear, commanded by Lord Sheffield, a nephew of Howard's. The Secretary of State, Sir Francis Walsyngham, set this particular hare in motion by briefing Howard personally. Howard, on going aboard, found his nephew in a hurry to get off to London. "And yet my Lord himself, as great haste as he had, made the barber, and three or four more which he suspected, to be sworn," stated Howard. "And so they were; and they utterly renounced the Pope's authority. After my Lord's departure, Mr. Ha. Sheffield, his lieutenant, took great pains and did examine the barber, and found that a two or three years agone, he was something inclined to papistry, but being matched by his wife with an honest race, as it seems, they converted him. I have talked with the man myself. He offers to receive, and to do anything that a good Protestant should do. This was the cause I think that bred the doubt in him. He had a book that was done by an English papist beyond the seas; a bad book; but he brought it to the preacher, with dislike of the book; and the preacher is counted to be a most zealous man and very honest."

The " bad book " may have been a pamphlet by either Father Parsons or Cardinal Allen, the English renegades at the Vatican, who argued that as the Queen had been excommunicated, no English Catholic could owe allegiance to her, or be guilty of treason against her. With war imminent, this would be dangerous material to possess.

But, Howard pointed out to Walsyngham, " The barber had many good books, as the New Testament, the Book of Common Prayer, the Book of the Psalms which he daily sang with the company. The man was prest by the Company of Surgeons, for he is a barber-surgeon, and not by my Lord; and he hath sailed often in her Majesty's ships, and accounted a very honest man. I think my Lord Sheffield will send you the party, and I believe you will not mislike him." Suspicion may have fallen further afield, for Howard thought fit to add that Lord Sheffield himself was " very earnest and zealous in religion," and had been heard to be " most vehement against Papists, so be-traitoring them, saying he that was in his ship that would not be sworn against the Pope, he would take him for a traitor, and so use him." This was a dire threat, for the penalty for treason was a frightful public butchery of the offender.

Howard was probably wise to ignore Walsyngham, and let the dubious doctor have the benefit of the doubt, for when it came to David Gywnn's turn to spread stories of treason, the most important man he named—was Walsyngham. Once suspicion was roused, there was no knowing where it would stop.

But by mid-July, they were more than sure of the temper of the fleet; morale was extraordinarily high, despite the inadequacy of the victualling and ammunitioning arrangements at the crucial moment. On 12 July, Howard and Drake entered Plymouth after their abortive sortie towards the Spanish coast; and on the same day, Medina Sidonia brought the Armada out of Corunna. On the stormy 17th, when the three remaining galleys of Portugal ran for shelter and were " seen no more," the English were furiously busy, writing.

Burghley, the Lord Treasurer, was complaining to Mr. Marmaduke Darell, that the ration returns for the fleet had been incorrectly rendered. " There was some fault in you, in that you made not your last certificate so perfect as had been requisite; for that you neither particularly mentioned the numbers of men, nor the vessels wherein they serve; which I pray you by your next certificate to reform." Poor Mr. Darell, who had been given the job of victualling more than a hundred vessels, virtually single-handed, with no proper organisation at all, probably wished Burghley to the devil for bothering him at this time, but could not very well say so. Howard could. At the same time as Burghley was writing to Darell, he was writing to Burghley.

" I have caused Sir Francis Drake and Mr. Hawkyns to consider of your charges, for that our company grow into great need, and many occasions in such an army both breed sundry great and extraordinary charges. I have sent therein enclosed an estimate thereof, praying your Lordship that there may be some care had that we may be furnished with money, without which we are not able to continue our forces together." Having fired that broadside at the Lord Treasurer, he wrote in more cheerful tones to the Secretary of State, Walsyngham: " But there shall be neither sickness nor death which shall make us yield until this service is ended. I never saw nobler minds than be here in our forces."

Also scribbling away to Burghley was Captain Thomas Cely, roundly demanding: "My good Lord, a sharp war and a short. The Queen's subjects doth desire it." He had a pet scheme of his own, which he was trying to push, without success. "When I have begun to enter into any matter of importance, one of them (the Council) told me and said this unto me: 'Cely, it is told me that you meddle with Councillors matters.' A rebuke I had, and so went my way. Another told me that if I could do her Majesty any service, so that it cost money, never speak of it, for she will not consent unto it. So I went my way with a flea in mine ear. My good Lord, I am a poor man, and one that hath been brought up without learning, and one that hath a patched carcase; for I had thirty-two sundry torments in the Inquisition; and eight years in prison lacking but two months; and in the King of Spain's most filthy galleys, and seven other prisons." Burghley probably sighed, and put it in the " pending " tray. However, Cely was to get suitable employment, in due course.

On 19 July, the Lord Treasurer took the whole matter to Walsyngham, effectively "passing the buck." He wrote: " I cannot conceal from you the causes which will shortly bring forth desperate effects. I have received letters from my Lord Admiral and Mr. Hawkyns, with a schedule declaring that they have great lack of money for wages, besides victuals; yet Mr. Quarles hath £6,000 this last week, and now Mr. Hawkyns' declaration that, to make a full pay to the 28th of this month, there must be paid £19,000! I marvel that where so many are dead on the seas the pay is not dead with them, or with many of them. A man would wish, if peace cannot be had, that the enemy would not longer delay, but prove, as I trust, his evil fortune: for these expeditions do consume us."

That same day, the gun smoke poured forth from the *San Martin*, to salute the first sight of England. There was news for Howard, too. "We had intelligence by one of the barks that his Lordship had left in the Sleeve for discovery, named the *Golden Hind*, wherein was Captain Thomas Flemyng, that the fleet of Spain was seen near the Lizard, the wind being then southerly or south-west; and the greater number of ships of the

English army, being then in Plymouth, with that wind were very hard to be gotten out of harbour."

The fleet in Plymouth was not the whole force, for some of the best ships were hundreds of miles to the east, guarding the Narrow Seas against Parma; they could never beat up against the wind in time, if at all. Worse, Plymouth Sound opens south-west; so that a south-west wind blows dead into it. The Armada had only to run swiftly before the wind, sail boldly into the Sound, and the English were caught in a deadly trap; unable to manoeuvre, they could be boarded where they lay by masses of the invincible Spanish infantry. It would all be over in a few hours, the greater part of the English fleet wiped out. Nothing then to stop the crossing of Parma's veteran army. Desperately, the English worked to extricate their ships. There may have been time for a game of bowls, and that was just the sort of gesture Drake loved; the incident may have taken place, but there is no mention of it in any of the contemporary accounts. The seamen were concerned only to get to sea.

Next day, 20 July, Medina Sidonia reported: "The Armada was very near the shore. We were seen by the people on land, who made fires and smokes." The warning beacons were blazing on the hilltops, carrying their message swiftly along the shore and inland: "The Spanish fleet is on the coast!" Men ran to arms, or checked the water in the leather buckets which had been provided for fire-fighting; and the church bells began their clamour, a strident warning across the countryside: "The Spaniards are coming, the Spaniards are coming!"

CHAPTER EIGHT

Hovering in the Wind

Saturday, 20 July

Upon Friday, being the 19th of this present month, part of the Spanish
navy, to the number of 50 sail, was discovered about the Isles of Scilly,
hovering in the wind as it seemed to attend the rest of the fleet . . .

Howard, *A Brief Abstract of Accidents*

SURPRISE WAS lessened by the bad weather; by appointing the
Scillies as rendezvous and then allowing the main body of the
fleet to lag behind, as it had done before during the abortive
June voyage, the Duke effectively "telegraphed" his coming.
While Don Pedro de Valdes "hovered in the wind," waiting
for his commander, every hour was of vital importance to the
hard-driven English, trying to work out of the deadly trap in
which they found themselves. At dawn on Saturday, 20 July,
with the beacons blazing their warning eastward from the Lizard,
Medina Sidonia was still tarrying as a result of the gale. This
time it was the flagship of the Neapolitan galleass squadron,
Don Hugo de Moncada's *San Lorenzo*. "I have now all the
Armada together, and I will set sail as soon as the flag galleass
has been put in order, her rudder being broken; these craft
are really very fragile for such heavy seas." Like a little grocer
counting cracked eggs with the shop on fire, Medina Sidonia
scurried around, accounting primly to his master. "The galleys
have not appeared, nor have I any tidings of them, which
causes me great anxiety," he lamented, in the first of several
letters which he wrote on this day. There is no sense of
urgency, no realisation that this dull and drizzly day would
decide all their fates forever.

The English at any rate were under no illusions as to
what might happen, if the Spaniards caught them in Plymouth
Sound. Thousands of men were labouring at the oars of their
boats, to tow the big, heavy ships out into the bay, where
their sails could be loosened, and they could stand out to sea
to the south-east. Barrels of victuals were left standing on

the quaysides. Better to starve than die like rats in a trap. Much of Mr. Darell's work in collecting the provisions was wasted, for he reported: " The haste of my Lord Admiral was such in his setting forth upon Saturday morning, as that divers of his ships had not leisure to receive the full of their last proportions." The casks of food and drink left behind were clear warning of how dire the emergency really was, but the English Admirals did not leave it at that; they thought that time spent in briefing their men was not time wasted. For, wrote Ubaldino, who talked to them later, they did not sail until " after the higher ranks had prudently and without ado, imparted to the lower information as to what should be done from hour to hour." The result, in Howard's words, was that, " although the ships of the English army with that wind were very hard to be gotten out of harbour, yet the same was done with such diligence and good will, that many of them got abroad as though it had been with a fair wind."

But to get some out was not enough, for the Armada outnumbered the entire English force then in Plymouth and could easily have destroyed a part of it, possibly even the whole of it; they had the advantage of the wind as well as of numbers. It was blowing straight into the Sound, and, had Medina Sidonia hurried ahead with his seventy warships and armed merchantmen, laden with soldiers, he could have blocked the Sound and brought on a confused melee at close quarters. Here was a chance of swift and crushing victory at the very start of the campaign, an opportunity to carry out his master's order, that " the object of our side should be to close and grapple and engage hand to hand." The Duke realised, or his advisers made him realise, this; what neither he nor they realised was that, not only was this the first chance the English would give them to get to close quarters, but it was also the last. It was now or never.

But the Duke was worried about the galleys, which would never return in any case, and hove to his whole vast force in order not to leave Don Hugo and his damaged galleass temporarily behind. And that was ironic, for de Moncada and his flagship were doomed anyway, as a result of what Medina Sidonia did not do on Saturday, the 20th of July. He cannot be blamed,

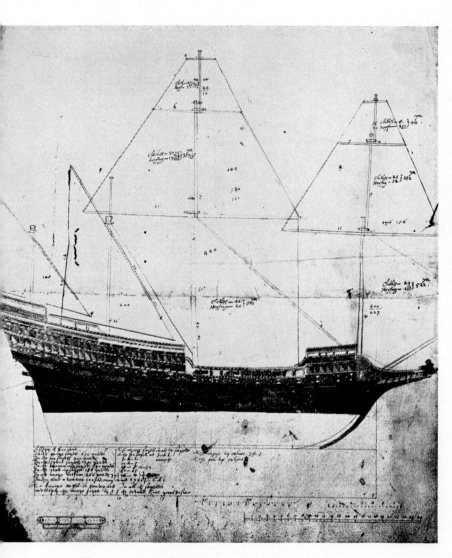

The new-type English galleon which beat the Armada. This draught and sail-plan were drawn by Matthew Baker in 1586. Compared to the *Great Harry*, she has the lines of a racing yacht. Drake's flagship, the *Revenge*, was of this design

ABOVE : The *Great Harry* or *Henri Grace a Dieu, from a coloured aquatint by R. Cruickshank.* She was an experimental battleship of about 1,000 tons, with two complete gundecks, a kind of floating fort; but slow and unseaworthy, capable only of operating for short periods in the Channel. BELOW : The *Ark Royal,* formerly the *Ark Raleigh,* Howard's flagship, *from a line engraving by C. J. Visscher.* Smaller than the *Great Harry,* with only one complete gundeck, and a much smaller bowcastle; a much faster and handier type of ship

for in attempting to decline the command, he had explained exactly why he knew himself to be incompetent in cases such as this. How, without experience, could he weigh the factors for and against? How could he even decide between conflicting arguments among his own expert advisers? Particularly when the King's own instructions to him were muddled and contradictory? If he found that he outnumbered Drake, he could fight him; but at the same time, he must go direct to the junction with Parma. He must join Parma; but must shelter in the Thames. " The enemy's object will be to engage at a distance, on account of the advantage which they have from their artillery; our side should close and grapple. . . ." No blame to the Duke, if, in all this uncertainty, he decided to act the part at least of good housekeeper and try only to hold his force together, intact if possible.

It was forty-five miles to Plymouth; by nightfall, the Armada had covered only twenty of them. The vast cavalcade of shipping, spread over miles of heaving sea, rolled slowly onwards at the speed of the slowest, the store ships huddled in the centre. The English had no leisure to savour the moment; their toil was too back-breaking. The Spanish sailors, long settled into their routine of watch-keeping, with its rhythm of broken sleep, thought little of it. But the soldiers, whose most onerous duty was that of cleaning weapons for inspection twice a week, were in the privileged position of spectators. With curious eyes, they watched the English coast go by. There were grim granite headlands, with thickly wooded valleys between them going down steeply to the shore, where the white waves flickered momentarily. A harsh and desolate land, seemingly, all grey tones under a grey, drizzling sky. It was hard to believe it inhabited, harder still to realise that their enemies were gathering. But they were being watched, all the time.

The first reporting centre was Falmouth castle, serving in 1588 the same role as the 1940 radar station on Hawk's Tor, behind Plymouth. But for the coast watchers, as for the early radar, it was hard to count the ships. The message which reached inland to Wellington was that " upon Saturday they were all, to the number of eight score and two sail, over against Falmouth."

For the Spaniards, the first sign that anyone was interested in them came during the afternoon, when there was a brief flurry as some of the Armada broke away from the formation. Few knew what it was all about, but Pedro Coco Calderon, the Chief Accountant, was privileged to learn. In the diary which he was keeping, he made the entry: "An English pinnace approached to reconnoitre, and Captain Ojeda with his ship and some pinnaces gave chase until she ran inshore." One of the Spanish pinnaces, carrying Ensign-bearer Juan Gil, made in her turn a reconnaissance towards the coast, and picked up a fishing boat from Falmouth, with four men in it, who were brought back to the Armada for questioning. There are two contradictory versions of what they said; the Duke's own War Diary, in which they are reported to have seen " the English fleet go out of Plymouth under the charge of the Admiral of England and of Drake," and a letter written by de Valdes to the King, in which they said that " the English fleet was at anchor." Medina Sidonia's entry, implying that there never was a chance to catch the English in Plymouth, suited best the reputation of Medina Sidonia; but equally, by the time he came to write the letter four weeks later, Don Pedro had good reason to cast aspersions on the Duke's handling of affairs.

A Council of War was held in the *San Martin* that day, either in the afternoon or evening, but the Duke kept very quiet about it; the subject was Plymouth. However, de Valdes wrote to the King: " The same day the Duke called to council, being within 10 or 12 leagues from Plymouth, where, by the report of the fishermen whom we took, he had understanding that the English fleet was at anchor. It was resolved: we should make to the mouth of the haven and set about the enemy, if it might be done with any advantage; if not, we should keep our course directly to Dunkirk without losing any time." When talking to Ubaldino later, as a prisoner, he added: " They had considered it an easy matter to seize Plymouth, for they had not imagined that they would have to meet at sea any force which they could not overcome, only an ordinary fleet for the guarding of the Channel."

De Valdes himself seems to have been against the proposal. He was questioned very fully on this point, according to a

standard questionnaire, of which Article 12 read: " Whether
they had any intelligence that the Lord Admiral was in Plymouth
before their departure from the Groyne? By whom had they
the said intelligence? Whether they had any meaning to attempt
anything against him there?" The English wished to penetrate
the Spanish spy network, and to discover any traitors among
themselves, if they could. De Valdes replied that " they received
advertisement in Spain that the English fleet was at Plymouth,
and should permit them to pass for to follow them." In short,
they did not expect the English to fight until both fleets, that
in Plymouth and that off Dover, were joined. He repeated the
story of the fishermen and their news that the English fleet was
in fact in Plymouth, adding: " Whereupon the Duke called a
council to consider of entering there and conquering the said
fleet. This examinate was of opinion that it was not fitting
to do so, because that the fleet was within the haven, whereof
the mouth is so strait as not more than two or three ships
could go in abreast, which was insufficient for that action."

The possibility of catching the English in Plymouth must
have been in the minds of many from the beginning; it was
as obvious to them as it was to the English, that a wind which
could carry the Armada to England must necessarily hamper
the English in any attempt to come out. But Medina Sidonia
had lost far too much time that day. The Armada was off
Fowey, with some twenty-five miles still to go, when the look-outs
reported an ominous sight. Sails, many sails, moving between
them and Plymouth, only half seen in the drizzle. In Don
Pedro's words to his King: " Within two hours after the council,
their fleet was discovered out of my ship four leagues off to
leeward of ours. . . ." The Duke had been debating, at his
Council of War, the situation as it had been in the morning,
and not as it was when the talking started. In fact, Howard's
ships had begun to clear the Sound by three o'clock that afternoon, and by evening, 54 out of 100 ships had escaped the trap
and were off the Eddystone reef. The Spaniards still held the
great advantages of superior numbers and the weather gauge;
but now, at least, these 54 ships could escape eastwards if hard-
pressed.

97

However, there was slight nervousness in the *San Martin*. The reaction of the Duke and his advisers was defensive, timid; definitely exasperating to the bolder spirits among the Spaniards. Nobody in the flagship was going to press those few English ships, helplessly downwind of them. Instead the Duke, like an anxious housewife frightened by burglars, went round locking all the doors. "As it was already late, and the weather was thick, we could not reconnoitre the enemy's fleet," wrote Calderon, an admirer of Medina Sidonia. " The Duke ordered Captain Uceda to go through the Armada during the night, giving instructions for the ships to be put into order of battle, as the enemy would be upon us in the morning. The Duke then gave orders for sail to be shortened, and remained awaiting him."

Not all the Spaniards were so passively minded. Pedro Estrade, a reinforcement infantry officer in the *San Marcos,* wrote: " In the afternoon we discovered about 76 sail and knew them to be the English fleet; they did bear towards the east, the wind being S.W. Then we amained until it was day and ran under our foresails only, which was a great oversight."

The Duke, however, was writing to the King for the second time that day. Obviously something other than Plymouth had been discussed at the Council of War. Having nerved himself to reinterpret his woolly instructions from Philip, which tended rather against any engagement until the Armada had joined with Parma, to the extent of contemplating an attack which had not come off, Medina Sidonia now flatly informed his master that he intended to alter the whole plan. " The object of the present letter is to say that I am obliged to proceed slowly with all the Armada together in squadrons as far as the Isle of Wight, and no further. All along the coast of Flanders there is no harbour or shelter for our ships. If I were to go from the Isle of Wight thither with the Armada our vessels might be driven on to the shoals, where they would certainly be lost. In order to avoid so obvious a peril I have decided to stay off the Isle of Wight until I learn what the Duke is doing, as the plan is that at the moment of my arrival he should sally with the fleet, without causing me to wait a minute."

Somebody at that council table must forcibly have put his finger on the weak point of the whole plan, the difficulties of the actual junction with Parma, which the King had insufficiently considered. And because what he said was sound sense, he must have carried the majority of those present with him. Certainly, the English were in complete agreement. Howard thought so, had thought so for months. There was in existence a very soundly reasoned intelligence estimate to this effect, which had been circulated. The English thought the Isle of Wight met three considerations which must be in the mind of the enemy: "First, where he may find least resistance, and most quiet landing. Secondly, where he may have best harbour for his galleys, and speediest supplies out of Spain, France and Flanders. Thirdly, where he may most offend the realm by incursions, and force her Majesty, by keeping many garrisons, to stand upon a defensive war." It was estimated that 8,000 men could "easily" take the island, which would serve as a perfect base for amphibious raiding forces, "so that all the castles and sea towns of Hampshire, Sussex and Dorsetshire will be subject to be burnt."* This extreme "nuisance" value was exactly what Philip expected of the Armada, if it should be free to operate following a successful landing by Parma, or if the invasion should fail or prove impossible. Then, he ordered it to take the Isle of Wight—after, not before, invasion had been attempted.

Therefore, from the evening of 20 July on, the entire operational plan of the Armada changed; it became more practical. The only factor unknown was the English fleet, and what it might do to try to prevent a landing in England direct from the Armada's own ships. For the English, there was no change; they already expected the Spaniards to attempt to force their way into Spithead and land troops on the northern beaches of the island.

---

* The last threat to the Isle of Wight had been in July 1545. The English fleet effectively defended the anchorage of Spithead by occupying it themselves. The French could land only small raiding parties at separated points—Seaview, Bonchurch, Sandown, and Whitecliff Bay. They were mostly repulsed by the local Home Guard, the cavalry component of which was mounted on cart-horses. Estimating that they would need to land 6,000 troops to occupy and hold the island, the French retired, having been defeated as much by the Home Guard as by King Harry's ships.

At midnight the weather was as dismal as it had been throughout the day; but at two o'clock in the morning of Sunday, 21 July, the moon came out. The cold, silver light sparkled on the waves and the slow wake of the ships as, hardly moving, they dreamed through the night under the few rags of sail needed to keep them on course. Calderon, looking out across the water, could just detect in the gloom, inshore of the Armada, and still downwind, five strange ships which must be part of the English fleet. They were all still there, he thought, still at a disadvantage; and would remain so tomorrow. That was comforting.

CHAPTER NINE

Not Half of them Men of War

Sunday, 21 July

Somewhat to the westward of Plymouth, we had some small fight
with them.

John Hawkyns to Walsyngham

IN SPITE of the unseasonable weather, it was summer; the days
were long. It was not completely dark until about 10 o'clock,
and it was growing light again between five and six. Consequently, at dawn on Sunday, 21 July, the Spaniards expected
to sight the English roughly to the north-east, scattered between
the Eddystone reef and Plymouth Sound, much as they had
been the night before. But eastwards, the sea was bare. The
only sign of the enemy was northwards, close in with the
shore, where a small group of ships was tacking repeatedly, zig-
zagging westwards into the teeth of the wind. The soldier,
Estrade, noted that there were seven of them. The Duke's
estimate was higher, as usual; he counted 11, " amongst which
were three great galleons that cannonaded some of our ships,
and continued turning to windward, the wind having shifted
to W.N.W." The sullen thudding of cannon fire rolled across
the sea, as the handful of English, outnumbered by more than
ten to one, even by Medina Sidonia's estimate, passed close
to the left wing of the Armada, methodically tacking; at each
seaward reach, which brought them within gunshot of Recalde's
Armada of Biscay, they contemptuously let fly at it. The
reason for their confidence soon became apparent; these were
better ships than the Spaniards'.

Actually, as they had only just got out, they were probably
some of the more unwieldy English ships, perhaps including
Frobisher's " high-charged " 1,200 ton *Triumph*, impressively
larger than any single ship in the Armada, and in direct line
of descent from Henry VIII's monstrous, experimental *Great
Harry*. But the most astounding thing which met the
Spaniards' gaze was a cloud of sails astern and to seaward of

the Armada, bearing down with arrogant ease on the four
squadrons of armed merchantmen which formed the rear of
its formation. The Spaniards regarded them with surprise and
alarm. Medina Sidonia put their number at eighty. Calderon
wrote: " The enemy's fleet, with the wind astern, bore down
on us. They had 20 great galleons, from 500 to 800 tons burden,
and 50 of from 200 to 300 tons, extremely well armed, rigged,
and handled. They came towards us in very good order. . . ."

In haste, the Armada shook itself out into battle order, and
the Royal Standard went fluttering up to the masthead of the
fleet flagship, Medina Sidonia's *San Martin*. There was very
little else he could do. The real striking force of the Armada,
the warships of the Castilian and Portuguese squadrons, as well
as the galleasses, were at the front, ready to bear the brunt of
an action against an English fleet caught ahead of the Spanish
might, downwind, where they should have been. Now, by
some devil's trick, they had in the few hours of darkness reversed
that position of disadvantage, and were attacking where the
Duke could not get at them. The Armada was arrayed like
an eagle: the two dozen real warships were the head and beak,
poised to strike ahead; behind them came the body of the fleet,
the ill-protected host of two dozen storeships; and attached to
the body at the rear, like two great, drooping wings, trailed
some forty armed merchantmen, the Armadas of Andalusia and
Biscay echeloned out to the left, towards the shore, the Armadas
of Guipuscoa and the Levant staggered out to the right, to
seaward. Except for their flagships, these squadrons were weakly
armed; against them, the English gun superiority would be
crushing. But how had they managed totally to outmanoeuvre
the Spaniards?

As the English came steadily on, their ensigns and red battle
flags flying for a fleet action, one answer became speedily
apparent to the most arrant amateur in the Spanish fleet. The
soldier, Estrate, wrote: " The English had the vantage by
reason of good powder, store of shot, and good ships of sail
and by a wind." The Duke noted: " The enemy's fleet, with
Drake on board, number 80 sail as far as can be counted,
some of them being excellent vessels, and all of them very rapid
sailers. Their ships being very nimble and of such good steerage,

as they did with them whatsoever they desired." The impression
of English superiority was overwhelming, when coupled with
the dreaded name of Drake, the legendary pirate Admiral who
had sacked their colonial cities, taken their treasure ships, sailed
into Cadiz, and blockaded the Spanish coast. The man of blood
and fire was upon them. Many were ready to panic without
further ado.

The English ships came plunging on, not 80 sail but only 54,
and bearing across the rear of the Armada to pick up the
inshore group, now beating out to sea across the stern of the
Spanish fleet to join them. When they were joined, they were
still only 67. There were 40 ships still in Plymouth, and
another fleet, equal in size, with some of the best of the new
ships, hundreds of miles away blockading Parma's invasion army
off Dunkirk. At this moment, the Armada outnumbered them
two to one in ships; in fighting soldiers its superiority was
overwhelming. The approaching English looked coldly out
on their enemy, trying to gauge its strength from the forest
of masts which stretched for miles across the sea. "At our
first meeting of them, which was within two miles of Looe in
Cornwall," wrote Richard Thomson, lieutenant of the 200
ton *Margaret and John* of London, " they were 136 sail of ships
and pinnaces, whereof 90 were very great ships, and the rest
of smaller account." Drake's experienced eye saw more clearly:
" The fleet of the Spaniards is somewhat above a hundred
sails, many great ships; but truly I think not half of them
men-of-war." Howard's report was detailed: "About 9 of the
clock in the morning, we recovered the wind of their whole
fleet which, being thoroughly descried, was found to consist
of 120 sail, great and small; whereof there are 4 galleasses
and many ships of great burden." The actual numbers of the
Armada varied somewhat, as swift pinnaces were despatched
ahead with letters for Parma, or back to Spain with reports
for the King; but it can have been little more than 120.

In none of the English narratives, diaries, and letters is
there any clue as to how the English had so swiftly turned
the tables on their enemies, and were now about to attack,
instead of being attacked. Howard passes it off as, " We did
what we could to work for the wind." Neither Drake nor

4*

Hawkyns, real seamen, even bothered to mention it. It must have been some commonplace trick, which any experienced mariner could manage in his sleep, if he had an English ship under him. The tidal stream in the Channel flows up to Dover, then turns and comes back; the times of the varying rates of flow at particular points are something that every seaman today knows by heart, since they can make a speed difference of four knots, and ships leave harbour timed exactly to catch a fast stream going in the right direction. Inside the great bays of the West Country there is little tide; it is necessary to go further out in order to pick up the current, and by sailing out beyond the Eddystone, as the English did, they would in fact enter the main stream. And since the bottom is not a flat desert, but on the contrary, a maze of submerged mountainous reefs reaching near, and sometimes above, the surface, some parts of the stream flow faster than others.* The currents in the depths are very complex, but leave surface signs which can be read, all the way from Bolt Head to the Lizard. To mariners who had sailed all their lives out of Plymouth, getting to windward of a dozing Armada on their own doorstep would be elementary. Much easier, in fact, than trying to explain to Walsyngham how the trick was done.

Now they bore down, their sails bellying out with the wind, the spray racing upwards from their bows; with the creak of timber and the shouting of orders as the gun-ports were opened and the long guns run out. The powder had been poured in, the shot rammed home on top of it; now the gunners, slow-matches burning, waited for the huge-hulled targets to loom into view through the ports. They were riding into action, strung out in loose line ahead, for the first gun battle of all time; there was no precedent, no history, no well-thumbed book of rules behind them. The last major engagement of fleets had been a galley action, as standardised as a dance; won by boarding, by soldiers swarming across bulwarks onto enemy decks; won by the Spaniards, at Lepanto, long ago. Now they would try what sails, and swift ships, and gunpowder could do.

* Near the East Rutts there is a vast natural amphitheatre of dolomite marble, with submerged cliffs 40 feet high.

Howard was not fond of putting pen to paper, except for brief exhortations for more money, more food, more powder, more shot; Drake loathed marshalling arguments to prove points which he knew already to be plain and undisputable; John Hawkyns wrote only mild business letters, and those seldom; Frobisher, although an educated man, could not write at all. Only Raleigh had the gift of coldly summarising essentials, and was spokesman for them all.

He wrote, contemptuously, for those who did not understand the new tactics: " Certainly, he that will happily perform a fight at sea must believe that there is more belonging to a good man of war upon the waters than great daring, and that there is a good deal of difference between fighting loose or at large, and grappling. To clap ships together without consideration belongs rather to a madman than a man of war; for by such ignorant bravery was (the Italian Admiral) Peter Strozzi lost at the Azores, when he fought against the Marquis of Santa Cruz. In like sort had the Lord Charles Howard, Admiral of England, been lost in the year 1588, if he had not been better advised than a great many malignant fools were. The Spaniards had an army aboard them, and he had none; they had more ships than he had, and of higher building and charging; so, that, had he entangled himself with those great and powerful vessels, he had greatly endangered this kingdom of England. For twenty men upon the defences are equal to a hundred that board and enter; whereas, contrariwise, the Spaniards had a hundred for twenty of ours, to defend themselves withal. But our Admiral knew his advantage and held it; which had he not done, he had not been worthy to have held his head."

His advantage was speed, mobility, range, gun power. And the fame of Drake and the English seamen. As the English galleons loomed larger and larger, effortlessly overtaking the Armada, the swift pinnace *Distain*, despatched by Howard, clapped on all sail and moved ahead. Into the great hollow half-moon formed by the two wings of forty armed merchantmen she came, all alone, among the slow-moving, high-castled Spanish ships; and her tiny pop-gun cannon roared out a

defiance across the waves. Then the first group of English
ships, not tight-packed in ranks like the Spanish squadrons, but
sailing line ahead, in follow-my-leader style, came racing past
the sterns of first, Bertondona's Levanters, and then Oquendo's
Guipuscoans, both under the general command of Don Alonso
de Leyva, in charge of the right wing.

As the English guns bore, they fired. Livid yellow flame
ran along the hulls, lighting up the gun-ports, and clouds
of smoke poured out over the sea, wreathing the oncoming
ships in a thick mist, and drifting down slowly onto the
retreating Spaniards. The whistle and whine of cannon balls
shrilling through the air, followed the broadsides; white columns
of water rose up from the waves, and collapsed; and the
crash, the ship-shaking shock of hits, and the piercing screams
of mutilated men, rent the disciplined calm of a moment
before, upon which the sound of the discharge, seconds later,
rode like a thunderclap.

By later standards, those broadsides were not so terrible.
The English ships were passing a few hundred yards away,
not lying gun-muzzle to gun-muzzle; the shot itself, when
loaded, was not a close fit within the bore, was likely to come
out at odd angles, so that the number of near-misses would
be high. The propellant powder was coarse stuff, not as potent
as it was to be later, and the cannons and culverins were of
no great weight. But such a barrage as this, at sea, had never
been seen or experienced before. The shock of a physical
charge, by mailed foot or horsemen, was a thing to which
the Spanish soldiers were well inured; it had behind it only
the strength of men like themselves, or of animals easily
frightened. But the shock of a fire-fight, the screaming, whining,
roaring, nerve-shattering sudden impact of heavy battery after
battery blazing away at a tightly-concentrated target, this was
something different. It was worse, far worse, than any cannon
fire on land, playing on a wide front against a whole army
—and, if truth be told, very often a private war between
opposing batteries. It did not matter that, in this case, the
guns were firing at masses of wood; for the men were tightly
packed within, and they could see, with the approach of each
English ship, twenty or more guns moving up to play upon

them, and they shrank when the muzzles bore, feeling that each and every shot was intended for them alone.

The Duke very nearly lost his Armada there and then, despite his vastly superior numbers; for its great defensive strength, its rigid, near-perfect military formation was momentarily rent. The right wing (styled the " Vanguard " in current military parlance) bulged and broke, despite de Leyva's efforts to rally them; or, as Calderon put it, " certain ships basely took to flight." In their efforts to get away, they fled before the wind and the rest of the oncoming English, and ran in amongst the ships on the other side of the half-moon formation, the left wing, under Recalde (styled the " Rearguard " according to military usage).

This availed them hardly at all, because the English were faster, and, as they swept across the arc of the dissolving half-moon, the smoking, fuming guns were being swabbed out and re-loaded. And the same nerve-shattering barrage broke on them all, reinforced by the broadsides of another group of English ships approaching from nearer to the land. In his turn, Admiral Don Martinez de Recalde found his command disintegrating; partly from the stabbing thunder of the English broadsides, partly from the rush of fleeing ships from the shaken right wing. The armed merchantmen of Biscay and Andalusia suffered the unprecedented cannonading in horror and dismay. From their high castles, they could beat off with ease any attempt to board; were themselves only too eager to swarm over the English bulwarks and into the enemy ships, if they could get at them. But the English never closed the range, and it was clear to all that unless the English wanted to board, no Spanish ship would ever get alongside them. Nor could these armed merchantmen fire back with effect; their guns were light, they had not many of them, and they were lacking in range as well as hitting power. Only the squadron flagships were strong. De Leyva's *Rata Coronada*, almost alone of the fleeing right wing, was trying to fight back, aided by Admiral Oquendo's flagship; and shortly after, Recalde in the *San Juan* was merely an isolated rallying point for a small group on the left wing, of which the most prominent was another strong vessel, the *Gran Grin*, vice-flagship of the Armada of Biscay.

The Duke of Medina Sidonia's description of that first shattering attack of the outnumbered English, the first massed use of their revolutionary new methods and equipment, made dismal reading in the War Diary of the Armada. " The enemy's fleet passed, firing on our van (right wing) under the charge of Don Alonso de Leyva; which drove into the rear (left wing) under the charge of the Admiral Juan Martinez de Recalde, who stood fast and abode the assault of the enemy, although he saw that he was being left unsupported, for that the ships of the rearguard were shrouding themselves in the main body of the Armada. The enemy assailed him with great discharging of ordnance, without closing, whereby his ship suffered much in her rigging, her forestay was cut, and her foremast had two great shot therein. In the rear, supporting him, were the *Gran Grin*, with Don Diego de Pimental and Don Diego Enriquez, the son of the Viceroy of Peru. The *capitana real* (Medina Sidonia's flagship) struck her foretopsail and let fly the sheets, and coming to the wind, awaited the rear to gather it into the main body of the fleet." According to Calderon, among the casualties in Recalde's powerful ship were Captain Pedro de Ycaina and other officers wounded; according to one of her crew, captured later, fatal casualties totalled fifteen.

The *San Martin*, the royal *capitana,* or fleet flagship, clumsily put her bluff bows round and began to work back, against the wind, towards the action raging in the rear, followed by some other galleons and the two galleasses which formed part of the " main battle," the fighting head of the Armada. As they turned out of line, the tight-packed mass of store ships came slowly past them, with the wind behind, and following them close, the hapless fugitives from the right and left wings. These, reported Calderon who was in the vice-flagship of the transport squadron, " were peremptorily ordered by the flagship to luff and face the enemy."

The Armada's meticulous defensive formation, in which lay its main strength, was coming apart, the disorder made more confused by the clouds of gunsmoke drifting slowly across the water, so that sometimes only the topsails of ships could be seen. No one witness can have seen the battle in its entirety, nor even half of it; nobody ever does, even when smokeless powder is used. Battle is essentially a personal experience. The witness is not looking at a game of chess, but at life and death; his life, possibly his death. Everything he sees is tinged with emotion, with the feeling of walking a deadly tightrope; no care for the future, for the future narrows down to now: will he, or will he not, survive the next five minutes? Or, worse even than death, will he, like Captain Priego's ensign in the flagship of Oquendo's squadron lie mutilated, bloody, and screaming on the deck, quivering with the shock of the hurtling iron ball that took off his leg? In many of the ships raked by the English fire, ploughboys, peasants, and fishermen, conscripted for war, were hearing for the first time the horrible, animal howling, high-pitched and inhuman, of human beings terribly hurt.

Two separate engagements developed, cut off from one another by the gunsmoke. Howard's *Ark Royal* spearheaded one attack, and he was probably followed by his kinsmen in *Golden Lion* and *White Bear*, among others. He reported: "The *Ark* bare up with the admiral (flagship) of the Spaniards wherein the Duke was supposed to be, and fought with her until she was rescued by divers ships of the Spanish army." But this battered flagship, whoever she was, could not have been Medina Sidonia's *San Martin*, which was in fact leading the rescue force.

No less than three English flagships were taking part in a simultaneous action with another part of the disorganised Spanish rear, for Howard reported: "In the meantime, Sir Francis Drake, Sir John Hawkyns, and Sir Martin Frobisher fought with the galleon of Portugal, wherein Juan Martinez de Recalde, vice-admiral, was supposed to be." Ubaldino adds the detail that this "Portuguese galleon was also accompanied by a squadron of several galleons of the same nation." Recalde's flagship was a large Portuguese galleon, the *San Juan* of Oporto; and she was in fact rescued by two other Portuguese galleons, Medina Sidonia's *San Martin* and the *San Mateo*. Almost certainly, Howard was disappointed in his belief that he had fought Medina Sidonia, who seems to have been engaged with Drake, Hawkyns, and Frobisher.

Calderon, who was also present, identified a big English ship as the enemy fleet flagship, and noted: "She struck her foresail, and from the direction of the land sent four vessels, one of which was the vice-flagship (presumably meaning Drake), to skirmish with our vice-flagship (Recalde's *San Juan*) and the rest of our rearguard (the Armada's left wing, commanded by Recalde). They bombarded her and the galleon *San Mateo*, which, putting her head as close up to the wind as possible, did not reply to their fire, but waited for them in the hope of bringing them to close quarters. The *Rata*, with Don Alonso de Leyva on board, endeavoured to approach the enemy's vice-flagship, which allowed herself to fall towards the *Rata*. But they could not exchange cannon shots, because the enemy's ship, fearing that the *San Mateo* would bring her to close quarters, left the *Rata* and bombarded the *San Mateo*. Meanwhile the wind forced Don Alonso de Leyva away, and he was prevented from carrying out his intentions; but he exchanged cannon shots with other enemy ships. Juan Martinez de Recalde, like the skilful seaman he was, collected all his ships whilst protecting his rearguard, engaging at the same time eight of the enemy's best ships. The Duke's flagship most distinguished herself this day, as she was engaged the greater part of the time, and resisted the fury of the whole of the enemy's fleet."

The soldier, Estrade, was somewhere there, amid the stabbing gun flashes and boiling powder smoke, in the Portuguese galleon *San Marcos*. He mentions some "very good artillery which the *Rat* had," but implies she was Don Pedro's flagship instead of De Leyva's, as she actually was. But the formidably armed oared galleasses were unmistakable, and their arrival concluded the engagement: "The vice-admiral of the galleasses (the vice-flagship *Zuniga*) went putting himself into our horn of Don Pedro de Valdes; and the English when they saw the galleasses to enter, they retired and went away all that they could. And the artillery ceased and we did apart ourselves."

Howard reported that he broke off the action at one o'clock, but Estrade says that there was some cannonading going on until four o'clock; possibly some of the English ships, which were operating loosely in small groups, could not resist the opportunity to dash in now and again and have a nibble at the straggling disorganised Spaniards, who were stretched over so many miles of sea that from one part of the battlefield a brief attack in another would come only as a distant thudding of gunfire. Howard reported the conclusion of the main engagement: " The fight was so well maintained for the time that the enemy was constrained to give way and bear up room to the eastward, to stop their leaks, in which bearing up, a great galleon, wherein Don Pedro de Valdes was captain, became foul of another ship which spoiled and bare overboard his foremast and bowsprit."

Up to that time Don Pedro's Armada of Andalusia, being in a less exposed position than Recalde's Biscayans, had got off lightly. He wrote: " Our ordnance played a long while on both sides, without coming to hand stroke. There was little harm done, because the fight was far off. When it had ended, I sent a pinnace unto Juan Martinez de Recalde, to know whether he had received any harm. His answer was that his galleon had been sore beaten, and that his foremast was hurt with a great shot. He prayed me that I would come to relieve him, for that other-ways he should not be able to abide any new fight if we were offered it the same day." Immediately, Don Pedro turned out of the line and began to work back upwind to the battered and dismayed Biscay squadron, their nerves still shattered from the cannonading they had received. Indeed, both squadrons had now become intermingled, and were trying to sort themselves out, with Recalde's splintered flagship lying far to the rear.

As de Valdes began to tack westwards, hauled close to the wind, there drifted down upon him a mass of ships, some his, some Recalde's, sailing on converging courses and working their sails. A Biscay ship loomed ahead among the Andalusians, leaving no room between her and the other ships for Don Pedro's vessel, the *Nuestra Senora del Rosario*, to

111

pass through the narrow gap; and no room either for him to turn away. As both ships swung under their helms, the bows of Don Pedro's big flagship smashed into the Biscay ship, destroying the spritsail and carrying away also one of her crossyards. The damage to the *Rosario* sent her partly out of control, for the steering of such heavy ships was done as much with the pull of the foresails as with the helm. As she pulled clear, a ship following the Biscayan loomed ahead also on a collision course. She was the *Santa Catalina*, one of Don Pedro's own squadron, and her presence, behind instead of in front of a Biscay ship, illustrated better than anything else the confusion and terror which had made most of Recalde's squadron " shroud themselves in the main body of the Armada." But now, there was no avoiding her and she drove heavily into the crippled *Rosario*, breaking her bowsprit, and bringing down the halyards and forecourse. Don Pedro's ship lay heaving on the waves, the rest of the Armada driving past her; and, as her crew took emergency measures to bring her under control again, Don Pedro fired a gun for help.

Hardly had it boomed out across the waters, and Medina Sidonia turned once again into the wind to wait for her, than an enormous cloud of black smoke, lightning lit by a brilliant yellow flash, poured up from the other wing of the Armada, where Oquendo's Guipuzcoans were re-forming. The thunder of the detonation followed seconds later. This was no cannon shot, it dwarfed even the roar of a broadside. Oquendo's vice-flagship, the *San Salvador*, had blown up. The hulk, reeking and streaming powder smoke, masts tottering, stern castles and galleries gone, upper deck blown to splinters, drifted sluggishly astern on the waves. From inside her came a low, persistent moaning, mixed with terrible screams, the agony of horribly burnt men.

It was now two o'clock, according to Calderon's very full and detailed diary; one hour after Howard had broken off the main action. An hour, with fast, modern ships, is a very long time; to re-impose order on straggling sailing ships, moving clumsily eastward at three or four knots, sixty minutes is a very short time. In spite of Spanish discipline, the Armada was not yet re-arrayed to the Duke's satisfaction. Preoccupied with re-forming his wings in battle order, he was confronted first with the crisis of the *Rosario* and, minutes later, with the shock of the *San Salvador* explosion. Both ships were drifting helplessly astern, and would be taken by the pursuing English unless he did something about it. Both ships were flagships; one was commanded by an admiral; both contained treasure essential to the fleet if it had to put into a foreign port where supplies would have to be paid for. The *Rosario* had 52,000 ducats of the King's money, to be paid out on behalf of the Andalusian squadron, apart from private treasure and plate belonging to the noblemen aboard. The *San Salvador* had far more, for the Paymaster General was aboard her, and had under his eye the largest single amount of money in any Armada ship, much greater than the average 50-55,000 ducats held in the flags and vice-flags of the squadrons. The Duke was very hard-pressed and, in the circumstances, did more for the *San Salvador* than for Don Pedro, who ever afterwards loathed him for it. He would hardly have succeeded, even there, had it not been for the galleasses which, with their banks of great oars, were independent of the wind, and were sufficiently heavily-gunned to make the English careful.

Apart from these cares and preoccupations, he knew now for a certainty that his master, the King, in his fighting instructions, had been aware of only half the truth. He had been right when he warned that: " The enemy's object will be to engage at a distance, on account of the advantage which they have from their artillery." By one reckoning in the *San Martin*, the English had fired more than 2,000 rounds at them that day, to which the Armada had replied with 720 round shot, entirely without effect, No one even so much as claimed to have damaged an English ship, whereas there was splintered planking and dead men in many of the Spanish ships. True it was, too, that the Spaniards had tried to carry out their King's imperative command " to close and grapple and engage hand to hand." The *San Martin's* consort, the *San Mateo*, had hopefully come up into the wind and held her fire, inviting Drake, Hawkyns, and Frobisher to come alongside and helpfully hang about while the great Portuguese galleon poured down her hundreds of armed men into them. And all they had done was treat her contemptuously as a battle practice target for their gunners, racing past her at rate she could not match. And poor Don Alonso de Leyva, the Lieutenant-General of the whole Armada, accompanied by the flower of Spanish chivalry in the great *Rata Encoronada,* he had not even been able to match the performance of the *San Mateo,* lumbering slowly after the nimble English vessels, for he had been unable even to come up into the wind; instead, when he had attempted to do so, he had simply drifted sideways in the opposite direction to the enemy. Whereas, as Medina Sidonia had noted, " The English did with their ships whatsoever they desired." This factor, the speed and handling qualities of the enemy's new vessels, had quite simply been left out of account by the planners back in Spain. There would be no grappling, unless the English desired it.

They did not. It would have been madness to press a close action, when less than half the English fleet was present, when time was on their side, when every day their numbers must increase. Indeed, even during the battle, reinforcements of men were being sent out from Plymouth by the Mayor, William Hawkyns, and hourly were being taken into the ships. The fight, as the Mayor reported to the Council in London, was in " plain view " of Plymouth, " which we beheld." The knowledge that they were fighting under the eyes of their countrymen, and not mere ignorant Londoners, but the people of a mariner's town, inflamed some of the English captains to the point where they would have taken unpardonable risks, had Howard allowed it. Henry Whyte, captain of the 200 ton *Bark Talbot,* wrote angrily to Walsyngham some weeks later: " The majesty of the enemy's fleet, the good order they held, and the private consideration of our own wants, did cause, in mine opinion, our first onset to be more coldly done than became the valour of our nation and the credit of the English navy; yet we put them to leeward, kept the weather of them, and distressed two of their best ships, whereof Don Pedro's was one."

The panic of the rearward Spanish squadrons, the way they crowded each other in their efforts to escape the gunfire, the bumping and boring which disabled Don Pedro's flagship, and the plight of the stricken *San Salvador*, must have prompted many to believe that this was the moment to press right home into that great formation and really carve it up. Howard, risking the kingdom on it, thought the time was not ripe; he had not enough strength for a knockout blow. The Spanish superiority in infantry was appalling; any attempt to break into the great half-moon from the rear would mean enveloping his forces in double their number of Spanish ships, where they could be surrounded, grappled, boarded, and taken.

The really experienced fighting admirals regarded the day's events as a mere preliminary canter, an interesting and inexpensive experiment with the new methods. " There hath passed some cannon shot between some of our fleet and some of them," commented Drake coolly, aware that they had been bombarding the armed merchantman and had yet really to test the best ships of the Armada bunched together. "As far as we can perceive, they are determined to sell their lives with blows," he added dryly. John Hawkyns, who was a business man at sea, when doing business at sea meant fighting, was briefly businesslike. He dismissed the battle as, " We had some small fight with them in the afternoon."

Howard had to be more forthcoming and justify his decision. " The Lord Admiral, considering there were forty sail of his fleet as yet to come from Plymouth, thought good to stay for their coming before he would hazard the rest too far." To Walsyngham, he wrote: " We durst not adventure to put in among them, their fleet being so strong." And he added, bearing out Drake's old warning that the ammunition allowance was good for about a day and a half: " Sir, for the love of God and our country, let us have with some speed some great shot sent to us of all bigness; for this service will continue long; and some powder with it." These, together with the lack of victuals, and the comparatively small number of English vessels present, were probably the " wants " referred to by Whyte of the *Bark Talbot*.

Howard then flew the flag for council, and the admirals came across to the *Ark Royal,* " where his Lordship's considerate advice was much liked of, and order delivered unto each captain how to pursue the fleet of Spain; and so, dismissing each man to go aboard his own ship, his Lordship appointed Sir Francis Drake to set the watch that night."

CHAPTER TEN

A Voice in Spanish Calling Us

Night of 21/22 July

MANY EYES in the English fleet must have been looking hungrily at the two distressed Spanish vessels, strong and important units of their respective squadrons. Don Pedro's *Rosario* was the *capitana,* or flagship, of the Armada of Andalusia, the *San Salvador* was the *almiranta,* or vice-flagship, of Oquendo's Armada of Guipuscoa. The crippled *Rosario* was now moving again, limping slowly towards the rear of the retreating Armada, while the *San Salvador* was surrounded by Spanish vessels, trying to take her in tow. No doubt some bold and rash spirits among the English, such as Whyte of the *Bark Talbot,* thought it " coldly done " when Howard made no move to interfere, but instead hoisted the flag for council. Yet, when it was over, Howard was able to record that his " considerate advice was much liked of." What had been talked about, and what had been decided, and why was it more important than the two potential Spanish prizes?

There are enough clues scattered about to make it plain. Ubaldino, the confidant of both Howard and Drake (and also Don Pedro), records that Howard's decision not to press the attack until he was no longer out-numbered, was ratified. This was plain common-sense, and, in the light of what the English actually did during the following week can probably be summed up as: " We can afford to wait, because we shall grow progressively stronger; by the time we reach the Straits of Dover, and join with the fleets of Seymour and Wynter, we shall have actual superiority; that will be the time to smash them." A vital factor in this decision must have been the serious inroads into the stocks of powder and shot caused by the brief action off Plymouth. Drake had forecast this situation exactly, and we know from many reports, mostly clearly expressed in Hawkyns' letter to Walsyngham, how large this problem loomed in their minds and how perilously close they came at times to complete impotence, from lack of ammunition. Their new methods of gun-fighting, instead of grappling, were too new; the industrial complex to support such intensive cannonading did not exist. Gunpowder then was as scarce and secret as uranium was recently, and master gunners as important to war then as nuclear scientists now; indeed, for security reasons, master gunners, at this moment, were not allowed to leave the country. The Armada, as yet, had no such worries; it had been stored and ammunitioned for a long campaign of many months, from the resources of a power far more wealthy than England, and controlling most of the existing powder factories. The English were going to be ammunitioned from hand-to-mouth, and from day-to-day, literally by whatever could be scraped from the bottom of the barrel and brought out to them from the shore.

A word from Howard, and the rhythm of the following week's fighting, tells the rest of the story. "We mean so to course the enemy as that they shall have no leisure to land," he wrote next day. The English would fight only in defence of possible invasion objectives, of which there were three to come after Plymouth. There were Torbay and Portland, mentioned in the November, 1587, invasion estimates, and the Isle of Wight, also listed but much the more likely objective for the Spanish army. The Spaniards would have to be "coursed," come what may, off all three places. How was this to be done? Again, commonsense and the week's events give a plain answer. Somebody would have to keep inshore of the Spaniards, while the rest put in "spoiling" and "fixing" attacks; that dangerous inshore station would have to be given to Frobisher, whose vast *Triumph* was eminently defensible, aided by the older, higher-charged English ships, particularly those of Howard and his kinsmen. The easily-taken but nimble new galleons of Drake and Hawkyns would be better employed where there was plenty of sea room, out to sea. As this is exactly what happened, and as the two coming battles were virtually duplicates of each other, and as, on each occasion, all the English leaders played and re-played the same distinctive roles, recognisable one from the other, an overall battle plan may be assumed. It could hardly have been an accident, when it makes so much sense;

remembering also that the men who attended Howard's Council of War were the cream of the fighting seamen of their time. They had good reason to be content, when they went down the side of the *Ark Royal* and into their boats. Here, despite the English " wants " in munitions and in numbers, was a workable scheme.

The Spaniards were much less happy; indeed, they had had a shock. They had expected the English artillery superiority, but had not been too worried because a little cannon fire was thought unlikely to sink a ship, or even cause many casualties. What they had not bargained for was the deadly combination of superior gun-power with superior speed and mobility, which meant that they would have to take continual punishment without effective reply. Not suspecting the English ammunition shortage, which would effectively curtail the cannonading, they foresaw a bleak future. Although outnumbered two to one, the English had panicked the rear of the Armada and endangered the whole Spanish formation; when the English fleet grew to its full strength, what could stop it? At the moment, the Duke was a little too busy with his cripples to give the matter effective thought, but he was to do so next day, when the Armada's battle formation was to be drastically altered and the ultimate disciplinary measure—death—threatened to any ship captain who emulated that disgraceful panic off Plymouth. Prisoners taken in the next twelve hours, their recollections fresh, were to supply the background to the Duke's decisions. Ubaldino reported, having talked to some of them: "After meeting the English fleet and seeing it get under sail so easily through the skill of the English, versed as they were in sea matters, and seeing that, with the type of ships they had which were a good deal smaller than the Spanish, they were able to get very near to the much larger ships and fight against them to their own advantage, the Spaniards confessed themselves greatly surprised and admitted that they had lost much of their hope in the victory of their fleet." Normally, it is wise not to take the depositions of prisoners at exact face value, but the events that evening, and the decisions taken next day, show that this was no great exaggeration.

At first, however, it seemed that the Duke had the situation in hand, and that there would be no prisoners. His own flagship

stood by the burning *San Salvador*, while four patches man-
oeuvred alongside, got a line across, and began to tow her after
the Armada. The fire on board was put out, and an unsuccessful
attempt made to remove some of the wounded to the hospital
ships. But the great carrack was such a reeking shambles inboard
that the task defied all human effort. " Both after decks were
blown up," wrote Calderon, who was in another *San Salvador,*
which helped to take off survivors. " More than 200 men were
killed, including Ensign Castenada, who was on watch; and the
ship was rent in both bow and stern. Many of the men jumped
into the sea and were drowned, but the four patches saved the
principal persons, including Paymaster Juan de Huerta, with
his staff papers, and some money in his charge." Captain Juan
de Villaviciosa, Vice-Admiral of Oquendo's squadron and the
senior naval officer on board, had burns; Captain Pedro de
Priego, commanding a company of 94 soldiers, was badly burnt;
the other two infantry captains, Don Francisco de Chaves, with
133 men, and Geronimo de Valderrama, with 92, were unhurt.
As there were in addition 64 seamen in the ship, she had therefore suffered more than 60 per cent. fatal casualties at one blow.
The shattered decks were littered with dreadful travesties of men,
blackened and pock-marked as if soot had been driven into
their flesh, their clothes still smouldering; flesh had run from
their faces and hands as if it had been liquid; some were still
alive, and moaning, but if anyone attempted to lift them, the skin
and meat came away at the touch, leaving the white bone
showing. For such wounds as these, the Armada was not prepared at all, let alone in such overwhelming numbers. How had
it happened? Sabotage, it was whispered.

Calderon, who next day reported that he had " received on
the flag-hulk Captain Villaviciosa and about 34 burnt men,"
had the opportunity to question survivors, including those who
had been in the vicinity of the explosion. He wrote: " It is
said that Captain Priego had beaten a German artilleryman,
who went below, saying that one of the pieces had got wet, and
would have to be discharged. He fired the piece and then threw
the port fire into a barrel of powder." A party of 14 Dutch
mariners then serving in the Armada, who later deserted when
off the coast of the Netherlands, had heard much the same story,

presumably from other survivors taken into different ships in the fleet. " She was set on fire by reason of the captain falling into a rage with the gunner and threatening to kill him if he shot no righter. The gunner cast fire into the powder barrels and threw himself overboard. In this ship, they say, was the treasure and five ensigns of Spaniards."

Apart from minor detail, these two first-hand stories are identical. But when Ubaldino came to write his history, there were two versions of the gunner's motive in circulation. "An army captain (i.e., Priego) had insolently beaten a Flemish gunner, it is not known whether on account of his work or of the wife of the gunner who was with him, as is the custom of his country; whereupon the poor wretch, despairing of his life and that of his wife, and perhaps even more of her honour, and that of his daughter, set alight to a barrel of gunpowder, thus avenging himself and his dear ones."

Ubaldino was merely reporting the two versions then current, both of which could conceivably be true; the gunner may well have had a double motive for his drastic action. It was with this very point in mind that Medina Sidonia had included in his Fleet Orders the instruction: "As it is an evident inconvenience, as well as an offence to God, that public or other women should be permitted to accompany such an Armada, I order that none shall be taken on board." Consequently, another historian, writing nearly four centuries later (Professor Mattingly, *The Defeat of the Spanish Armada*), roasted Ubaldino for his credulity in believing that there might have been women in the Spanish ships; disdainfully, he dismissed the possibility as " poetic licence." What he was doing, in effect, was to lecture a sixteenth-century historian on the customs of the sixteenth century.

But poor Ubaldino was at least as conscientious in his research as his American rival; and he was better informed. He knew what the English had found in the ruin of the *San Salvador*. A few Spaniards, mostly of " the common sort," for the senior officers had been rescued, plus " two Frenchmen, four Almains, and one Almain woman." Here, possibly, was the wife or daughter of the " German artilleryman " beaten by Captain Priego, according to Calderon. Ubaldino stands accused, therefore, at the worst, of confusing a Fleming with a German, no great error, if error it was. His twentieth-century successor, however, disappears inevitably into the pit awaiting those scholars who fail to do their homework, for the official inventory of the *San Salvador*, certified to the Council by George Trenchard and Francis Hawley, justices of the peace for Devon, still survives, in one of the two main source works for the Armada campaign. Among the living, they found this "one Almain woman."

While the treasure was being taken out of the *San Salvador*, Don Pedro de Valdes had brought up near the rear of the Armada, to repair the damage to the *Rosario*; and was soon totally, instead of partially, disabled. "While I was in this case," he wrote, "the sea did rise in such sort that my ship, having struck sail and wanting her halyard of the foremast, being withal but badly built, did work so extremely as shortly after, and before it could be remedied, her foremast brake close by the hatches, and fell upon the mainmast, so as it was impossible to repair that hurt but in some good space of time. I did again send word thereof several times to the Duke, and discharged three or four great pieces, to the end all the fleet might know what distress I was in, praying him either to appoint some ship or galleass to tow me ahead, or to direct me what other course I should take." And all the fleet did take note of his distress. Don Jorge Manrique, Inspector-General of the Armada, later coldly reported to the King: "The Armada passed on, leaving her behind in sight of the enemy; and what subsequently became of her and her crew is not known." Estrade, writing when more had been learnt, recorded: "Then again she shot off four pieces, but there were none that came to succour her, for that the wind did blow much, the sea was grown, and the English did follow us. At prayer-time we left her, for that the Duke of Medina did shoot off a piece with a bullet by which we proceeded on our way. After, we understood that she was boarded with five galleons, who did much harm unto Don Pedro and slew all his people."

There were seven Englishmen in the *Rosario*, and knowing what their fate would be, if captured, four of them got into the pinnace which Don Pedro sent to the *San Martin* to ask for aid; but three remained behind, taking their chance. In the pinnace also went the friar, Bernado de Gongora, who had to stay in the Duke's ship and watch the final desertion of his friends. "The Duke continued on his course, leaving them in the power of the enemy, who always followed a league astern; and in the ship was good old Vicente Alvarez, the captain, and what has been done with them God knows."

The rage among the Spaniards may be imagined, directed, not at the English, but at Medina Sidonia and his advisers in the *San Martin*. But their fury was as nothing to Don Pedro's. "Nevertheless, although he was near enough to me, and saw in what case I was, and might easily have relieved me, yet would he not do it; but even as if we had not been Your Majesty's subjects nor employed in your service, discharged a piece to call the fleet together, and followed his course, leaving me comfortless in the sight of the whole fleet, the enemy being but a quarter of a league from me."

The Duke's version of the affair is rather different; it records a half-hearted attempt to save the disabled flagship and her treasure. Half-hearted because, the Duke was advised, he would risk losing the whole Armada if he tempted another battle with the English so late in the day. "As it was now night," he reported, "Diego Flores told the Duke that if he took in sail and stood by her the rest of the Armada would not perceive it, as most of the ships were far in advance, and he would find himself in the morning with less than half the Armada. Diego Flores was of opinion that the Duke ought not to risk the whole of his force, as he was sure that if he stood by he would lose the day." Personally a brave man, but quite unable to judge the technical merits of the case, and impressed as they all were with the alarming effectiveness of the English fleet, Medina Sidonia gave way. "In face of this advice the Duke ordered Captain Ojeda to stand by Don Pedro's flagship, with four pataches, Don Pedro's vice-flagship, Diego Flores' flagship, and a galleass, to attempt to pass a hawser on board and tow her, or else take the men out of her." The attempt failed, and Medina Sidonia fired the recall gun. Don Pedro was left behind, in the night, to the mercy of the English. Two hours later, recorded Calderon, out in the darkness over the heaving black waters behind them came the sullen rumble of gunfire, three or four shots only. Then silence. "Nothing further is known of Don Pedro," Calderon wrote.

In the minds of every man was shame, coupled with the knowledge that Don Diego Flores de Valdes was the cousin of Don Pedro de Valdes, that they were known to dislike each other, and that it was Diego Flores who had advised that his kinsman be left to his fate.

In fact, Medina Sidonia, in his War Diary, exaggerated both the size of the force he sent to help the *Rosario* and the urgency of the English threat; at any rate, only one ship made for the crippled Spaniard, the rest swept on after the Armada with silent guns. This lone vessel was the *Margaret and John* of London, 200 tons, 90 men, Captain John Fisher. Her master was John Nash and her lieutenant was Richard Thomson, who probably did the actual composing of their joint petition for a share in the prize money. Thomson must have been a smart man for, within a week, he took part in the capture of two Spanish flagships. The *Nuestra Senora del Rosario* was his first.

"We only, with our ship," he wrote, "as all the fleet can testify, bare romer with the (Spanish) ship, being accompanied neither with ship, pinnace, or boat of all our fleet. At our approach, we found left by her, for her safeguard, a great galleon, a galleass and a pinnace, with order either to help her repair her masts, and so follow the Spanish army, gone before, or else to bring away the men, treasure and munition thereof, and to fire or sink the ship; all which three, upon the sudden approach of our ship, only forsook Don Pedro, leaving him to the mercy of the sea. And this much hath Don Pedro himself confessed, condemning and exclaiming much upon those that were left for his comfort, in that they forsook him, upon the coming of one small ship."

"About 9 of the clock the same evening we came hard under the sides of the ship of Don Pedro, which by reason of her greatness and the sea being very much grown, we could not lay aboard without spoiling our own ship. And therefore, seeing not one man shew himself, nor any light appearing in her, we imagined that most of the people had been taken out; and to try whether any were aboard or not, we discharged 25 or 30 muskets into her cagework, at one volley, with arrows and bullet. And presently they gave us two great shot, whereupon we let fly our broadside through her, doing them some hurt, as themselves have and can testify.

"After this we cast about our ship, and kept ourselves close by the Spaniard until midnight, sometime hearing a voice in Spanish calling us; but the wind being very great, and we in the weather (upwind), the voice was carried away, that we could not well understand it, but were persuaded by our mariners, to be the voice of one swimming in the sea; whereupon we put off our ship boat with 8 oars, to seek, call, and take them up; but found nobody."

It must have been an eerie experience, locked alone on the night sea with the great, blacked-out Spaniard, her high castles towering above them, and all inside as quiet as death. Obviously, Don Pedro had doused every light, in the hope of being unmolested, so that he would have time to repair the damage and perhaps rejoin the Armada. The *Margaret and John* left him shortly after midnight, to follow Howard. Drake, in the *Revenge*, had the post of honour that night, leading the pursuit throughout the hours of darkness. Very shortly, however, the glow of his stern lantern vanished abruptly, as if wiped off the face of the night with a duster. Howard, puzzled, moved up to find out what had happened, but could see in the gloom no sign of his Vice-Admiral. Then the moon came out. On all the sparkling expanse of silver sea ahead and around, there was no ship that could conceivably be the *Revenge*, only the huddled forest of masts and white sails in front that was the Armada. Howard closed up to within culverin shot of them, followed at some distance by the *White Bear* and the *Mary Rose*, and sailed on steadily through the night, just out of range of the enemy's guns.

At dawn next morning, Monday, 22 July, Howard found himself alone on the waters off Berry Head, by Torbay, with only these two English ships, and the Armada, for company. Far astern, half-mast high, came the next English ship; and the rearmost was quite out of sight. Still, there was no sign of the *Revenge*. One of the first ships to come up with Howard's

Ark Royal was the *Margaret and John* of London; she must have had a very pretty turn of speed. " We went aboard the *Ark*," wrote Thomson, " and certified his Lordship in what distressed state we had left the ship our enemy; praying leave that we might be permitted to return to finish our attempt; or that his Lordship would send a pinnace to Dartmouth or Plymouth, that some shipping might be set forth to fetch her in."

While they were making their report, with one eye on the prize money, no doubt, a fast pinnace came creaming up from astern, the water sheering back from her bows; and she also came alongside the English flagship. Out of her came Captain Thomas Cely, jubilant, less conscious of that " patched carcase " of his, the souvenirs of his time in the Spanish prisons and the galley at St. Mary Port less than ten years before. Curiously enough, Puerto Santa Maria, with its groves of orange trees, was where the Duke of Medina Sidonia had his estates. Cely's news would not please him. " Up came one Captain Cely," wrote Thomson, " certifying his Lordship that Sir Francis Drake, staying behind the fleet all night, had taken the said ship of Don Pedro de Valdes, with 460 men in her, full of artillery, munition, and treasure." So that was where Drake had got to—cunning beggar!

Howard, accepting that Drake always had uncanny luck where treasure ships were concerned, reported simply: " Our own fleet were disappointed of their light, by reason that Sir Francis Drake left the watch to pursue certain hulks which were descried very late in the evening." If he had seen strange sails to seaward, it was certainly his duty to find out what they were; and if he had to do it personally, with the flagship, to extinguish his stern light before he turned off course, in order not to lead the rest of the fleet astray. Other people, notably Martin Frobisher, the sanguine Yorkshireman who commanded the *Triumph*, were not so easily satisfied with the truth of the story; or if true, that it was the whole truth. It was not until some weeks later that Frobisher had the satisfaction of telling one of Drake's officers, to his face, what he thought of Sir Francis.

The officer, Mathew Starke, deposed that Frobisher's diatribe had gone as follows: " Sir Francis Drake reporteth that no man hath done any good service but he; but he shall understand that

ord Charles Howard, Earl of Effingham.
From an oil painting by D. Mytens

Sir Martin Frobisher. *From a line engraving
by C. van de Passe*

John Hawkyns. *From an oil painting by
an unknown artist*

Sir Francis Drake. *From an oil painting by
an unknown artist*

The Battle of Plymouth, showing the small English Western Fleet attacking the Armada, which is sailing in crescent formation. The artist has inserted, lower left, the later incident of the capture of the *Rosario* by the *Revenge*; one of the small ships is possibly Captain Cely's. *From a line engraving by J. Pine after C. de Lempriere*

others hath done as good service as he, and better too. He hath done good service indeed, for he took Don Pedro. For after he had seen her in the evening, that she had spent her masts, then, like a coward, he kept by her all night, because he would have the spoil. He thinketh to cozen us of our shares of fifteen thousand ducats; but we will have our shares, or I will make him spend the best blood in his belly; for we hath had enough of those cozening cheats already."

" Then he demanded of me if we did not see Don Pedro over night or no. Unto which I answered: ' No.'

" Then he told me that I lied; for she was seen to all the fleet. Unto the which I answered: ' I would lay my head that not any one man in the ship did see her until it was morning, that we were within two or three cables length of her.'

" Whereunto he answered: 'Ay, marry, saith he, you were within two or three cables length; for you were no further off all night, but lay a-hull by her.'

" Whereunto I answered: ' No, for that we bare a good sail all night, off and on.'

" Then he asked me to what end we stood off from the fleet all night. Whom I answered that: ' We had descried three or four hulks, and to that end we wrought so, not knowing what they were.'

" Then saith he: ' Sir Francis was appointed to bear a light all that night; which light we looked for, but there was no light to be seen; and in the morning, when we should have dealt with them, there was not above five or six near unto the Admiral, by reason we saw not his light.'

" Then saith he: ' I have no more to say unto you; you may depart.' "

The phrase " when we should have dealt with them " was significant; for on the morning of 22 July, the Armada was off Torbay, one of the listed possible objectives. Clearly, the English had intended to give battle; but Drake's action had saved their powder, for the Armada kept steadily on. Now there were only two possible invasion points left—Weymouth, by the Bill of Portland, and the Isle of Wight.

CHAPTER ELEVEN

Hang Any Captain . . .

Monday, 22 July

THE FIRST man into the *Rosario* was Nic Oseley, civilian, business man, and spy. Among the English State Papers are accurate reports concerning the mobilisation of the Armada; some of these were the work of Oseley, who under cover of his business as a merchant in Spain, took on in 1588 the adventurous task of riding from port to port to gain information, in spite of the fact that he was known as an English agent, having previously been imprisoned for it. On his return to England with the latest news, just before the coming of the Spaniards, Walsyngham had sent him to Lord Howard. But it was Drake who took him on board, as up-to-the-minute adviser on the Armada, and it was Drake who put to use his knowledge of Spanish, on the morning of Monday, 22 July. And he was, of course, much the best person to put to the commander of this powerful ship Drake's terms of surrender. "Aboard they had much evil order, as I did see," reported Oseley, "who by Sir Francis' commandment was the first went to them."

"Finding myself in so bad case," was Don Pedro's version, "void of all hope to be relieved, and Sir Francis Drake, admiral of the enemy's fleet, bearing towards me with his ship, from whom there came a message that I should yield myself upon assurance of good usage, I went aboard him, upon his word, to treat of the conditions of our yielding."

According to Ubaldino, who had it first-hand from Sir Francis, Drake's offer was brusque and brutal: " surrender unconditionally or give battle." There was a pointed reference to " the rules of war," and " that they should surrender to his will, because otherwise he did not wish to waste his time, and perhaps lose sight of his fleet." The rules of war, then, were that mercy was shown to an opponent, by land or by sea, only if he laid down his arms without fighting. Once blood had been shed, no quarter was given to men of the " common sort "; the senior officers, however, could expect to survive because of their ransom potential. Therefore, Don Pedro's own life was not in question, nor that of his officers, but only those of his men. He had a high-charged ship, which would give the English some trouble to take; he could delay Drake and keep him out of the fight for a little time, and there was his own honour at stake. But the gaping gun-ports of the *Revenge*, and the " hurry up, no bloody nonsense " attitude of her admiral, decided him. The crippled *Rosario* would not last long. Drake would simply lay the *Revenge* across her bow or stern, from which only a few Spanish guns could reply, and batter her with his broadsides until half her men were dead or dying. As for his honour, no one could be ashamed of surrendering to the most famous fighter then at sea; indeed, there was even a certain distinction in it.

Therefore, wrote Don Pedro, " the best conclusion that could be taken was the safety of our lives and courteous entertainment; for performance whereof Sir Francis Drake gave us his hand and word of a gentleman, and promised he would use us better than any others that were come to his hands, and would be a means that the Queen should also do the like; whereupon I thought good to accept of his offer." The promise was carried out to the letter, and 10 days later Don Pedro and his senior officers found themselves guests in the house of Richard Drake, a kinsman of Sir Francis; " about forty of the better sort besides bestowed in divers men's houses in London," the rest remaining in the captured ship. Even as prisoners, however, the Spaniards could still do some good for Spain. The men Nic Oseley questioned told him, straight-faced, that the Armada numbered 150 sail. And Don Pedro, "talking courteously and in a familiar way" to Ubaldino, presumably at Richard Drake's house, stated that the number was 142, of which, of course, he quickly added, a mere 110 were fighting ships. To make these estimates more credible, he gave a number of details—the presence of hospital ships, the detaching of the galleys, and so on—which were accurate, but of no particular value to the English.

In fact, before surrendering, he had given most probably a quick security briefing to his men, guessing that they would be thoroughly interrogated, as in fact they were. Drake, having just reported the Spanish fleet as " somewhat above a hundred sails, not half of them men of war," no doubt smiled politely. For, " after having converged together a brief space, Vice-Admiral Drake expressed the wish that Don Pedro should always eat at his table, thus honouring him as a foreign friend, and he desired him to sleep in his cabin." To make even greater show of hospitality, Drake " allowed no violence to be done to the persons of the Spaniards on board the prize, nor did he allow anything to be taken or touched of the goods belonging to Don Pedro. Of course the money that was found there, amounting to 50,000 escudos, belonging to the Royal Treasury of Spain, was taken and later given to the Lord Treasurer of England," adds Ubaldino. And therefore it came about that Don Pedro, although a prisoner, did not miss the fighting after all; indeed, he was to be in the thick of it throughout, watching the defeat of the Armada from the stern cabin of Drake's flagship—a grandstand seat if there ever was one.

Of course, Drake's main motive must have been the sheer interest of being able to talk to someone on the opposite side who was nearly, if not quite in his own class, for Don Pedro was an Admiral of reputation who had held high command in the Portuguese campaign. At the same time, he had put his opponent into a good humour and could hardly help picking up information of importance. But that cut both ways, and the English Government were alarmed when they heard of it, thinking that some of the " secrets of the services " might be revealed. Consequently, they ordered Don Pedro out of the *Revenge* and into house arrest in custody of Richard Drake. There, on 4 August, he was examined according to a carefully drawn-up questionnaire headed *Articles to be ministered to Don Pedro de Valdes and his associates.* Don Pedro fenced delightfully with his interrogators.

" What was the end and purpose of the King of Spain his sending so great an army by sea into these parts?"

" The King sent this armada to the Prince of Parma for to clear the way, so as he might land in this kingdom and conquer it," replied Don Pedro, blandly.

" With what honour and conscience could the King do the same?" enquired the interrogator, with a touch of English self-righteousness.

" It lieth not with me to answer if the King did well or ill, being a subject, and unable to judge the actions of his prince," replied Don Pedro, making a point which may still be debated.

But these were only sighting shots. The Government's main preoccupation was with the potential, and perhaps mythical, fifth-column. " What princes Catholics were parties to this enterprise, and what support did they look for out of France, from whom, and from what place?" Don Pedro shook his head. He knew nothing about that, he said. " Which were their two places where they should have made their descent here in this realm; and what party did they look for here?" pressed the interrogator. But Don Pedro would say only, that the selection of a landing place was left to the Duke of Parma, except that they intended to anchor at the Isle of Wight, if necessary, to repair damage. He knew nothing of any support to be expected from Englishmen. The interrogator came back to that point a few minutes later: " Which of the Englishmen in the army were privy to the secrets of the enterprise?" "None of them," replied Don Pedro. On military matters, he definitely tried to mislead them, but not so grotesquely as would make it apparent. There were in the Armada, he said, about 140 ships, and 29,000 men; and the Duke of Parma had 36,000 horse and foot. On the *Rosario's* treasure, he went the other way, and under-estimated. " Near 20,000 ducats, as also vessels of silver worth another thousand," he said. Perhaps he had made a little under-the-counter bargain with Drake; we shall never know. We know only that, when facing his interrogators, Don Pedro de Valdes was still fighting for Spain.

Most of the Spanish prisoners seem to have maintained the same unbroken front. Vicente Alvarez, captain and owner of the *Rosario*, stated that the Armada had consisted of 152 sail when it left Corunna, and had been depleted only by the four galleys and two pinnaces despatched to carry letters. But he gave away the "River of London" as the invasion objective, and stated that " it was commonly bruited amongst them that a third part or one half of the realm of England would join to their aid so soon as they should enter on the land." He admitted that seven or eight Englishmen had been serving voluntarily in the *Rosario*, some of whom had been captured with her, but "the rest, William Stucley, the pilot of the ship, Richard Brierley, and one more, passed forth of the ship before they were taken, promising to fetch them more aid." The English renegades serving in the Armada knew, naturally, what their fate would be, if taken, and escape was probably the main motive of these men. Alvarez put the King's Treasure at 52,000 ducats, more than double Don Pedro's estimate.

A much more detailed and accurate report came from Gregorio de Sotomayor, who stated that his family were well-off Portuguese: "Trade or occupation, we have none; but do live by our goods and rents." Medina Sidonia's worries about deserters are partly explained by his statement that: "when the Spaniards embarked themselves, they commanded 2,000 Portingals to go aboard upon pain of death." He did not know of any traitors in England, but "as a good Portingal," would gladly have helped the Queen by naming them, had he known. The treasure, he said, was in the various flagships, naming them; particularly rich was "a Venetian ship in whom came for general Don Alonso de Leyva; this ship brought great store, for there came in her the Prince of Ascoli, and many other noblemen." He concluded this voluntary confession, which was additional to the questionnaire, by giving a most important piece of information: "I declare further that King Philip did command that the fleet should be victualled for 6 months, but Luis Hezar and Francisco Duarte of Cadiz did victual them but for 4 months, and with that which was nought and rotten. For which occasion the King commanded them to be apprehended; and so they remained prisoners in Portugal at our coming away. And this is the very truth."

It was. On the day he was taken, it hardly mattered, but within a few days of his being questioned, it was vital. And by that time there was independent corroboration.

Drake's *Revenge*, when she closed with the *Rosario*, had been accompanied by the *Roebuck*, 300 tons, 120 men, under Captain Jacob Whiddon, one of the armed merchantmen of the Western Squadron. Whiddon was told to take the prize into Dartmouth, but the crippled *Rosario* would not go in that direction, which was dead into wind, and Whiddon therefore brought her into Torbay. A colourful description of the scene eventually reached the King of Spain from his agents in England. "Two English couriers, who embarked at Rye on 26 July, report as follows: After they had left port they fell in with some fishermen, who told them that shortly before a large Spanish ship, with many oars on each side, and full of Englishmen, had passed. They said she bore a banner of Santiago, and another flag of the Queen of England over all. The people on board had spoken with them, and had told them that the English fleet had encountered the Spanish fleet on Sunday, and fought it. They said they had fought, but did not say whether they had been victorious, or were beaten. The English ambassador is troubled, as it is thought that their fleet is defeated. . . ." The Spanish official, who interpolated this piece of wishful thinking, was only one of many to make the same mistake; the Armada may not have been invincible, but the optimism of its supporters was.

Before the *Rosario* had even reached Torbay, it was first come, first served. Whiddon had out of her 10 of the best brass guns for his own vessel, muskets and calivers for his own men, barrels of wine and oil for everybody; he had some of the powder and shot, too, but no-one could prove it afterwards, because he blued that on the Spaniards. A Plymouth pinnace, which encountered her next, sent by Howard to get the powder and shot out of her for use in the English fleet, came away with two fine brass guns as well. The *Samaritan* of Dartmouth, 250 tons, 100 men, had to be content with a single brass gun, 10 muskets, and 10 calivers. Then she came into Torbay, and the natives swarmed over the bulwarks.

When the Deputy Lieutenants of Devon, Sir John Gilberte and George Cary, hot-footed it down to Torbay to take over the prize and make an inventory, an appalling spectacle met their eyes—rows of empty gun carriages in a looted ship. Many of those guns which remained were old-fashioned iron types, not worth the lifting. Cary wrote bitterly to Walsyngham: " I was never much experienced in these causes before this time; but now I find that all these sea goods are mixed with bird-lime; for no man can lay his hand of them, but is limed, and must bring away somewhat. Watch and look never so narrowly, they will steal and pilfer." The remaining stock of small arms they had moved to the shore, " lest it be embeaselled away."

However much it may have annoyed those two gentlemen at the time, it is obvious in retrospect that the seamen were performing merely their strict patriotic duty, to defeat the civil service at any cost, and the Spaniards, too. For Gilberte and Carey received a request from Mr. Carew Raleigh, brother of Sir Walter, for six of the guns to be placed in his footling fort at Portland; and passed it, for action, to the Council. The place for the guns, now, was in the ships fighting the Armada at that moment; the seamen had a use for them and the land men had not. However, Gilberte and Cary did their main job, which was to despatch 88 barrels of fine-corned Spanish powder and 1,600 Spanish round shot to Howard's munition-starved ships.

A month later, they had got the *Rosario* into Dartmouth at last, under tow of eight boats, and, by now, were sincerely regretting Drake's promise to the Spaniards " for the safety of their lives and courteous entertainment." Cary grumbled to Walsyngham: " We would have been very glad they had been made water spaniels when they were first taken." The *Rosario's* own store of provisions was rotted already: " their fish savours, so that it is not to be eaten, and their bread full of worms "; and " the people's charity to them (coming with so wicked an intent) is cold; so that if there be not order forthwith taken by your Lordships, they must starve." He added an interesting comment: " The pilot of the ship is as perfect in our coasts as if he had been a native born."

Of the Englishmen taken in her, he said nothing; but another report by a Spanish agent tells their story: " Don Pedro has been captured, and two Englishmen with him, one of them named Browne, have been hanged."

The capture of the *Rosario* was an unexpected windfall for the English, helping to make good the laggard processes of government by which they were starved of ammunition. But what turned the tide was the taking, a few hours after her capture, of the damaged *San Salvador* also, complete with another great store of powder and shot. In fact, the Duke was thoughtfully re-ammunitioning his enemies. All he rescued

from the *Rosario* were a few frightened English traitors, before
he abandoned her "in sight of the enemy," in Don Jorge
Manrique's ominous phrase. Now, he did it again. The precipi-
tate abandonment of this second flagship, in something like a
panic, is made clear by Calderon's diary, for he was very closely
concerned. "She continued her voyage with great difficulty," he
wrote, "until Monday (22 July), in the morning, when the Duke
ordered the people to be taken out of her and the ship sunk.
The captain, however, was badly wounded, and the men in a
hurry to abandon the ship, so that there was no one to sink
her; besides which, she had many wounded and burnt men on
board, who could not be rescued as the enemy was approaching."
This latter phrase was pure loyalty, for the English fleet, that
morning, consisted of Howard's *Ark Royal* and about half-a-
dozen other ships, the rest having been scattered and delayed
by Drake's much-debated gambit which had resulted in the
capture of the *Rosario*. Howard's own report was: "Very many
were out of sight, which with a good sail recovered not his
Lordship before it was very late in the evening." There was
therefore no good cause for the panic, except the battering the
Spaniards had taken the previous day off Plymouth. The *San
Salvador* was not even obviously sinking, for Calderon hazarded:
"It is believed that the enemy will have put a hawser on board
and towed her to a port on the coast."

The Duke, of course, covered himself (and Diego Flores de
Valdes) by entering in the War Diary: "At eleven o'clock the
captain of Oquendo's vice-flagship came and informed the Duke
that the ship was foundering, and had become unmanageable."
Actually, she was still afloat nearly four months later, albeit
with 10 men continuously working the pumps, and not in a very
seaworthy condition, for then she sank at last, in a November
gale, 70 miles further up-Channel, taking with her part of her
prize crew and some of the men who had sailed her from Spain.
However, the men in the Armada did not know of these little
military deceptions; they saw only, as Estrade did, that "We
left her, and the English went to her, shot off a gun, and went
aboard." "In sight of the Armada she was captured by the
enemy," wrote the historian of the galleass *Zuniga*. "Abandoned
in sight of the enemy," reported Don Jorge Manrique to the

King. Knowing how small the English fleet was at that moment, it must have been a depressing sight for the Spaniards.

The first English vessel alongside her was a small skiff from the *Victory*, Hawkyns' flagship; in it was Hawkyns himself and Lord Thomas Howard, of the *Golden Lion*. "They saw a very pitiful sight," wrote the Lord Admiral, "the deck of the ship fallen down, the steerage broken, the stern blown out, and about 50 poor creatures burnt with powder in most miserable sort. The stink in the ship was so unsavoury, and the sight within board so ugly, that they shortly departed." They had found, to their relief, that she had been abandoned in such haste that her ammunition stores were intact; and the *Bark Flemyng*, presumably the ship of that Captain Flemyng who had first sighted the Armada, was ordered to tow the reeking derelict into Weymouth. That is to say, she was to follow the Armada and the handful of pursuing English on their "headland to headland" course across the wide mouth of Lyme Bay. The Spaniards, therefore, had the unexpected pleasure of seeing the *San Salvador* still keeping on her course up-Channel, but under English management. However, she soon lagged behind, because Flemyng's ship was only of 50 tons, and the *San Salvador* by English estimation 600 tons (958 tons by Spanish reckoning).

Her munitions were so vital to the English (and soon were to be equally needed in the Armada), that Howard sent a message ashore to Richard Pitt, Mayor of Weymouth and Melcome Regis, ordering him to tie up the loose ends. Pitt therefore wrote to all mayors along the coast: "His Lordship hath taken two great carracks or ships from the enemy, sent to the shore, wherein great store of powder and shot in either of them; and requireth that all the said powder and shot be sent unto his Lordship with all possible expedition, for that the state of the realm dependeth upon the present supply of such wants. These are, therefore, in her Majesty's name, straitly to charge and command you, forthwith, upon receipt hereof, you make diligent enquiry to what place the said carracks or ships are gone. . . ." That was on Wednesday, 24 July, and received a prompt reply from the Mayor of Lyme Regis: "Received this same day by 9 of the clock in the morning, and have sent out for the same purpose to seek out the same ships; and we see one great ship

alone to lie in sight of this town of Lyme, and we think it is
one of the ships. John Jones, Mayor."

The Government, however, was much slower off the mark
here than they had been in the case of the *Rosario*; a full week
passed before their representatives, George Trenchard and
Francis Hawley (the latter was deputy vice-admiral), boarded the
San Salvador to compile an inventory. They complained that
they had been " greatly delayed by reason of the far distance of
the ship in the bay from this town of Weymouth, and by high
winds . . . the carrack is so great that she cannot be brought into
this haven. We think it also part of our duties not to conceal
from your Lordships the notable spoils that were made upon the
ship; the disorder growing so far, as we could very hardly repress
it ourselves, the great repair from all places being such. The
bolting out of particularities our commission reacheth not unto,
but, surely, in the stealing of her sails and cables, etc., the disorder
was very great. It is credibly thought that there were in her
200 Venetian barrels of powder of some 120 pounds weight
apiece, and yet but 141 were sent to the Lord Admiral. This
very night some inkling came unto us that a chest of great weight
should be found in the forepeak of the ship the Friday before
our dealing; and all search hath been made sithence our coming,
but no treasure can be found, and yet we have removed some part
of the ballast. We find here no Spaniards of any account, but
only one who calleth himself Don Melchor de Pereda, and nine
others of the common sort; two Frenchmen, four Almains, and
one Almain woman; and since their landing here, twelve more
are dead. We humbly beseech your Lordships to give some speedy
direction what shall be done with them, for that they are here
diseased, naked, and chargeable."

The revenge of the " German artilleryman " had not even yet
run its full course; the *San Salvador* still had many lives to
claim.

Medina Sidonia, patient, well-meaning man that he was, had
been concentrating during that disastrous Monday of 22 July
on what he thought were major issues, beside which the loss of
two flagships, shameful though it was, seemed unimportant. The
panic and disorder into which the attack of only some seventy
English ships had thrown the rear of the Armada, was a clear

warning to re-organise and re-impose discipline. His advisers produced a theoretical formation much better able to deal with such attacks in future; he approved it, and had it distributed round the fleet, for " action that day." With the order, went the hangmen. The Armada's War Diary records: " The Duke summoned the whole of the sergeant majors (senior military policemen), and ordered each one to go in a patache, and take his instructions round to every ship in the Armada, specifying in writing the position which they should respectively occupy. Orders were also given to them, in writing, to immediately hang any captain whose ship left her place, and they took with them the Provost Marshals and hangmen necessary for carrying out this order."

As the Armada re-grouped in this new formation, Nic Oseley, for one, was impressed. " They are divided, as I do see, twelve in a squadron, and do keep such excellent good order, that if God do not miraculously work, we shall have wherein to employ ourself for some days." It was a brave threat, and a brave piece of work, from a timid and vacillating leadership; which that night put in a timid and vacillating attack on the English. " The night fell very calm," wrote Howard, " and the four galleasses singled themselves out from their fleet, whereupon some doubt was had lest they might have distressed some of our small ships which were short of our fleet, but their courage failed them, for they attempted nothing." He was now content, for thanks to Medina Sidonia and the advice of Diego Flores, the English were sure enough of their ammunition supplies to mount a battle in the morning, and to " course " the Spaniards safely past Portland.

CHAPTER TWELVE

Forced to Flock Together Like Sheep

Tuesday, 23 July

Athwart of PORTLAND, *we had a sharp and long fight with them, wherein we spent a great part of our powder and shot.*

John Hawkyns to Walsyngham

HAWKYNS HAD dismissed the Battle of Plymouth, during which the Spanish rear had panicked under the new-style bombardment attack as " some small fight." But the Battle of Portland, he said, was " sharp and long." Hawkyns had been a professional fighting businessman all his life, a slave trader among other things; even the excellence of the English ships was mainly his work. His cold verdicts on the Armada battles are not those of an excited tyro, nor are they separated in time, for they all occur in his brief report on the campaign, written for Walsyngham's benefit, on 31 July. He meant exactly what he said, neither less nor more. He could have told much more, of course, which would have been very helpful to historians; but he got paid for fighting, not writing. And, with Drake, his former protege, he was in the thick of the fighting, timing his attacks to perfection. But in his report he mentioned those points only which seemed to him vital; and in his brief summaries, the ammunition state, the " powder and shot," is emphasised after every battle, except the first one at Plymouth. Clearly, it was the limiting factor in three out of the four battles. Despite their numerical inferiority, the English could have done much more at Portland, had they not had to hoard ammunition, not knowing how many battles they had yet to fight. The stores of the *Rosario* and the *San Salvador*, 1,600 round shot in the former alone—nearly as much as was expended by the whole English fleet off Plymouth—enabled them to fight one battle more than they had expected; but how many battles were still to come? On the morning of Tuesday, 23 July, when the Battle of Portland began, the bulk of the captured powder and shot had not yet arrived, or been distributed; but it was money in the bank against present expenditure. The Lord Admiral could afford to loose the reins a little, and allow his men to fight.

Frobisher and associates, the great *Triumph* leading, began to beat up for Portland Bill, working their way inshore into the teeth of the dawn land breeze. They intended to work the fast-flowing Portland " race " against the Spaniards, and to hold them off from any attempt to get into Weymouth Bay. Howard and kinsmen, plus Hawkyns, also in powerful ships, stood eastwards, parallel to the general lie of the land, but at right-angles to the giant dragon's back of the jutting Bill of Portland; they were headed for the heart of the Armada, to " fix " it, hold it in position, while Frobisher made his difficult and dangerous cast shorewards. The " old firm," Drake and the fast ships of the Western Squadron, went racing out to sea, aided by the northeast wind, ready to swing round when the wind steadied, and put in at the exactly calculated moment a " spoiling " attack on the seaward wing of the Armada, " rolling it up " shorewards in increasing confusion. In fact, a fairly standard and formal sort of plan on military lines, confusing only to naval students long afterwards, obsessed by the semi-comic impasse of two fleets trying to fight each other in " Fleet Line Ahead." But that was still very much in the future, and no one engaged off Portland that day had ever heard of it. If anyone had suggested any such thing, they would have dismissed it as irrelevant. The English, in their reports and correspondence, refer with perfect indifference, sometimes to the Spanish " army," sometimes to the Spanish " navy," meaning in both cases the Armada; and they talk indifferently of the English " army " and the English " navy," meaning in both cases the English sea forces. In fact, they made no distinction: to them, war was indivisible.

So it was to the Spaniards also, although they were a little old-fashioned, behindhand in taking hold of the new-fangled artillery weapon; they still placed much of their faith in " conventional " forces—horse and foot. Whereas the English, with no great military tradition to hinder them, were experimenting with the new " hardware," to see what it would do and how it could best be used. To the more hidebound of the Spaniards, the artillery was an " ignoble arm," uncolourful, unmanly, and not really fair. Now, having had a taste of it at sea, they had hurriedly revised their formation; but it was still military.

As originally planned, back at Lisbon, and as actually used off Plymouth, it was standard stuff, consisting of the two basic formations used by any formed body of troops: " Marching Order " and " Battle Order." This explains the (to us) infuriating habit of the Spaniards, when they refer to their rear as the " Vanguard." Their nomenclature was based on the " Marching Order " and not the " Battle Order." What happened in land operations was this: the army was strung out along a road in four divisions, the Vanguard leading. Behind it came the Centre, or " Main Battle," including the army commander's H.Q., the support weapon groups, and so on. Behind that coiled the baggage train, sometimes a siege train too, and in the rear, where it ought to be, the Rearguard. As armies spent most of their time marching, not fighting, everyone thought of this formation as the normal one. Then, from up front, came the shout: " Enemy ahead—under effective fire!" or whatever the current jargon was for that exciting moment. Immediately, three things happened. The Centre, or " Main Battle," on the word of command, came to a crashing halt on the left foot. The Vanguard about turned, and doubled back, inclined out to the right, to take post on the right of the Centre, so forming the right wing. Simultaneously, the Rearguard came up at the double from behind, inclined out to the left, and took post on the left of the Centre, thus forming the left wing. The baggage, or siege train, shuffled to a halt behind the Centre, and looked scared. The army was now arrayed in Order of Battle.

This, with modifications, was what the Armada did off Plymouth on the Sunday, when Medina Sidonia hoisted the Royal Standard to his maintop. The main modification was one imposed by sea warfare (or desert warfare for that matter); there wasn't a front or a rear in reality. Instead, there was "All Round Defence," familiar phrase. The Spaniards knew there was one English fleet at Plymouth, and another off Dover; they expected to be between them, and to have to fight facing both ways.

Therefore, although the baggage train (the store ships) was in the middle, the Centre, or " Main Battle," under Medina Sidonia, remaining in position ahead of it, the Vanguard and Rearguard both went to the rear, inclined outwards and backwards in echelon, theoretically able to hold off the Plymouth fleet.

In the event, they were able to do no such thing; and began streaming away in panic and confusion from the English cannonade, so that Medina Sidonia, leading the " Centre " (which now was actually the head of the fleet), had to double right round to the rear with some of his best ships before he could bring pressure to bear where it was needed. It was this long detour which the new formation, worked out on the Monday, was designed to avoid; it was more compact, very much more "All Round " in its defence capabilities. The Plymouth formation was described by the English as a " half-moon," an apt picture of the backward sloping right and left wings formed by the Vanguard and Rearguard respectively. The formation from Portland on, they called a " plump," or " roundel," again a descriptive term.

What had been forced on the Spaniards was a total re-organisation. The store ships remained in the middle, as before, but everything else was changed, with the main weight of the Armada at the rear instead of at the front. There were two compact fighting divisions now, in place of three separate, loose formations. There was, at the rear, what we may call the " Battle Group Alonso de Leyva," composed of both the former vanguard and rearguard, stiffened by three of the galleasses, plus four strong ships—*San Mateo, San Luis, Florencia,* and *Santiago* —detached mainly from Medina Sidonia's own squadron. The rest of the fighting ships of Portugal, plus Diego Flores' Castile squadron, and one galleass, remained in front, under the Duke, forming what we may call the " Battle Group Medina Sidonia." Don Alonso's appointment was temporary, for he was not an admiral but a general, the Land Forces Commander of the Armada; Recalde was the senior seaman, but his flagship had been so battered by the English off Plymouth that she could not go into action that day, at any rate. De Leyva commanded, wrote the Duke, " pending the repair of Juan Martinez de

Recalde's ship." The actual positioning and alignment of the ships is not stated, nor does it matter; the main point was to be able to bring a strong force to bear, at the right place, at the right time. And that was the intention of the English also.

The actual processes of the battle are bloated and distorted, in the two main narratives, those of Howard and Medina Sidonia, because neither really knew what he was doing (both were acting under instructions from their juniors), and because they had neither of them been in such an action before. The real fighting experts had their coats off and were working away like blacks, too busy to write reports, so that the flights of description were left to the amateurs. Consequently, the Duke and the Lord Admiral, thrilled to the core at their own courage, tell their tales on the level of, " There was I, upside down, at 40,000 feet." There is a happy, patriotic optimism about them that smacks of the first despatch from the front of a brand new war correspondent.

Few of the eminent scholars who have tried subsequently to find a pattern to the battle have had much success; most of them approvingly quote Camden's baffled, " It was managed with confusion enough." Largely, this was because they were looking backwards from the standpoint of fully developed sailing ship warfare between nearly identical fleets, instead of looking forwards with the Elizabethans to a very different problem, solved on military lines. The essence of the tactics developed later was for rival fleets to sail in line ahead past each other; two rulers, placed parallel on a table, would represent that formal encounter. Such battles were rarely decisive, because the fleet which turned in towards the other lost the advantage of its broadside guns. Nelson broke this impasse by going back to the first principle of war—overwhelming numbers at the point of attack. His method varied with the nature of each particular problem, but the object was the same, and it was sound.

The Elizabethans had a particular problem, quite different to any set Nelson, but when the moment for decisive battle came, they used exactly the same principle as he did. But the Channel encounters were not meant to be decisive. The English object was to knock the Spaniards off balance at the right moments and so prevent a landing. And the method they used was the orthodox military one of beating the enemy, not so much by fighting, as by disorganising him. Even the finest troops in the world lose most of their effectiveness when some are jammed tightly together, others are scattered, and all cohesion is lost. One way of doing this is by deep penetration, separating front from rear; the Blitzkrieg is the most modern example. Another, equally classic method, is the " Cannae "—the double-envelopment. The enemy's attention is held or " fixed " in the centre by a dummy attack, while his flanks are rolled up by simultaneous attacks on both wings; if this comes off, his formations are so jammed together that they cannot fight effectively and, if the pressure can be kept up, eventually become a mere struggling mob. Viewed in this light, which was a normal one for Elizabethan times, both the Portland and Isle of Wight battles suddenly make sense; the obvious confusion is explained.

Naval historians normally fall back upon the weather as a cause for confusion; their narratives explain this move or that by reference to an unexpected change in direction of the wind. This extreme capriciousness of their wind lends excitement and drama to the story, as they describe how so-and-so found himself in consequence in some unexpected and intolerable situation. Poor Frobisher is blackguarded right and left, and Drake seems somehow a magician, always in the right position at the right moment, as if he had a crystal ball handy. In fact, of course, he had; they all had. It is only the scholars who find the repeated changes in wind direction unexpected.

The truth, less suspenseful perhaps, but more satisfying, is that summer winds in the Channel form a pattern which is about 98 per cent. predictable. Yachtsmen tend to put off at the last civilised moment, between 9 and 9.30 in the morning, with the last of the land breeze from the north. Then they expect a spot of calm lasting for half-an-hour or an hour, before the standard south-westerly gets up. Motorised amateur divers study wind force and direction, too, because these are vital factors in predicting probable underwater visibility and may mean the cancelling or diversion of a previously planned expedition. And all along the line from Looe, in Cornwall, to Brighton, in Sussex, their logbooks record the present-day facts: twice only, perhaps, was the prevailing wind from the north, the best direction for diving; on every other occasion the wind was in the southern arc, usually south-west. Steadily, monotonously, infuriatingly from the south-west. Just as it was for the Armada. Absolutely standard. You could bet on it.

Obviously, Drake bet on it, too. He probably had an alternative plan as well, but as it turned out, he had no need to use it. The usual interchange of warm land air with cold sea air took place as the sun rose, and a gentle breeze blew from the north-east. Theoretically, that gave the Spaniards the weather-gauge, for what it was worth; actually, it gave the galleasses a chance to see what they could do, light winds or dead calm being their designed operating conditions. The English fleet split into three, and then four sections, which positively made the Spaniards' mouths water. The whole fleet first stood north-west, across wind, towards the shore. The Armada obediently followed, upwind of the English; the Spaniards were chasing the English, the English were running! The crowd of under-employed spectators in the Spanish fleet, from Medina Sidonia to Estrade, began to get excited. Then orders crackled in the English fleet, sails flapped momentarily, they spun round in their tracks in a large reversal of course, and approached the Spaniards at an angle, luffed very close to the wind. There was going to be a battle! They were going to be able to board! They were going to wipe out the disgrace of Plymouth!

The Duke was urging on his men in a surge of happiness he had not believed possible. Bertondona was the first favourite. There he goes! in the great *La Reganzona*, 1,249 tons, he's closing their flagship, yes, he's got her, she's turning away, he's pressing alongside, no, he isn't, oh well, he got quite near anyway. Ah, here come the rest, they'll catch her! *San Marcos, San Luis, San Mateo, La Rata, Santa Ana, San Felipe, San Juan de Sicilia, Florencia, Santiago,* the *San Juan* of Don Diego Enriquez (newly appointed to command Don Pedro's old squadron), and straining along in the rear, the giant Levanter *La Trinidad Valencera,* flagship of the Battle Group Don Alonso de Leyva. The Duke's heart swelled with patriotic Spanish pride, as the great galleons

145

and carracks, with their high castles and glistening, glittering
paintwork, bellying sails and stiff banners snapping in the breeze,
bore down on the enemy flagship; he noted the names of them all,
as they went down to the attack as if in review, and the battle
smoke went bellying across the sea from the mouths of a hundred
guns.

They were broken, the English! there was a group of them,
huddled under the land, cut off from the rest of their fleet. Prey
for the galleasses! They could be boarded and taken, every one!
He was going to win a naval battle, he, the quiet gentleman
who preferred the land! But he would deserve it! He would
intervene! He had a personal direction sent at once to Hugo
de Moncada's flag galleass *San Lorenzo*, to get that great English
ship, probably a Portuguese Indiaman, cut off there with her
consorts under the land. And he waited with feverish impatience
for de Moncada to run her alongside, and let the Spanish infantry
swarm up over her insolent bulwarks, and have that English
flag run down.

The excitement of the action infected everyone on the Spanish
side, for the English ships in the centre were accepting battle,
close battle, and the scene was constantly shifting. "We gave
chase to the enemy," wrote Estrade enthusiastically, in the *San
Marcos*, "the galleasses with some other ships wearing into
them, playing with their ordnance, turning in the wind from
the south-west to the south-east, fighting with us, and there was
great store of cannon shot. The flagship of Juan Martinez de
Recalde came entering in from the south-east, and with him
and Juan Gomez de Medina, in the *Gran Grifon*, flagship of
the hulks, and other ships, we came so nigh unto the enemy
Vice-Admiral that with one piece of cast-iron we shot two
bullets into the Vice-Admiral of the English, and there was
great shot of ordnance." Even the store ships were fighting the
English! It was incredible! In fact, so excited were the Spaniards
that two gunners in one of the hulks forgot their gun drill,
neglected to sponge out the gun after firing, and shoved a fresh
powder bag down the hot muzzle, still reeking with fragments
of blazing powder. They lived, but were badly burnt. Two

gunners in Calderon's ship, the vice-flag hulk *San Salvador*, did the same thing, and the resulting explosion killed both of them.

In fact, the "holding" force in the centre under Howard and Hawkyns, had done its job, and "fixed" the bulk of the de Leyva Battle Group. *Ark Royal*, *Golden Lion*, *White Bear*, *Elizabeth Jonas*, *Victory*, and *Nonpareil*, firing with better guns far better served, gave better than they got; and with their speed and mobility, even in light winds, ran the Spaniards close alongside without allowing them to board. Drake was not present; he was going fast out of it, seaward, under cover of the southward drifting gunsmoke of the main battle. Soon, fifty English ships, shrouded in the clouds of smoke from the cannonading, had gone out to sea with the last of the land breeze.

Meanwhile, the battle under Portland Bill had been going on for an hour and a half, and de Moncada had achieved nothing. Frobisher had got himself into a position from which he could block any Spanish attempt to break into Weymouth Bay; apart from the *Triumph*, he had five of the London ships with him, including the *Margaret and John*. The four galleasses, urged by the Duke to get alongside them with "both sail and oar," had now been backed up by a horde of great ships—Gaspar de Sosa's *Florencia*, Oquendo's *Santa Ana*, Garibay's *Begona*, Maldonada's *San Juan Bautista*, and Don Alonso de Luzon himself in *La Trinidad Valencera*. The furiously impatient Medina Sidonia could see the galleasses swept by the racing, boiling current very close to the *Triumph*, their oars flailing the water, but never actually closing to board. In fury and disgust, he had the bows of the *San Martin* turned in that direction and bore down to give a hand himself, but it was too late. That night, he sent a written reprimand to Don Hugo de Moncada: "A fine day this has been! If the galleasses had come up as I expected the enemy would have had his fill."

But de Moncada was a galley man, which was why he had been chosen to command the Neapolitan galleass squadron, and he was used to tideless smiling seas. What Frobisher had made him try to negotiate was Portland Race which, on a high spring tide, runs up to seven knots. It can be done, of course, but to "work" it as Frobisher was doing required local knowledge of a highly specialised kind, and a good deal of cold nerve. Given understanding of its mechanism, a "race" and its accompanying "eddy" gives effortless power of movement in two opposite directions; in fact, it was to Frobisher at least as helpful as a bank of oars either side of the *Triumph*. If one can imagine three moving roadways, the outside one doing two knots in one direction, the middle one doing seven knots in the same direction, and the inside one doing one knot in the opposite direction, one sees the possibilities. But to penetrate the powerful, driving curtains of water—for they descend vertically downwards with sharply defined faces—is initially intimidating. Further, the eddy and the race are linked like the tracks of a tank, and the speed difference between them is absorbed by circular "boilings" which are the opposite of whirlpools, boiling up in the centre, sliding down under at the sides. To venture a heavy ship into that, within a stone's throw of a rocky shore, would be enough to make a stranger catch his breath. Frobisher could do it, because he knew for certain that he had deep water close inshore. Today, the sides of Portland Bill slope down very steeply underwater, covered with large rocks and boulders fallen probably from the cliffs above, to a depth of between 60 and 70 feet and, eventually, out in Weymouth Bay, merge into a flat, sandy bottom; in Frobisher's time it was probably much the same. De Moncada cannot have understood, for Frobisher repeated the trick two days later, and got away with it again.

According to the diarist of the galleass *Zuniga*, which was engaged against Frobisher, they first went into action at 8 o'clock. According to Howard, the galleasses "were very well resisted by those ships (Frobisher's) for the space of an hour and half, when at length certain of her Majesty's ships bare with them, and then the galleasses forsook them." The diarist of the *Zuniga* agrees: "While we were attacking the great ship of the enemy and two other ships, five of the enemy's galleons bore down upon our galleasses; the wind at this time having suddenly shifted, so that the enemy had it astern whilst we had it against us, and consequently none of our ships could come to our aid. The galleasses therefore had to run and join the rest of the Armada." According to Calderon, "at ten o'clock the wind shifted to the south "; i.e., at the usual time for the wind change.

Howard agrees: " The wind then shifted to the south-east-wards and so to SSW, at what time a troop of her Majesty's ships and sundry merchants' assailed the Spanish fleet so sharply to the westward that they were all forced to give way and to bear room. Captain Vanegas, an Armada witness, agrees: " The enemy's *capitana* with fifty other ships got the wind of us, and that they could well do because of their extreme nimbleness and the great smoke that came from the artillery; and they charged upon the right wing of our Armada."

There it was, then, the standard land battle fought at sea, in the standard wind conditions of the English Channel. The left wing (Frobisher) working round the enemy's inshore flank, to prevent him edging into Weymouth Bay; the centre (Howard and Hawkyns) fixing the enemy with a close battle which sucked in most of his best ships and held them there for ninety minutes; while Drake and " the merchant ships appointed to serve westwards under his charge " escaped under cover of the smokescreen provided by the battle in the centre, and were ready, when the wind swung round to south-west, to put in a spoiling attack on the enemy's seaward flank and roll it up. Which it certainly did, in spite of Medina Sidonia's brave and desperate efforts to stop it.

This was the final phase of the action, in which Howard and Medina Sidonia at last encountered each other gun muzzle to gun muzzle but not, as the Duke hoped, quarterdeck to quarter-deck. The immediate cause of their encounter was that the left wing of the double envelopment—Frobisher's ships—was nothing like strong enough for that classic task, and probably the English had nothing so ambitious in mind. He was to act merely as " longstop," a kind of sliding longstop, riding up and down on the race or the eddy, able to go sweeping into Weymouth Bay at high speed simply by moving twenty yards from one current to the other, if he so desired. Anyway, at this moment, as Drake's seaward attack developed and began to roll up the right wing of the Armada shorewards, Howard thought Frobisher hard-pressed. So, in order to take the pressure off him, and simultaneously "fix" the centre of the Armada so that Drake's move could have maximum effect, he attacked directly eastward at the centre of gravity of the enemy fleet. He did not go directly towards Frobisher; that would be "wet hen" tactics. And as this was the decisive moment, which would crumple up the Armada and remove any threat to Portland, he made clear that the punch must have weight behind it.

"His Lordship called unto certain of her Majesty's ships then near at hand and charged them straitly to follow him, and to set freshly upon the Spaniards, and to go within musket-shot of the enemy before they should discharge any one piece of ordnance." There is always a tendency, at first, to fire too soon in a blaze of happy optimism; everyone does it, whether he is commanding an Elizabethan ship or flying a Spitfire or huddled behind an anti-tank gun. That the English leaders had already realised this and were trying to check the tendency, Ubaldino makes clear, for after paraphrasing Howard's order to close to musket-shot range, he adds, what he must have learned from Drake and Howard: "because that was the true method of helping friendly ships with the greatest damage to the enemy." There was one other good reason for really closing with them now. If a lucky Spanish shot should disable an English ship now it did not matter in the least; the Armada would soon be in no position at all to snap her up as a prize. Had that happened earlier in the morning it would have mattered a great deal.

Howard's close-fight orders were, he recorded, "very well performed by the *Ark*, the *Elizabeth Jonas*, the *Galleon of Leicester*, the *Golden Lion*, the *Victory*, the *Mary Rose*, the *Dreadnought* and the *Swallow*—for so they went in order into the fight." They must have made a brave sight—Howard was obviously stirred—as the great English galleons, heeled over to port under the pull of their stiff-bellying sails, slid through the waves with the silver spray creaming back under their bows and tumbling astern; for the breeze was stiffening, and the English ships worked best under these conditions. Compared to the Spaniards, they looked like racing yachts. There the comparison ended, for the green and white paint of their sides was abruptly broken by double rows of gun-ports, heavy guns on the lower deck, lighter pieces on the upper deck. That threat did exactly what it was intended to do. "Which the Duke of Medina perceiving," wrote Howard, "came out with 16 of his best galleons, to impeach his Lordship and stop him assisting of the *Triumph*."

Medina Sidonia's own narrative shows how it looked to the other side: "Soon afterwards, the enemy's ships returned, with the wind and tide in their favour, and attacked Juan Martinez de Recalde in the rearguard. Don Alonso de Leyva reinforced him, and my flagship, which was in the midst of the main squadron, sailed to the support of those ships of the rearguard which were mixed up with the enemy's rearguard (Frobisher and his reinforcements) and were separated from the mass of both fleets." The Armada was in a fine old tizzy, with the Battle Group Medina Sidonia forced to help de Leyva, who was helping Recalde, who was soon in bad trouble. "The Duke ordered Captain Marolin de Juan (the Armada's fleet navigator) to go in a feluca and try to guide the vessels which were near the Duke's flagship to the support of Juan Martinez de Recalde. When this was effected, the enemy left Juan Martinez, and attacked the Duke's flagship, which was isolated and on her way to the assistance of the said ships."

By this day both sides had got their enemy's flagships sorted out; they now knew roughly who was who, whereas, off Plymouth, any large and important looking ship was judged to be the enemy leader. So when Howard's battle group left Recalde and bore down on the *San Martin*, the Duke knew that here was his chief opponent, a nobleman of his own rank and station, who, judging from the closeness of the action, might let him grapple and board; but he was terribly disappointed. "When my flagship saw that the flagship of the enemy was leading towards her, she lowered her topsails, but the enemy's flagship passed her, followed by the whole of his fleet, and shot at her, ship by ship, as it passed. Our guns were served well and fast. . . ."

"The *San Martin* returned their fire with so much gallantry," wrote Don Jorge Manrique, "that from one side alone she fired off 100 shots, and the enemy did not care to come to close quarters with her."

"She was reinforced by Oquendo's flagship, which managed

to join her and help her gallantly in her brave fight," wrote Calderon. "The *San Martin* fired over 80 shots from one side only, and inflicted great damage on the enemy. The latter shot at the Duke at least 500 cannon balls, some of which struck his hull, and others his rigging, carrying away his flagstaff and one of the stays of his mainmast."

"The galleon *San Martin* did bear room with us, and played with her cannon almost with all the whole English army in such sort that for more than one hour we could not see her for smoke," wrote Estrade, enthusiastically.

"My flagship was in the hottest of the fight," wrote the Duke; and although she was eventually reinforced by Recalde, de Leyva, Oquendo, and the Marquis de Peñafiel in the *San Marcos,* he added, complacently, "they did not come up until the hottest fury was passed."

"The Lord Admiral was always in the hottest of the encounter," wrote Howard proudly, of his own part in the action, "and it may well be said that for the time there was never seen a more terrible value of great shot, nor more hot fight than this was; for although the musketeers and harque-busiers of crock (manning heavy muskets on a mounting) were then infinite, yet could they not be discerned nor heard for that the great ordnance came so thick that a man would have judged it to have been a hot skirmish of small shot, being all the fight long within half musket shot of the enemy. At which assault, after wonderful sharp conflict, the Spaniards were forced to flock together like sheep."

The plan had worked, and Drake's seaward attack had rolled up the right wing on the centre, but Howard singled out for praise only one man: "William Coxe, captain of a small pinnace of Sir William Wynter's, named the *Delight,* showed himself most valiant in the face of his enemies at the hottest of the encounter; he afterwards lost his life in the service with a great shot." Of course, this happened under Howard's own eyes; the battle smoke was so dense that the whole scene, so terrible and novel to these men, could not be made out by any one witness. They were stunned, deafened, utterly weary with the day-long cannon-ade and the continuous work and excitement, the typical nervous drain of battle. That was the end of the action, except for a small Spanish sortie in the evening, by four or five ships, which was beaten back by the *Mayflower* of London and some other ships, showing, as Ubaldino remarked, " great daring, tempered with prudence." The rest, with that strange joy that comes of being still unexpectedly alive after passing through an inferno of shrieking, howling, whining missiles, had leisure at last to discover, as usual, that the damage, for all that, was relatively light.

Don Jorge Manrique, Inspector General of the Armada, reported: " The enemy retired, without having inflicted any notable damage on us." The Duke claimed, doubtfully: " The enemy admiral shortened sail, having as it seemed to us, sustained some damage." The main English preoccupation, however, was not with damage, but the ability in the future, the very near future, to inflict it again on the enemy. For, Hawkyns grumbled, " We had spent a great part of our powder and shot, so that it was not thought good to deal with them anymore till that was remedied." They had " coursed the enemy " off from all chance of landing in Weymouth Bay, had he intended to do so; in so doing, they had shot away most of their ready-use ammunition; and the Armada was now within very close distance of the Isle of Wight, where a landing must definitely, not just possibly, be expected. Back in June, a month ago, Howard had warned: " The Spanish fleet may come to the Isle of Wight, which for my part I think they will attempt." In fact, on this very day, Admiral Seymour in the Narrows, having just received a report from Drake of the Battle of Plymouth, written in haste immediately afterwards, was himself writing to the Council: " I do send your Lordships Sir Francis Drake's letter, by the which you shall understand the state of the Spanish army, how forward they be; and as to our opinions here, we conjecture still their purpose may be to land in the Isle of Wight, to recover the same —which God forbid. Thus humbly praying your Lordships to send us powder and shot forthwith, whereof we have want in our fleet, and which I have divers times given knowledge thereof, I humbly take my leave. From aboard the *Rainbow,* at anchor a quarter seas over against Dover, the 23rd of July, 1588, at 11 of the clock at night."

The ammunition state was critical, not merely in Howard's part of the fleet, but in those squadrons also which lay still ahead of them, blockading Parma.

CHAPTER THIRTEEN

To Win an Honourable Death

Wednesday, 24 July

ON WEDNESDAY, 24 July, there was a lull. The winds were light, the English almost out of ammunition. The two fleets drifted slowly eastwards along the coast of Dorset, until at evening the southern cliffs of the Isle of Wight were visible ahead. The moment of decision was approaching. Dorset was almost frighteningly rugged: great, grey cliffs reared up hundreds of feet, the lines of the rock strata distorted into a crazy pattern of arcs smeared here and there with green patches of vegetation; great natural arches sprang straight out of the cold, clear depths. Inland, the hills were high and forbidding. There was no landing here. In the distance, the chalk cliffs of the Isle of Wight shone white; there was no landing there, either. The anchorage and the landing place were beyond the island, between its northern coast and the mainland at Portsmouth. Therefore, the Armada kept " the direct trade," the headland-to-headland course that led from the seaward tip of the dragon-backed Bill of Portland to the looming bulk of Dunnose height, higher even than the white cliffs below it that formed the southern cape of the island. 352 years later, exactly, in July, 1940, the radar station on Dunnose was picking up the first Luftwaffe formations to venture into the area on business; and four days after the anniversary of the Armada fight, another desperate battle took place under Dunnose, as the roaring formations surged in and, one by one, like high-divers plunging from a board, the *sturzkampfers* of Richthofen's Fliegerkorps peeled off and went screaming down on a battered British convoy, until all the water south of the Wight, for many miles, was littered with strange wreckage—boats, coke, oil, even a bullet-torn wheelhouse. And above, the thunder of the guns, the white puffs of blossoming smoke, the shrill whine of diving fighters and the drum-roll of machine-gun batteries. But the fighter pilots who went down that day on the bombers, and the seamen caught in the exploding chaos of an erupting sea, fought with Drake, and Hawkyns, and Howard behind them. They fought for an inviolate island, that had never been conquered, and would not be, even now.

But Drake, and Hawkyns, and Howard, and Frobisher, too, had no such tradition behind them. Instead, they had a tradition to reverse—that England fell easily into the lap of a conqueror, and that the Isle of Wight was especially vulnerable. It was only forty-three years since, in King Harry's time, that a French fleet had penetrated into St. Helen's, and had barely been prevented from making good their landing, Henry's brand-new *Mary Rose* capsizing during the action. The towns of Portsmouth and Southampton, and villages without number that lay inland of the easy, sandy beaches of the low-lying coast to the eastward, had been stormed, sacked, and burnt by soldiers landing out of enemy ships. And dead men lay in the ditches, where they had been cut down by the invaders, merciless enough in the swift and brutal way of soldiers; but not followed, as the new Spanish professionals would be, by black-garbed torturers guided by renegade Englishmen, perhaps even helped by Englishmen ashore. Sir George Carey, commander of the Wight garrison, with his headquarters centrally placed at Carisbrook Castle, had his watchers out on the southern cliffs to look for their coming, and the troops of this most important outpost camped and assembled, ready to "impeach" a landing. The mainland opposite was held by Henry Ratcliffe, Earl of Sussex, styled "Constable of Portchester Castle, Warden and Captain of the town, castle and isle of Portsmouth." His equivalent, in a similar situation 352 years later, was to be Lieutenant-General Sir B. L. Montgomery, commanding an equally improvised force, just as ill-equipped, on the then more vulnerable Sussex beaches.

Reluctant as they were to strip their forces to the point of impotence, both responded to Howard's appeals. Two days later, Sussex was to write: " I have sent him so much powder and shot as that I have altogether unfurnished myself." As he was Howard's first-cousin, he probably replied to the appeal more readily than is usual in modern times. Carey had sent Howard

" four ships and a pinnace sufficiently furnished with mariners and soldiers " on the very day of the Battle of Portland, and this day, 24 July, sent " another pinnace unto him with an hundred men; but he returned them unto me with great thanks, willing the captain to tell me that he had as many men as he desired or could use."

In London, the Council directed, " that in the county of Kent a good number of the best and choicest shot of the trained bands in the said county should be sent forthwith to the seaside, that they be brought out to double man the ships." The Council wanted prizes, they wanted to hear of captured Spanish vessels, so they were sending Howard the pick of the coastal Home Guard, whom Howard in due course returned, with thanks, as he had Carey's company sent out in the pinnace.

In fact, war fever was running high. Leicester, with 4,000 men, was at Chelmsford, north of the Thames, ready to repel a landing on that side of the estuary; the Thames boom was being hurriedly strengthened, to prevent the heavy Spanish ships from breaking it by ramming. Great events were imminent, threatening the very capital of England. So intense was the feeling of standing in the open on a great stage, for which the play was even now being composed by a more than human dramatist, that all sorts of people suddenly began stampeding for the footlights. The most surprising characters succeeded in joining the fleet. On 24 July, Sir Horatio Palavicino, a Genoese banker high in the confidence of the Government, and a personal friend of the chief Spanish intelligence agent in London, wrote to Walsyngham that he no longer wished to serve with the Earl of Leicester, declaring: " The greatness of my zeal, which desireth to be amongst those who do fight for her Majesty's service and for the defence of her kingdom, doth constrain me, with an honourable company, to depart as this night toward Portsmouth, there to embark and join the Lord Admiral, where I hope to be present in the battle, and thereby a partaker in the victory or to win an honourable death. . . ." And so Sir Horatio, with his " honourable company," rode through the night towards the battle, and, before they even reached Portsmouth, must have heard the sound of the guns, thundering out in the Channel.

While the citizens of London readied their leather fire-buckets, with which each household had been provided—for the "fire" in "fire and sword" was no idle word—the worthies of Torbay watched Spanish soldiers marching through the town, the brown-burned men of the "tercios," or regiments, a word as ominous as "Panzer Division" was to be 352 years later. Women watched them, old men, children—but hardly any Englishman of martial age; for the men of Torbay were mariners, and every mariner that England had, be he ocean explorer or inshore fisherman, was with the fleet. In fact, the *Rosario* was being worked into Torbay by her Spanish crew, under armed guard; there were not enough English seamen left to do it. But the marching Spanish soldiers were received with hatred. George Cary of Cockington, the Devonshire Cary, not to be confused with the Hampshire Carey who was holding the Isle of Wight, reported to the Council the "greatest discontentment of our countryside, that a nation so much disliking of them, our vowed enemies, should remain amongst them." Don Pedro de Valdes, however, later testified that many of the "said poor people were raised by them and were their neighbours, and came in this employment for the love and zeal that they bear unto them"; which was doubtless true. The English, however, were in no mood to consider why the Spaniards had come, but only that they had come.

From the Bill of Portland to the Isle of Wight is forty miles. But since the Needles Channel is narrow, the Armada would certainly and in fact was, making for the Spithead entrance by St. Helen's, a distance of a further twenty-five miles. With light winds lasting all day on the Wednesday, 24 July, and the rival fleets making less than two knots, anyone who cared to could have kept easy pace with the ships by walking along the cliff tops from Lulworth to Swanage, or obtained a grander panorama from along the crest of the Purbeck Hills; and doubtless, many did. From the heights of Chale, Bonchurch, and Dunnose, in the Wight, the coming of the Spaniards could have been seen for half the day.

But there was very little to see, apart from a brief flurry of gunfire at first light, when some English ships made a dawn attack on the rear of the Armada, in which Medina Sidonia claimed

ABOVE: The Battle of Portland, *left*, and the re-organisation of the English fleet into four squadrons, *centre bottom*, according to Adam's Chart No. 6, a contemporary document. BELOW: The Battle of the Isle of Wight, under Dunnose cliff, the English ships being towed into action by their boats in a dead calm, and the Spanish galleasses rowing to the rescue of the *Duquesa Santa Ana*, *bottom left*. From a line engraving by C. J. Visscher

ABOVE: Launching the fire-ships against the Armada off Calais on the night of 28/29 July; the scratch crews returning in rowing boats to the English fleet, *centre*. BELOW: The fight for the flag-galleass *San Lorenzo* off Calais. Boats and pinnaces attack while Howard waits out of range, *bottom left. From line engravings by J. Pine after C. de Lempriere*

hits on an enemy flagship. He gives details, but Howard reported merely: " There was little done, for that in the fights on Sunday and Tuesday much of our munition had been spent, and therefore the Lord Admiral sent divers barks and pinnaces unto the shore for a new supply of such provisions." He also, as we know, sent back Carey's pinnace and its one hundred men; and was to reject in turn the soldiers of the trained bands of Kent. We know that he was short of victuals, as well as powder and shot, and he probably thought both food and powder would pay better dividends if fed to his mariners and gunners than if shared out also among a host of semi-trained soldiers. But this was to get him into trouble at Court, later on. Just as Lord Dowding had to face a court of enquiry after winning the Battle of Britain, so Howard had to face his accusers after he had beaten the Spaniards. In both cases, London expected too much. They wanted annihilation; and they did not get it. The Luftwaffe was beaten, but still in being, after the Battle of Britain; the Armada was beaten, but still in being, after Howard, Hawkyns, Drake and the rest had finished with it. But only numbers can annihilate; and by order of the Council, a substantial group of formidable English ships were being deliberately immobilised, " half seas over from Dover." Howard was still outnumbered. Even if he had not been, a handful of half-trained infantry did not allow him to board a fleet of high-charged ships carrying something like 18,000 soldiers, 10,000 of them highly-trained professionals. England had no such force, nor could she afford one.

Both sides made use of the pause on that peaceful Wednesday, for a re-organisation. The Spaniards, because Recalde's *San Juan* had been made battle-worthy again, divided their rear into two squadrons—one commanded by de Leyva, the other by Recalde, but with Recalde in overall command; Medina Sidonia still commanding the battle group at the head of the formation. The Armada was now divided, so to speak, into one powerful battle group under the Duke, with two " Don Columns " of twenty ships each in the rear. The English, on the other hand, rationalised their three existing, untidy battle groups—Frobisher and some of the London ships; Drake and the Western Squadron; and Lord Howard and kinsmen, with Hawkyns in close attendance to see that he didn't do anything foolish. Howard had obviously passed the test now, for they left off holding his hand, and formed four squadrons.

We know Frobisher commanded the inshore squadron, we know that Howard had sole command of the next squadron in line, we know that Hawkyns was next to him and to seaward, therefore Drake was on the extreme seaward wing, as far away from Frobisher as they could get him, and also in the most vital position from the point of view of the intended battle plan. Very probably also, Frobisher, an explorer with nothing like the fighting experience of Drake and Hawkyns, had special tidal knowledge and could make best use of the various " races " in which this stretch of water abounds. Once again, the personal factor had to be considered; as it obviously was by the Spaniards, in allowing de Leyva to retain part of his temporary command. He had great prestige as a chivalrous soldier, and had serving with him in the *Rata Encoronada* the pick of the younger sons of the nobility of Spain.

The English must have been satisfied with the success of their battle plan, as it had worked off Portland, for they now intended to employ it off the Wight, but with greater weight on the right wing. Adams's Chart No. 6, published in 1590 to illustrate both the Battle of Portland and the re-organisation of the English fleet into four squadrons on the following day, shows clearly what it was; indeed, it is obvious enough already, from a study of the combined English and Spanish narratives, and the chart serves merely as additional confirmation. It has always puzzled Nelson-fixated naval experts, because Nelson didn't do anything like that; nor is it contained in the traditional " Fighting Instructions " which Nelson disregarded. Without exception, the nautical experts lay great stress on the " military " organisation of the Armada, derived, obviously, from the parade-ground manoeuvres of galley fleets. But so stunned and delighted are they with the beginnings of sailing ship warfare, that they quite fail to notice that the plan which the English are using is military also. As indeed it would have to be, given the tough hedgehog formation for all round defence into which the Armada had been re-organised after Plymouth.

It is the typical double-envelopment plan, familiar to military students from Hannibal on, and still used at all levels, from

Army Group to platoon. It has survived all weapon changes, because it works—given sufficient force. A Spaniard, in the coming battle of the Wight, obviously recognised it, because he refers to the heavy fighting that followed the English assumption of "the half-moon formation." If the force available is some-what weak, the result is not annihilation, but a crowding together of the enemy's ranks which makes it very difficult for him to manoeuvre. Put in at the right moment, when the Armada was preparing to land troops on defended beaches—an operation requiring exact spacing and timing of the assault formations—the landings would be thrown completely out of gear and could not in fact be attempted without the risk of complete disaster. The particular variant of the plan used by the English was the obvious one, when one flank of the enemy is jammed up against an immovable or impassable obstacle; in this case, the English cliffs with a tide race at their foot. Then, the main weight is directed at the other, exposed flank, so that the enemy is squeezed laterally against this immovable obstacle. In this context, a "right hook." A Spanish witness off Portland thought the right hook had 50 ships in it, but he probably exaggerated in his excitement—large formations always look much larger than they really are. The Adams's Chart of the battle shows the main weight employed in the centre by the holding force; he is probably right, for at Portland the centre consisted not of Howard's group alone, but Hawkyns as well. No doubt, after that battle, and with the far more vital battle of the Wight still to come, Drake and Howard must have said, with von Schlieffen: "Keep the right wing strong!" And the new formation of four squadrons would allow that: Frobisher taking up the "stop" position under the cliffs, Howard attacking in the centre with the holding force, and not less than two squadrons, those of Drake and Hawkyns combined to deliver the all-important roll-up punch from seaward—the "right hook." All perfectly possible, provided the wind kept to the routine pattern of the Channel. But it did not, and because the fate of England might hang on this conflict, the English had to resort to desperate measures to get the battle going as planned.

In fact, the wind died away altogether on the night of 24/ 25 July, thus frustrating an English night attack which was to have been put in by twenty-four armed merchant ships—six from each of the four squadrons. This, if it could have been done, would at minimum risk and cost, have kept the Spaniards on the jump all night and so have facilitated considerably the main assault early next morning.

When the sun rose up behind the hills of Wight on Thursday and drove away the shadows from the gently stirring sea, both fleets, with flapping sails, and in no great order, lay motionless on the waves for many miles, stretching southward from the island almost out of sight.

CHAPTER FOURTEEN

South of this Island Six Leagues

Thursday, 25 July

By the occasion of the scattering of one of the great ships from the fleet, which we hoped to have cut off, there grew a hot fray, wherein some store of powder was spent.
John Hawkyns to Walsyngham

" This morning began a great fight betwixt both fleets, south of this island 6 leagues," wrote Sir George Carey at dusk that night of 25 July. " It continued from five of the clock until ten, with so great expense of powder and bullet, that during the said time the shot continued so thick together that it might have been judged a skirmish with small shot on land than a fight with great shot on sea." Carey was in a hurry when he scribbled that note to the Earl of Sussex, and neglected to make his meaning crystal clear. " Stretching as far south of this island as 6 leagues," would have been more correct, fitting the statements of witnesses and also a contemporary picture, showing Frobisher close in under Dunnose. Or perhaps he meant that the opening phase of the battle took place far out to sea, which it did. The immediate cause of the action was the lagging behind during the calm of the night of two Spanish ships.

According to Estrade, " at the break of day, the hulk of Pedro Meras was so nigh unto the enemy that more than twenty came shooting at her very strongly, but none of them did lay her aboard, although they were very near." The list of the Andalusian Squadron shows a number of large vessels classed simply as " ships," including the ill-fated *Rosario* herself, plus one " patache," one " galleon," and one " hulk " owned by Pedro Meras, the 900 ton *Duquesa Santa Ana*. The patache was for scouting and for conveying orders and messages; the role of the " hulk " is not really clear. She may have been a storeship attached to the squadron, or just a particularly tub-like merchant vessel, but she did carry 280 soldiers, more than any other vessel in that squadron, except for the lost *Rosario*, which had 304.

In fact, there were more soldiers in just this one Spanish squadron than in the whole of the English fleet.

Although Estrade mentions only one hulk in distress, Calderon says there were two: " The weather was calm, and the hulks *Santa Ana* and *Doncella* fell astern. The enemy attacked them with some of their ships, which they towed within range." The *Doncella* is the only " hulk " listed in Oquendo's Guipuzcoan squadron, the rest being described as " ships "; she was of 500 tons and carried 156 soldiers. The Duke, however, wrote: " The hulk *Santa Ana* and a galleon of Portugal had fallen somewhat astern, and were fiercely attacked by the enemy." Such discrepancies are not terribly important, illustrating merely that, after five thundering hours of confused battle, memories are liable to err a little and that, often, a witness could describe with fair confidence only what happened in his own immediate vicinity. In this battle, for instance, Howard's report concerns mainly the doings of his own squadron, and has only fringe references to Frobisher and Hawkyns, and none at all to Drake by name; which means that Drake was operating at some distance from him, on the seaward wing, possibly some six leagues out to sea, if we can accept Carey's estimate. That would be about nine miles south of some point of the island, which is diamond-shaped.

Howard reported that one of the lagging Spanish ships was to seaward of him, opposite Hawkyns. " There was a great galleon of the Spaniards short of her company to the southwards. They of Sir John Hawkyns his squadron, being next, towed and recovered so near that the boats were beaten off with musket shot. Whereupon three of the galleasses with an armado issued out of the Spanish fleet." The " armado " was presumably de Leyva's flagship *Rata Encoronada,* being towed into action by the galleasses for the sake of her extra gun power; both the Duke and Calderon mention her as engaged. The diarist of the *Zuniga,* who was present, wrote: " The English would certainly have captured the hulk *Santa Ana* if the three galleasses, *San Lorenzo, Zuniga,* and *Girona* had not at once gone to her rescue. In order to save her, they had to engage over thirty of the enemy's ships. . . ."

While Hawkyns was having his ships towed into action by their boats, into the fierce musketry fire of the soldiers massed behind the bulwarks and castles of the *Duquesa Santa Ana*, Howard strove to cover him by engaging the oncoming galleasses, their oars rhythmically beating to froth the oily calm of the heaving sea. The *Ark Royal* and the *Golden Lion* also launched their longboats, and began to tow the two big ships into action, a fairly desperate measure. The Spanish rowers were under cover, the Englishmen in the open boats were not; the galleasses were the most heavily armed ships in the Armada, mounting 50 guns each, any one of which was capable of knocking a longboat into splinters. At the last moment, the boats hauled round hard, to bring to bear on the galleasses the broadsides of the *Ark* and the *Lion*. "There were many good shots made at the galleasses in sight of both armies," wrote Howard, " which could not approach, it being calm, for the *Ark* and the *Lion* did tow to the galleasses with their longboats. They fought a long time and much damaged the galleasses, that one of them was fain to be carried away upon the careen; and another, by a shot from the *Ark*, lost her lantern, which came swimming by, and the third his nose. At length it began to blow a little gale, and the Spanish fleet edged up to succour their galleasses, and so rescued them and the galleon, after which time the galleasses were never seen in fight any more, so bad was their entertainment in this encounter."

The " little gale," that freshening sea-wind which usually breaks up a calm in these waters, and was doubtless expected, enabled the English to get their battle plan moving faster; and this day, they took extreme risks. Frobisher went inshore, as he had at Portland, to work the tide race under the cliffs; Howard pressed the Spaniards hard in the centre; and the squadrons of Drake and Hawkyns swung round to deliver the " right hook " from seaward. Overall, the plan was the same as that which had worked at Portland, but complicated, and made difficult, by the peculiar wind and tidal conditions of the Isle of Wight area; yet possibly paying a much greater dividend if matters could be managed right. The whole of the English movements, from dawn onwards, show a desperate desire to get things moving at almost any cost. The expedient of towing their ships into action alone is sufficient indication. Why? Obviously, because there was a time factor involved. The Armada had to be in such-and-such a position, in a given state of disorganisation, at a definite time.

Although the two fleets were motionless, relative to the sea, they were not motionless relative to the land; the east-setting current was drifting them steadily north-east, parallel to the cliffs, towards Bembridge Foreland. The Armada had only twelve miles to go; then it could sweep round Bembridge Ledge and into St. Helen's, anchoring between there and Spithead in a great arc, from behind the cover of which the boats could put away for the shore with the assault troops. Any wind from the southern arc would be favourable all the way, for, when it hits the barrier of the Isle of Wight, it divides and flows round the island and into Spithead. So, too, does the tide, at the right time; but there is a period when the Channel tide continues east along Bembridge Ledge, and meets there a tide race setting outwards from St. Helen's, and also, a little further east, a fast, south-east going stream consisting of the mass of water previously locked up in Southampton Water and the three wide harbours of Portsmouth, Langstone, and Chichester. That stream runs three to four knots; so long as it was running near its peak speed, the Armada could not make headway against it, being tied to the speed of the slowest of the hulks. If the English could hustle the Spaniards past the Spithead entrance at the right time, the Armada would never have a chance to get into the anchorage, but be drifted away beyond the submerged tip of Selsey Bill. If the Spaniards tried too hard, the English might even get some of them embayed inside the wide sweep of Hayling and Brackles-ham, or at any rate on the barely submerged remains of the Selsey peninsula.

This coast, which both fleets were now approaching, was completely different in character to anything they had passed before. The West Country cliffs are high and steep, rising from comparatively deep water and a rocky bottom; very clear, cold water. But the coasts of the Hampshire/Sussex border are low-lying and sandy; for many miles from the shore there is, at low tide, no water to float a ship of any size. Two hundred years before, much of it had been dry land; then the floods of the thirteenth and fourteenth centuries, caused by a drastic change in sea level, had inundated large areas, including villages and

churches. The old rivers, both those which had existed in
pre-historic times when the Wight was not yet an island, and
those which had largely disappeared from sight after the inunda-
tions of the late Middle Ages, were still there, grooves in the
seabed, and formed the intricate network of undersea channels
which ships used to come into the harbours; but the average low
tide depth over the greater part of the area is today often no
more than 10 to 15 feet, less than the draught of many Armada
ships. In fact, it was the same sort of coast that the Spaniards
were to meet again off Dunkirk, with the same built-in hazards
to an unwieldy fleet. But it had in addition the most complicated set of tides, unlike any others in the British Isles, caused
by the setting of the Isle of Wight, diamond-shaped, off a mainland which followed its contours. The result is that slack water
occurs in some places at high tide, in others one hour before and
one hour after high tide, and others again, at low tide; to use the
waters of this notoriously difficult area as part of their defences,
would be an obvious measure. Depending on exact timing.

But if the English did not get the Spaniards past Bembridge
Ledge on time, the tide would work for the enemy, taking them
easily and directly to their intended anchorage, with the assistance
also of the wind. Hence the English attacks from dawn onwards.
These had the effect of holding back the Spaniards, and delaying
them, for Medina Sidonia himself was sucked into the fighting,
together with his ships of the vanguard group. It had the
additional effect of disrupting the Armada, so that, if anything
went wrong with the timing and the enemy was in fact able to
turn into the anchorage off St. Helen's, it would do so off-balance.
Any attack, if caught in the forming up area short of the start-
line, will waver and may collapse, and doubly so if it is a landing
operation launched from ships against defended beaches. No
one then alive had more experience of amphibious operations
than Drake and Hawkyns, who were therefore the two men best
fitted to deliver the blow against one. In the absence of a
complex signalling system (on land or at sea) greater responsibility devolved on individual commanders, without noticeable
loss of cohesion; and in any case, there was nothing that Howard
could profitably tell Drake or Hawkyns; indeed, it was a
providential mercy that primitive communications prevented

Walsyngham from conducting the campaign at long range from a London office.

Of course, nautical experts invariably lament, when they consider how much better things could have been organised, if only Howard had had a communications system as good as that of Jellicoe at Jutland; but this comes from too much sailing of desks round Greenwich offices. Manoeuvres don't matter. What matters is to get good equipment, good men, good training; and then point the lot in the right direction. They do the rest. As a matter of record, Rommel's operation order for the battle of Kasserene, which nearly, but not quite, threw the Americans clean out of Africa, was: "So-and-so Division—right of the road; so-and-so Division left of the road." It proved more than adequate.

All that Howard had to do, this morning of Thursday, 25 July, was to get stuck into the centre of Armada and bring on such a battle as would suck into it the fighting ships at the head of the enemy formation, as well as their rear. Once he had done that, once the enemy centre was firmly held, Frobisher could try to get round their shoreward flank close under Dunnose, while Drake and Hawkyns carried out their enveloping manoeuvre out to sea. And it went off like clockwork. Even Howard's narrative, focused on the battle in the centre, shows that the two wing movements were near enough simultaneous. The diarist of the *Zuniga* makes it more than plain to everyone not operationally obsessed with sailing ship tactics devised a century later. He says: "Some of our ships got mixed up with the enemy's fleet, and there was a great deal of fighting *on all sides,* as the English had assumed the *half-moon formation.*" An admirably brief appreciation of the situation, which he obviously recognised, because it was familiar to him. If the tactics had been brand-new, revolutionary, that would not have been the case.

The English moves followed on as a result of the counter-attack by Howard on the three galleasses, *San Lorenzo, Zuniga,* and *Girona,* lying somewhat to seaward of centre; during this action, the wind freshened and enabled Howard to dispense with the boats which had been towing his ships. "The Duke's flagship, with the vanguard, came to their assistance," wrote Calderon, tactfully omitting to mention that the Duke himself was absent, having got separated from his own battle group, and was near the shore, close under Dunnose, accompanied only by the fourth galleass. "Finding the flagship alone, except for the galleass *Patrona*, and to windward of the line of battle," writes Calderon without a blush, "the enemy selected some of the best ships in his fleet to deliver a combined attack on the flagship, the rest of his vessels being left to engage the rearguard." The latter was Howard's group, the "combined attack" on the *San Martin* being led by Frobisher in the *Triumph*, at the head of the inshore, left-flanking squadron. "The plan would have succeeded if Oquendo had not kept so close a luff, and sailed towards the flagship with other vessels following him, and thus covering her and receiving the chief brunt of the attack, which was very heavy."

"They came closer than on the previous day," wrote Medina Sidonia, "firing off their heaviest guns from the lowest deck, cutting the trice of our mainmast, and killing some of our soldiers." A number of the Spanish ships rallied to their distressed leader, including Recalde and Don Diego Enriquez, and two of the stronger galleons. There is no doubt about where they were, for the Duke recorded that: "Oquendo placed himself before my flagship, as the current made it impossible for him to stand alongside." Frobisher was working "race" tactics again, using this time the notorious St. Catherine's race, which can reach eight knots on a spring tide, and pours, heaped and heaving, down past Dunnose to join the Bembridge race at right-angles. Once again, as at Portland, Medina Sidonia thought he'd got Frobisher; and once again, he was vastly mistaken; and this time he had no one but himself to blame.

The Spaniards, seeing Frobisher's *Triumph* apparently pinned by the wind to leeward of them, came down confident of the kill; in fact, by the odd way she was moving, they thought they had crippled her. "This enemy flagship had suffered considerable damage," wrote the Duke, "and had drifted to leeward of our Armada." "Her rudder was injured and useless," said Calderon. "My flagship then turned upon her," reported the Duke, "supported by Juan Martinez de Recalde, the *San Juan de Sicilia*, the flagship of the galleons of Castile, the *Gran Grin*, and the rest of our ships. To windward of us was the enemy's fleet coming up to support this flagship, which was in such straits that she had to be towed by eleven longboats, lowering her standard and firing guns for aid. My Royal flagship and vice-flagship were gaining on her so much that the rest of the enemy's vessels stood towards her, to support her, and we were sure that at last we should be able to succeed in boarding them, which was our only way to victory." Calderon thought so, too. For when the "ten longboats from the other ships took her in tow, and, the wind freshening, our flagship and other ships sailed towards her; but she got out so swiftly that the galleon *San Juan* and another quick sailing ship—the speediest vessels in the Armada—although they gave chase, seemed in comparison to her to be standing still." Captain Vanegas added: "We had already got the enemy flagship almost within musket shot, when nine launches got her under way and conveyed her out of our hands with such rapidity, that it was a thing of wonder."

These phrases are usually quoted to show the superior sailing qualities of the English fleet as a whole; but the *Triumph* was one of the old-fashioned high-charged ships, not a low-built galleon like the *Revenge* or the *Victory*. In fact, the description reads perfectly for what happens when a ship, or for that matter a swimmer, moves into a tide race or eddy—and suddenly goes sliding smoothly away without effort. The change from one sliding roadway to the other is made by going diagonally across the stream, and through the "boilings," a matter of twenty yards or so; which is probably what Frobisher was using the boats for. The Duke's description of Oquendo's ship being unable to come alongside him, due to the rushing power of a current which was moving a 1,000 ton ship like a log of wood, makes it virtually certain.

And there, on that note of near-victory over Frobisher's flagship, the official Spanish record of the battle abruptly ends. Medina Sidonia (or was it Diego Flores?) entered her in the War Diary as Howard's flagship, knowing perfectly well she was not, for the *Ark* had already been correctly identified off Portland. Don Jorge Manrique, reporting later, knew this, for he described her as "the largest ship in the enemy's fleet," not as the English fleet flagship.

But it was not the end, not even of this particular phase of the action, for the English fleet flagship, Howard's *Ark Royal*, was bearing down steadily on the *San Martin* and the other Spanish ships fruitlessly chasing Frobisher. He wrote, having described vaguely some action of the Drake and Hawkyns squadrons going on simultaneously: " During which time, over against Dunnose, the Lord Admiral, espying Captain Frobisher with a few other ships to be in sharp fight with the enemy, and fearing they should be distressed, did, with five of his best ships, bear up towards the admiral of the Spanish fleet; and so breaking into the heart of them, began a very sharp fight, being within two or three scores paces one of the other, until they had cleared Captain Frobisher and made them give place."

Neither Medina Sidonia nor Calderon care to describe this, and instead they sing out in unison, like trained song-birds. " Seeing that in the proposed assault the advantage was no longer with us, and that we were now near the Isle of Wight, the Duke discharged a gun and proceeded on his course, the rest of the Armada following in very good order, the enemy remaining a long way astern," was how Medina Sidonia put it. And Calderon piped up with: " This being seen by the Duke, and the weather being fair, he proceeded on his voyage."

In what " proposed assault " was the advantage no longer with him? The chase after Frobisher? On the contrary, the assault was that outlined in the Duke's letter to the King, dated off Plymouth: " I have written to Your Majesty clearly, and the object of the present letter is to say that I am obliged to proceed slowly with all the Armada together in squadrons as far as the Isle of Wight, and no further, as all along the coast of Flanders there is no harbour or shelter for our ships." Something had happened to cancel that assault, and as the assault anyway was against the King's orders, it would be best to let the matter lie, and not put himself in the ridiculous position of admitting failure to carry out a forbidden enterprise.

In fact, the Frobisher action was widely hailed as a victory, and much heartened the Armada; the *Zuniga* diarist wrote: " It was asserted that during the day the enemy suffered much damage, especially their flagship. They had at this time 90 vessels all told. . . ." The master of a Seville ship wrote: " Off the Isle of Wight, we found the wind fair and were aweather of them, going very near of them and they flying. We had them broken and the victory three parts won, when the enemy's *capitana* turned upon our Armada, and the galleon *San Mateo* which had the point of the weather wing gave way to it, retreating into the body of the Armada." The " weather wing " of the Armada was, of course, many miles out to sea, virtually out of sight of Howard, who refers merely to the *Nonpareil* and the *Mary Rose* striking their topsails " very bravely " during the extrication of Frobisher; these ships were of Drake's and Hawkyns's squadrons respectively, and this meagre hint is all the information he gives us about the progress of the " right hook." The Seville captain is more informative. When the seaward wing of the Armada was driven in by it, the *San Mateo,* one of the genuine warships, being hustled into the body of the fleet, there was a general attack. " Seeing that, the enemy took heart and turned with his whole fleet or the greater part of it, and charged upon the said wing, in such wise that we who were there were driven into a corner, so that if the Duke had not gone about with his flagship, instead of conquerors that we were, we should have come out vanquished that day. Seeing that, those of his Armada that had been cut off, bore up to rejoin."

It is not clear what he means by " driven into a corner," but the success of the Drake/Hawkyns " right hook " is clear; the seaward wing of the Armada was rolled up more effectually even than at Plymouth, when the Spaniards " were forced to flock together like sheep." For, in this case, the Armada had actually been cut in two—and by an inferior force of some 90 ships. This could easily have happened, if the Spanish formation had been pressed in close against the coast, for then the inshore ships would be in a faster current than those offshore; the current itself would tend to tear the Armada apart. In the jostling confusion, some of the ships might have been in danger of running onto the submerged rock ledges which stretch out a long way seaward between Culver Cliff and Bembridge Foreland; and perhaps this is what the Seville captain meant by a " corner." On the other hand, once well clear of the tip of Bembridge Ledge, there would have been little, tide permitting, except their own disorganisation to prevent the Spaniards from bringing up to their anchors inside the Spithead anchorage. It is more likely that they were swept past the point of Bembridge Ledge in some confusion, and there found themselves being jammed, not against a coast, but against a fierce, outgoing current, and then, as they tried perhaps to come in, were swept bodily away by the main south-east going stream towards the long arc of the Selsey peninsula. That would certainly fit the description of a " corner," particularly if Drake and Hawkyns were continually pushing them northwards at this time, for the whole battle would then drift very fast to the north-east, and Medina Sidonia would certainly have to " go about with his flagship," or have most of his Armada put onto Cymenes-ora, the then recently submerged Bill of Selsey, now known as the Owers banks. The tide off the Isle of Wight does set towards the Owers at certain times, the sunken River Looe, now the Looe Channel, drawing off part of the converging streams, and keeping the current brisk even in dangerously shallow water close by the shore.*

The Armada navigators must have realised early that they had been out-manoeuvred, for they were soon back on course to clear the tip of the Owers, so that Sir George Carey could conclude his letter: " The fleets kept the direct trade and shot into the sea out of our sight by three of the clock this afternoon; whereupon we have dissolved our camp wherein we have continued since

* It was Corbett who first suggested that Drake's intention may have been to strand the Armada on the Owers, and this has been accepted by Lewis and Mattingly, among others, as a complete explanation. A very small map might allow this, but not personal experience of the area, both above and under water. What they do not explain is what factor prevented the Armada from sweeping round Bembridge Ledge directly into the anchorage they desired to take up. In most narratives, the Armada is off Dunnose one minute, and nearly onto the Owers the next. The present author, with Corbett's explanation in mind, once timed this distance while travelling in an 11-knot coaster. The time taken to cover the distance was 2½ hours. If the impression given by Lewis and Mattingly is correct, then the Armada would have hit, not the sandbanks, but the sound barrier. Mattingly nearly grasps this, for he begins to doubt that the Duke's intention was still to take the Isle of Wight; but we know from Parma's correspondence that he was still hankering after the Wight, even when anchored off Calais. Mattingly believes also that the Spanish galleons drew 25 to 30 feet of water which, by present-day standards, means a really big ship; the only genuine galleon extant is the *Vasa*, a very large vessel, and we know quite definitely that she drew 14 feet forward and 16 feet aft. In the present actual state of the seabed (not always the same as that shown by Admiralty charts), such a ship could be neatly embayed anywhere between Horse Sand, off Portsmouth, and Selsey Bill. In short, the English may have been trying to push the Armada, not onto the Owers, but inside them.

Monday. And so praying your Lordship to send this enclosed by post, I humbly commit you to God. From Carisbrook Castle, this 25th of July, at 8 hours in the night." The soldiers of the Wight garrison could now stand down with safety; the Armada's last port of refuge was gone.

CHAPTER FIFTEEN

A Device of Firing of Ships

Friday, 26 July-Sunday, 28 July

Near to CALAIS, my Lord Admiral, with firing of ships, determined to remove them.

John Hawkyns to Walsyngham

ADMINISTRATIVELY, AS the two fleets cruised past the Sussex beaches that evening after the battle, the Lord Admiral and the Duke thought as one. Reinforcements and more ammunition. The cast of their thought was, however, quite different. Howard looked forward with confidence to the junction of his four squadrons with the two additional squadrons off Dover, which would at last give him numerical superiority, and to receiving fresh supplies of powder and shot. He wrote: " Now, forasmuch as our powder and shot was well wasted, the Lord Admiral thought it was not good in policy to assail them any more until their coming near unto Dover, where he should find the army which he had left under the conduction of the Lord Henry Seymour and Sir William Wynter, knight, ready to join with his Lordship, whereby our fleet should be much strengthened, and in the meantime, better store of munition might be provided from the shore." This was no idle expectation, for he had written such a letter to the Queen, that Walsyngham had been rocketed into action.

On Friday, 26 July, while both fleets lay becalmed all day off Hastings, Walsyngham noted: " I find by a letter written from my Lord Admiral unto her Majesty that, for lack of powder and shot, he shall be forced to forbear to assail and to stand upon his guard until he shall be furnished from hence. There is 23 last of powder sent unto him with a proportion of bullet accordingly. There are letters sent to the Lord Wyllughby, and in his absence to Sir William Russell, to send over 1,000 of their best shot for the furnishment of the ships. I hope there will be an 100 sail of Hollanders and Zealanders at the least to assist the Lord Admiral within these three days."

As a result, Howard was able to report: "All this day and Saturday, 27th July, the Spaniards went always before the English army like sheep, during which time the justices of peace near the sea-coast, the Earl of Sussex, Sir George Carey, and the captains of the forts and castles alongst the coast, sent us men, powder, shot, victuals and ships to aid and assist us." Some of the ammunition taken from the two captured Spanish ships also arrived. In fact, Howard celebrated Friday the 26th as a victory already. He staged a ceremony in his flagship, knighting Hawkyns and Frobisher, his own kinsmen Lord Thomas Howard and Lord Sheffield, also Roger Townshend and George Beeston, a venerable officer of the regular navy. This was " in reward of their good services in these former fights, as also for the encouragement of the rest." Apparently, he was very pleased at their success in having hustled the Spaniards past the Isle of Wight, when his force was so small.

In the Duke's letters, however, there is a distinct note of anxiety. For the first time the Spaniards were beginning to be worried by shortage of ammunition; not powder, they still had enough of that, but cannon balls. They had been provided with enough to last for six months of operations, including a land campaign, and had shot most of it away already in three sea battles. The reason was, that they had expected to win by boarding, after only a brief, preliminary cannonade to cow the enemy; and, at that, they had expected only one sea battle to take place, for the English would hardly fight, they had thought, until both their fleets were united off Dover. In the evening of 25 July, immediately after the Isle of Wight battle, Medina Sidonia sent a fast pinnace on ahead to Parma, with letters and a liaison officer, Captain Pedro de Leon of the *tercio* of Sicily, to arrange for the junction of their two forces. In the covering letter, the Duke explained how he had done his best " to induce one of the enemy's ships to grapple and so begin the fight; but all to no purpose, as his ships are very light, and mine very heavy, and he has plenty of men and stores. My stores are running short with these constant skirmishes; and if the enemy continues his tactics, it will be advisable for your Excellency to load speedily a couple of ships with powder and balls of the size noted in the enclosed memorandum, and to despatch them to me with the least delay."

Having slept on it, the Duke sent away yet another pinnace to Parma, pleading for help. He wrote: " Friday dawned calm, the fleets being in sight of each other; and the Duke despatched a pinnace to the Duke of Parma with the pilot Domingo Ochoa, to obtain from him shot of four, six, and ten lbs., because much of his munition had been wasted in the several fights; praying him also eftsoons to send 40 flyboats to join with this Armada, that he might be able with them to close with the enemy, because it had been impossible to come to hand-stroke with them." The Duke must have been a very worried man. The Armada's planned role had been to convoy Parma across the sea to England; now, the Armada was asking the army commander, not only for powder and shot, but for ships as well, with which to hold off the English and enable it to keep the sea. . . . It was a very strange reversal of roles, for which, naturally, Parma was neither prepared nor equipped. He had told the King, time and again, that his " fleet " consisted of Dutch canal barges, which might just be able to stagger across the Channel on a very calm day, if protected by the Armada. But the Duke had persuaded himself, or been persuaded by someone else, that the answer to the English fleet was flyboats, and that Parma had them. Fly-boats were not the answer; and Parma did not have more than a dozen of them anyway, for the bulk of the flyboats serving on that coast were sailing under the flag of the Dutch rebels—the " 100 sail of Hollanders and Zealanders " mentioned by Walsyngham. They were keener even than Medina Sidonia to see Parma's " fleet " come out; but their motives were rather different, for they confidently expected to be able to sink the lot. As Parma very well knew.

The Duke's demand for " shot of four, six, and ten lbs." to replace his wastage gives a good indication of the light armament with which most of the Spanish ships must have been fitted; although the flagships probably had some heavier guns, judging by their performance. Or so the original Armada historians thought, Professor Laughton among them; and, really, the Duke's ammunition indent on Parma cannot be made to read as evidence of anything else. However, another nineteenth-century historian, Corbett, took the English artillery superiority ludicrously too far, and this, in turn, has recently sparked off an equally extreme reaction. Professor Lewis has tried to show that the Spaniards had an enormous superiority in heavy, short-range cannon, and that the English superiority was in the lighter, long-range culverin. His argument is a multi-stage affair, each proposition being based on another and depending on it. Due to the scarcity of technical facts about the two fleets, belief in the validity of some of his propositions requires an act of faith. For instance, there were more than half-a-dozen systems of weights and measures simultaneously in use in the Spanish dominions. The professor decides that some one system must have been devised for the Armada, and states which one he thinks it was. If he is right on both counts, well and good; but if he is wrong, the whole structure comes down with a thunder and roar. Similarly, he outfits all the English merchant ships with guns, admitting that we do not actually know the armament of a single one of them. His calculations are based on scrappy records of guns issued from the Tower of London during the period, with no indication to whom they were issued—the Queen's ships, the merchant ships, the forts and castles along the threatened shore, Leicester's army, or the mobile army in the north threatening the Scots. The professor duly makes his guess, and outfits the merchantmen accordingly, but this may well be pure fiction. As originally published, in a series of articles in the *Mariner's Mirror*, Professor Lewis was modest enough to admit that the whole, ingenious, multi-structured affair was guesswork, and might be wrong. But subsequently, his theories having been well received, the Professor claimed that his work had " established " the facts.

There is a much less technical sequence of explanations for the apparent indecisiveness of the first three battles, which, moreover, has the all-important support of the people who actually took part in them. Firstly, the English were out-numbered, but knew that the odds would be on their side once they reached Dover. Secondly, the English offensive power was limited throughout by a shortage of ammunition. Thirdly, the English (and the

Spaniards, too) were over-estimating the effective ranges, from sheer inexperience of such fighting. This recalls Lord Dowding's ruling, in 1940, that the guns of his fighters were to be synchronised at 450 yards, which was soon disregarded by the pilots, who set them to create a cone at 200 yards instead, but even then, regarded that as the distance for a sighting shot; the kill was not to be made until you could " see the rivets " at 50 yards. To begin with, many of the Elizabethan captains must have tended towards Lord Dowding's error. In fact, we know they did. Ubaldino implies it, and a Spanish witness reported little damage done in the Channel battles because " they shoot very far off."

Fourthly, the effect of cannon fire on the structure of a ship, even at very short range, was not particularly dramatic. Professor Lewis talks of " ship-smashing " or " ship-killing " guns; but this is a misnomer. It is most unusual, even today, for a powerful ship actually to be sunk by gunfire. Anything substantial succumbs, if at all, only to underwater explosions—to torpedoes, for instance. And not just to one torpedo, but a salvo; or even several salvoes. The Elizabethans did have the equivalent of a torpedo spread—wind and tide being right, they could loose a salvo of fireships at the enemy; but this standard weapon of the time could not be used in a mobile battle, only against a fleet at anchor. A development of this device so new and so terrible that it ranked virtually as a " secret weapon " was what the top level Spaniards called the *maquinas de minas* (the " mine contrivance "), which was referred to by the lower ranks as, simply, the "Antwerp hell-burner." This may have been what the King of Spain had meant when he had warned Medina Sidonia, months ago, about the English " offensive fireworks." Fire weapons at sea had a long history, and by the sixteenth century much detail had been forgotten; the secrets of Greek Fire, either shot by catapult in projectiles or pumped out by a device not unlike a flame-thrower, had been lost long ago, although the dreadful name still lingered. But now, the reality of the new *maquinas de minas,* used at Antwerp for the first time three years ago, made these old tales seem but the playings of children.

The Antwerp hell-burner, devised by the Italian engineer Giambelli for use against the investing Spanish forces on the

Scheldt estuary, was not a simple incendiary device, it was explosive. A small ship was loaded with gunpowder barrels; a covering of heavy stones was placed on top of the barrels; and a time mechanism, consisting of clock-operated flintlocks, was laid. When the fire reached the powder, after the set interval, the resulting explosion was virtually that of a " block-buster," made far more deadly by the sharp fragments of stone which spewed across a wide area like shrapnel. The Spaniards before Antwerp had lost a thousand men, and Parma himself had been wounded, from the explosion of just one such weapon. That was largely from the surprise effect—they had crowded round the apparently harmless ship and were standing up, in the open, when the explosion occurred; consequently, like others since, the new secret weapon had instantly acquired a reputation more terrible even than that warranted by the facts. Giambelli was known to be in England in 1588, but his talents were being unproductively employed in strengthening the Thames defences. The preparations being made at Dover were for simple fire-ships.

The men of the Cinque Ports, mostly fishermen from Rye and Hastings, sent 30 boats to the Queen's representative at Dover Castle, Rychard Barry, together with bundles of brushwood and barrels of pitch. Barry outfitted 19 of them as fire-ships, loading as well an additional 72 barrels of pitch sent down to him for that purpose by Walsyngham. This work was going on in Dover harbour, in anticipation of the Armada coming to anchor off the opposite coast, some twenty miles across the water, when, on Saturday, 27 July, both fleets were seen in the Straits, moving slowly off Boulogne towards Cap Gris Nez with the south-west wind which had sprung up again after the calm of the previous day. Ammunition boats were also being loaded, ready to go out to Howard's ships, and one of the more peculiar passengers who went aboard was an Irish student from Armagh, a Catholic sympathiser who by the aid of his compatriots at Oxford University, had obtained a passport to go to France. The sailors told him they were bound for Calais, so he took their word for it, and next day was transferred to Howard's flagship, together with the powder and shot, and was consequently a spectator of what the English did to what he called " our Armada." Similarly placed, of course, were Don Pedro de Valdes and the other Spanish guests in Drake's *Revenge*, about whom the Government was beginning to get restive, in case they should learn " the secrets of the services intended." Spectators gathered on both sides of the Straits, a natural amphitheatre, in anticipation of a battle, as they were to do again in 1940. On this occasion, one of them was the Governor of Calais, Monsieur Gourdan, who drove down to the shore in a coach with his wife, in order to have a grandstand seat for the affair.

The Spanish fleet, now on the French side of the Channel, passed close under the looming bulk of Cap Gris Nez, and sailing a few miles further on towards the open roadstead off Calais, suddenly came to double anchor like a squad of soldiers halting on a single word of command. " We kept the wind of them, which is a very great advantage and special safety for the weaker part," wrote Richard Tomson of the *Margaret and John*. " By that means, to the great annoyance of our enemies, we have so daily pursued them at the heels, that they never had leisure to stop in any place alongst our English coast, until they came within two miles of Calais, where in the evening, very politicly, they came all upon a sudden to an anchor, purposing that our ships with the flood tide should be driven to leeward of them; but in happy time it was soon espied, and prevented by bringing our fleet to an anchor also in the wind of them."

The Armada had now arrived at the point of no return. The Straits of Dover are the meeting place for the tides which sweep in from the Atlantic and divide to pass round the British Isles, one stream going past Scotland and so down into the North Sea, the other flowing up-Channel. To pass from one stream to the other, in the Straits, is very tedious, and with the prevailing south-westerly winds, awkward indeed for sailing ships. Medina Sidonia reported that " there were divers opinions as to whether we would anchor there off Calais or go on further; but the Duke, understanding from the pilots who were with him that, if he went on further, the currents would carry him out of the English Channel and into the North Sea, he resolved to anchor off Calais, seven leagues from Dunkirk, from whence the Duke of Parma could join with him."

The Armada had boxed the compass of English history; history past, and history still to be. It had fought a battle off the Isle of Wight, in the very same waters where the dive-bombers were to destroy an English convoy in a battle equally decisive; it had then passed, beaten off from a landing, through the fringes of " Piccadilly Circus," the junction of the roadways of steel ships which were to pass to and from Normandy like a conveyor belt in the summer of 1944; and it had anchored now exactly under the cliffs where the German command post was to be hastily sited at Wissant (in an old omnibus fitted out with telephones) for the Channel battles of 1940, in preparation for another proposed invasion which failed. And, " seven leagues " distant, was Dunkirk, then a little fishing haven; but in 1940 to be wreathed with the black plumes of burning oil tanks, under which the Royal Navy and a host of amateur-manned auxiliary craft ferried off a trapped and defeated army from the beaches. Another point also was different, and this was to be the turning point for the Armada; Dunkirk was held by Parma, but France was neutral. There was no shelter for the Armada on that coast; Parma had to come out quickly, or not at all. The Duke wrote at once to Parma : " The enemy's fleet is on my flank, and able to bombard me, whilst I am not in a position to do him much harm. I beseech your Excellency, if you cannot at once bring out all your fleet, to send me the 40 or 50 flyboats I asked for yesterday, as, with their aid, I shall be able to resist the enemy's fleet until your Excellency can come out with the rest, and we can get together and take some port where this Armada may enter in safety." The Duke sent his secretary, Arceo, in a pinnace with the letter and a verbal message that Medina Sidonia "could not tarry there off Calais without endangering the whole fleet." None of this was the Duke's fault, nor was it Parma's; it was solely the responsibility of the King, who had failed to think out the problem in sufficient depth, or had perhaps thought that the Armada could easily brush aside English opposition at sea. But now, it was less than ever able to do so.

The English fleet was no longer " the weaker part " numerically; it was now the stronger. Admiral Sir William Wynter, in the *Vanguard,* had brought his squadron into the Downs, hoping that there would be time to revictual his ships, which had rations only for three days more, when a pinnace arrived from Howard, ordering a rendezvous off the French coast. " We forthwith made sail and gat out," wrote Wynter, " and by the time we could recover over, which was about seven of the clock in the afternoon, the Spanish army was anchored to the eastward of Scales Cliffs, very round and near together, not far from the shore." Admiral Lord Henry Seymour, in the *Rainbow*, received the same message and led his squadron to the rendezvous with Howard, " and met with his Lordship off Scales Cliffs, about eight in the evening, where both the armies anchored against the other, and we somewhat to the westward." The little force of 67 ships which had met the Spaniards off Plymouth, had grown to a something over a hundred before reaching the Straits, and now, anchored off Calais, numbered more than 140. Many of them were small private ships, volunteers, like those which, centuries later, were to help evacuate the B.E.F. from Dunkirk; but nevertheless, a formidable sea force was gathered to windward of the Armada that Saturday night. Calderon thought there were 160 of them; the soldierly Estrade thought not so many. " So this day," he wrote, " with such ships as came unto them along the coast there were above 150 sail, yet in that which I did see and others likewise there were but 18 good galleons, or 20, of 300 tons, and the rest small, which did amaze me. The English did well accomplish their business (but with the secrets of God)."

To the Spaniards, this quiet massing of force seemed very ominous; the English, now, had nearly three times as many ships as they had had a week ago, and the Armada was the weaker by two flagships. A gentleman of Medina Sidonia's household, Don Luis Miranda, wrote: " We rode there all night at anchor, with the enemy half a league from us, being resolved to wait, since there was nothing else to be done, and with a great presentment of evil from that devilish people and their arts. So too in a great watching we continued on Sunday all day long."

The strain was too great for some in the Armada. There began that evening the first of a series of desertions from the doomed Spanish force. The first to go were Simon Henriquez and Juan Isla, master and pilot respectively of the hulk *San Pedro el Menor*, which had taken part in the only victorious battle the Armada had ever fought—that off the Scillies, against the two little barks, Scottish and Irish, back in June.

But to some of the English, particularly those whose first sight of the Armada this was, the assembly of high-charged ships, grouped closely round the hulks and pinnaces like a protective wall, seemed immensely strong and hard to breach. Wynter wrote: " Immediately, so soon as my Lord Admiral's ship was come to an anchor, he sent his pinnace aboard my ship for me, commanding me to come aboard his Lordship, which I did; and having viewed myself the great hugeness of the Spanish army, did consider that it was not possible to remove them but by a device of firing of ships. His Lordship did like very well of it, and said the next day he would call a council and put the same in practice. His Lordship and I were reasoning of this matter in his Lordship's cabin, when there did drive with the tide aboard my Lord's ship her Majesty's ship the *Bear* and three others, who were all tangled together, so as there was some hurt done by breaking of yards and spoil of tackle." Estrade and Miranda might have amended somewhat their opinion of the "devilish arts" of the English, had they seen this accident, involving the Lord Admiral and his noble kinsmen; and what Drake and Hawkyns thought about it may be imagined. Medina Sidonia saw only the fact of the powerful reinforcements, under Seymour and Wynter, which he thought were commanded by John Hawkyns, who ranked second only to Drake as a Spanish legend. " The enemy's fleet was reinforced by 36 sail, including five great galleons," he wrote in the War Diary. " This was understood to be the squadron which Juan Acles had under his charge before Dunkirk." He sent Captain Heredia ashore to the Governor of Calais, to explain why the Spaniards had anchored in French waters, and Heredia shortly returned, having found Monsieur and Madame Gourdan sitting in a coach by the beach, waiting for the battle to begin.

But nothing happened that night, except the first trickle of desertions from the Armada; and nothing happened all next day, Sunday, 28 July, except a continual coming and going of pinnaces and small boats, among the English fleet, and between the Armada and the shore. The Duke was becoming desperate, as well he might, with the whole enterprise hanging in the balance. Monsieur and Madame Gourdan sent out to him a present of some fruit, and a message that the Armada's anchorage " was extremely dangerous, because of the strong cross currents of the Channel." Captain Don Rodrigo Tello, sent ahead in a pinnace by Medina Sidonia three days after the Armada had left Corunna, so as to give Parma plenty of warning, now rejoined with news of the invasion preparations. " He reported that the Duke of Parma was at Bruges, where he had visited him, and although the Duke expressed great joy at the arrival of the Armada, he had not come to Dunkirk up to the night of Saturday, when Tello had left, nor had the embarkation of men and stores been begun." That evening, the Duke's secretary, Arceo, reported in similar terms from Dunkirk: " Parma had not arrived there, the stores were still unshipped, and he, Arceo, thought that everything could not be ready under a fortnight." During the day, a stream of messengers left the Armada for the shore. First, a provision party with 6,000 ducats to spend in Calais; and lastly, the Inspector-General of the Armada in person, Don Jorge Manrique, to stir up Parma's headquarters and get him to come out at once with his invasion barges to engage the English fleet and sail across the Channel to the mouth of the Thames. The Duke's last letter to Parma, written late that day, read: " I represent to you the urgent need of providing a port for the Armada, without which it will doubtless be lost as the ships are so large. Besides that, it is impossible to continue cruising with this Armada, as its great weight causes it always to be to leeward of the enemy, and it is impossible to do any damage to him, hard as we may try." Clearly, the Duke was at the end of his tether, predicting disaster, a few hours before the process actually began.

But Parma was sitting tight. He was not going to be involved in the ruin of the enterprise. He made his explanations, not to the Duke, but to the King, that same day from his H.Q. at Bruges. " The enemy has a large force of armed vessels on this coast to oppose our coming out, but doubtless they will depart when the Armada arrives," he wrote, blandly. " But to judge from what the Duke says, it would appear that he still expects me to come out and join him with our boats, although it must be perfectly clear that this is not feasible. Most of our boats are

only built for the rivers, and they are unable to weather the least
sea. It is quite as much as they can do to carry over the men
in perfectly fair weather, but as for fighting as well, it is evident
they cannot do it, however good the troops in them may be."

In the English fleet, the movements of boats were between the
squadron flagships and Howard's *Ark Royal*. Wynter wrote:
" Upon Sunday, being the 28th day, my Lord put out his flag
of council early in the morning; and after the assembly of the
council it was concluded that the practice for the firing of ships
should be put in execution the night following, and Sir Henry
Palmer was assigned to bear over presently in a pinnace for
Dover, to bring away such vessels as were fit to be fired, and
materials apt to take fire." Wynter apparently did not know
that the fireships had already been prepared, and probably still
thought the idea was his, the discussion with Howard the previous
evening having been so rudely interrupted. But, in the event,
they were not used. On Sunday, at midnight, there would be a
spring tide running strongly down from the west towards the
Armada; and the wind was still from the west, gusty, with rain, as
it had been for the last two days. Conditions then would be
almost perfect for the firing of a fireship salvo at the Spaniards.
We do not know who pointed that out, but after Palmer had
left for Dover in the pinnace, Wynter recorded, " it was seen he
could not return that night, and occasion would not be over
slipped, it was thought meet that we should help ourselves with
such shipping as we had there to serve that turn."

Captains Yonge and Prouse were given charge of the preparations, and among the eight small ships they selected were Yonge's
own 140 ton flyboat and the 200 ton *Bark Talbot,* commanded
by Henry Whyte, the captain who had been critical of the
Plymouth attack as " more coldly done than became the value of
our nation and the credit of the English navy. After that," he
allowed, " our fleet increased daily; and as men and ammunition
came, we plied them every day with more courage than other,
until they came to an anchor before Calais. There it was devised
to put them from their anchor, and ships were allotted to the
fire to perform the enterprise; among the rest, the ship I had in
charge, the *Bark Talbot,* was one; so that now I rest like one

that had his house burnt, and one of these days I must come to your Honour for a commission to go a-begging."

Such stores as could be got out, were removed; but the guns were loaded so that they would explode in due course with the heat. Incendiary material was placed and the skeleton crews still aboard waited for the gun shot which would be the signal for the attack to begin. At midnight, with the tide pouring relentlessly down towards the tight-packed Spaniards, it came. "About twelve of the clock that night," wrote Wynter, " the ships were brought and prepared with a saker shot, and going in a front, having the wind and tide with them, and their ordnance being charged, were fired; and the men that were the executors, so soon as the fire was made they did abandon the ships, and entered into five boats that were appointed for the saving of them." In close line-abreast, fire flickering up their rigging and the roar of the flames beginning to burst from their decks, they drove down on the anxious, sleepless Spaniards.

"At midnight," wrote Medina Sidonia, " two fires were seen kindled in the English fleet, which increased to eight; and suddenly eight ships with sail set, and fair wind and tide, were seen coming straight for my flagship and the rest of our fleet, all burning fiercely." " They came towards us all in flames," wrote Calderon, " burning furiously in the bows, with the mainsails and foresails set, and the rudders lashed." The flames heated the metal first of this gun, then of that, and the powder began to explode; flaming, thundering, they rode down on the Armada. " Spurting fire and their ordnance shooting," wrote another Spaniard, " which was a horror to see in the night." There was not a single witness in the Armada, so far as we know, who took them for ordinary fireships. " Fire machines or mines," thought Medina Sidonia. "Artificial fire," judged Don Balthasar de Zuniga. "Artificial machines," wrote both Calderon and Manrique. The boom of the explosions, and frightful gout of flame when the deck of one of the fireships fell in, convinced them— these were floating mines, the hell-burners of Antwerp come again!

The Duke had put out a screen of pinnaces, under one of his own officers, Captain Antonio Serrano, for just such a contingency as this. Serrano, a notably brave man in a gallant company of soldiers, had the desperate task of flinging grapnels onto the fireships and towing them aside, risking both fire and explosion while he did it. But the captains of the Armada did not wait to see what luck he had; they did not even stay for the capstans to get their anchors out of the ground; they simply cut their cables and ran, drifting with tide and wind in hopeless confusion all the way from Calais down to Dunkirk. "The eight ships, filled with artificial fire and ordnance, advanced in line at a distance of a couple of pikes' lengths between them," wrote a Spanish witness. "But by God's grace, before they arrived, while they were yet between the two fleets, one of them flared up with such fierceness and great noise as were frightful, and at this the ships of the Armada cut their cables at once, leaving their anchors, spreading their sails, and running out to sea; and the whole eight fireships went drifting between the fleet and the shore with the most terrible flames that may be imagined."

In the confusion, some of the unwieldy ships crashed into each other; Don Hugo de Moncada's flag galleass *San Lorenzo* was rammed by one of his own squadron, the *Girona*, and by Don Alonso de Leyva's flagship, *Rata Encoronada*. The crippled *San Lorenzo*, her rudder smashed, began to creep towards the shore. "Fortune so favoured the English," snarled an angry Spanish officer, "that there grew from this piece of industry just what they counted on, for they dislodged us with eight vessels, an exploit which with one hundred and thirty they had not been able to nor dared to attempt. When the morning came they had gained the weather gauge of us, for we found ourselves scattered in every direction."

And bearing down on them, for the kill at last, came the six fast squadrons of the united English navy. Howard, Drake, Hawkyns, Frobisher, Seymour, Wynter. Heeling over before the wind, their flagships led the last attack. *Ark Royal, Revenge, Victory, Triumph, Rainbow, Vanguard*. Behind them their squadrons, and, eager to be in at the death, all the little ships and pinnaces, too. *Pippin, Scout, Moon*, and *Nightingale;* the *Bark Bonner* and the *Bark Buggins;* the *Rat of Wight* and the *Virgin, God Save Her. Pansy, Prudence, Jewel, Lark, Dolphin, Distain.* Crowding down came the *Brigandine, Black Dog,* and *Hearty*

Anne, the *Handmaid of Bristol,* the *Crescent of Dartmouth,* the *Greyhound of Aldborough.* Timbers groaning, guns run out, musketeers manning their sides, white bow waves bursting from the heaving seas, they went racing down to the battle off Dunkirk. This day, there would be no holding back.

CHAPTER SIXTEEN

Fourteen Chests of Very Noble Spoil

The Fight for the *San Lorenzo*, 29 July

THE MOST surprised man, on the morning of Monday, 29 July, was the Prince of Ascoli, reputedly King Philip's natural son, who found himself at dawn, in a Biscay fishing smack, in the middle of the English fleet streaming down to attack the Spaniards. He was one of a group of trustworthy officers whom the Duke despatched during the night, in light, fast vessels which the Spaniards called zabras, to carry orders to the scattered ships of the Armada. Having delivered the instructions, Ascoli returned to the *San Martin,* to find the Duke's flagship no longer there, nor any other Spanish ship, for that matter; but only the hulls of the eight fireships, still blazing on the shore. And as the grey light of the new day revealed his dangerous isolation, and the English did not bother to turn aside for so trivial a prize, he very shortly found himself in the rear of both fleets, completely cut off from his friends. Soon afterwards, he saw a Spanish pinnace in the same plight for much the same reason; she carried two members of the provost staff who had been sent round the Armada to give the captains the order to rally. As she was a better proposition from the fighting point of view, he transferred to her, and followed in the wake of the battle. And ran straight into trouble, from a cause which he could not have foreseen.

The order of the English attack had been decided the previous day. Howard, the titular leader, was to go in first with his squadron; followed by a big battle group under Drake, which included the squadrons of both Hawkyns and Frobisher; followed by the two squadrons of Seymour and Wynter, Seymour commanding. The Spaniards were to be caught before they could re-form, and individual ships overwhelmed by mass attacks at close range. One English ship against one Spanish ship could not secure a quick decision; but four or more English against one Spaniard would be a very different matter. In short, the Armada was to

THE GUNDECK OF A GALLEON

This is the main battery deck of the Swedish galleon *Vasa*, sunk in 1628, and raised in a good state of preservation 333 years afterwards

One of the formidable gates of the fortress town of Bruges, in
the Spanish Netherlands, headquarters of the Duke of Parma

be destroyed in detail, the obvious and orthodox method; and, because this coast, like that of Hayling-Bracklesham-Selsey, was also a drowned land, it may well have been their intention to scare the Spaniards pell-mell shorewards until they grounded on the treacherous banks. The wind now, still at around south-west, was on this coast slightly offshore, so that it favoured a Spanish escape; the Armada would have to be hard pressed at the critical moment, if it was to be run aground. It would have to be hard-pressed anyway, to take full advantage of the few hours of confusion. And it was at this moment, at the vital onset of the battle, that Howard made for the English their one great mistake of the campaign. Medina Sidonia's faults were those of a gentle scholar, uncertain always of what was really best to be done, and doing nothing, or doing something too late. Howard's error was the opposite: the rashness of a fighting man with little experience, who had perhaps been prodded too often from Westminster to board and take some of the Spanish ships.

He had with him now newly joined volunteers from the court, aching for action, who must have brought with them stories of the Government's displeasure at his failure to board, for the clerk of the Council was to put these complaints officially, and on paper, within forty-eight hours. And the very first thing they saw, at daybreak that Monday, was the crippled flag galleass *San Lorenzo*, limping close inshore for the shelter of Calais Harbour, her rudder gone, but steadied by a foresail and trying to steer with her oars. She was one of the most powerful units in the Armada and, as a flagship, must hold many noblemen of Spain as well as a rich treasure chest. True, she should not have been allowed to escape, but the swarms of English small craft could have settled the business. Already some of them were heading towards her. Howard then made a breathless mistake; he swung his whole squadron out of the line of advance, bore down on the crippled galleass, which he could not approach because she drew less water than the *Ark Royal*, and launched his longboat under the command of his lieutenant, Amyas Preston. Into her poured a crowd of gentlemen adventurers, including two courtiers, Thomas Gerard and William Harvey. In a moment, full of armed men, she was surging across the shallows towards de Moncada's flagship, while the big ships of Howard's squadron

7

looked on out of range, unable to intervene; and also, out of the battle at the moment when maximum weight was required.

Admiral Seymour's report seems dryly critical of his superior. "It being resolved the day before that my Lord Admiral should give the first charge, Sir Francis Drake the next, and myself the third, it fell out that the galleass distressed altered my Lord's former determination, as I suppose, by prosecuting the destruction of her, which was done within one hour after." Sixty precious minutes gone. . . . "In the meantime," Seymour went on, "Sir Francis Drake gave the first charge upon the Spanish Admiral, being accompanied with the *Triumph,* the *Victory,* and others." Captain Vanegas, who was in the *San Martin,* confirmed it: "The enemy's fleet seized the occasion by the forelock, and seeing the flagship alone and the rest of the Armada to leeward, charged upon her with three *capitanas* leading." These were the flagships of Drake, Hawkyns and Frobisher. Medina Sidonia was soon in desperate trouble, so Seymour with his two squadrons swept past the gunsmoke of her brave defiance, and smashed into the rest of the Armada, still to leeward, and trying to come to the help of their flagship. "Myself, with the *Vanguard,* the *Antelope,* and others," he wrote, "charged upon the tail, it being somewhat broken, and distressed 3 of their great ships; my ship shot one of them through six times, being within less than musket shot." The implication seems to be that some of the high-velocity culverin balls were penetrating the enemy from one side to the other, when fired from such close range.

In those Spanish ships now, mostly the best commanded and strongest, men were falling in heaps, guns were dismounted, cage-work shattered, sails rent to ribbons, and the dismal clanking of the pumps amid the roar of battle told of shot holes low down in their hulls. Soon, only the work of the damage control parties, which included divers, was keeping some of them afloat. Nevertheless, the moment of decision was passing, as part of the Armada started to reform, with splendid discipline, into some sort of order. Howard, meanwhile, was three miles away, intent on preventing the escape of the galleass into Calais; in that, at least, he succeeded.

"At the break of day," wrote Richard Thomson of the *Margaret and John,* we espied riding within shot of the town of

Calais the greatest of the King's galleasses, the rest of the Spanish
fleet being two leagues to leeward of her. My Lord Admiral
began to go toward the galleass with his ship, the *Ark,* but finding
the water to be shallow, other ships of less draught bare in with
her and shot at her; whereupon she let slip and run the galleass
aground hard before the town." Some of these small ships were
Seymour's, hoys and pinnaces by his account, which were of no
great use in battle and could be spared for this operation. They
were better suited to it than the 200 ton *Margaret and John,*
which also ran aground in trying to get near enough to the
galleass to bring her guns to bear. Howard's bigger ships had to
remain further out still, or, as Wynter put it: " My Lord Admiral
did stay off and on, with some good ships with him, to give
comfort and countenance to our men."

The *Margaret and John,* however, had no choice but to
remain where she was, aground on Calais bar near the galleass,
because the tide was going out, at half-ebb, and she could not
be refloated until the flood, many hours later. As the tide fell,
so the great galleass heeled over on the landward side, so that,
to seaward, some of her bottom planks were showing, and her
guns pointed helplessly at the sky. The crowd of hoys and
pinnaces closed in to batter her with their light pieces. " She
was assailed by 15 or 20 English ships, small vessels of 30 or 40
tons," wrote an anonymous Spanish witness who, judging by the
detail he gives, was probably in or near the *San Lorenzo* at the
time. " She was nearly surrounded by these small English ships,
which fired off about 100 cannon shots at her upper parts. The
guns on the galleass could not reply, as she had a list to land-
wards. But she was still very sound, as not one of the English
cannon shots pierced the hull, but only her upper planks above
the oars."

In the *Margaret and John,* Richard Thomson was arming himself to join her boarding party, of which he may have been the
leader. Anyway, it was he who wrote the report on the storming
of the *San Lorenzo.* " My Lord Admiral, seeing he could not
approach the galleass with his ship, sent off his longboat unto
her with 50 or 60 men, amongst whom were many gentlemen as
valiant in courage as gentle in birth, as they well showed. The
like did our ship send off her pinnace, with certain musketeers,

amongst whom myself went. These two boats came hard under the galleass sides, being aground; where we continued a pretty skirmish with our small shot against theirs, they being ensconced within their ship and very high over us, we in our open pinnaces and far under them, having nothing to shroud and cover us; they being 300 soldiers, besides 450 slaves, and we not, at that instant, 100 persons." So it appeared to Thomson. The anonymous Spanish witness did not agree, for he wrote: " The Italian sailors and artillerymen, with some others (presumably Spanish soldiers), were the first to escape and fly to shore; and so many went that not more than 50 men stood by the captain to defend the ship."

The popping and banging of musketry continued, mixed with the screams and cries of the galley slaves who manned the now useless oars, until a single lucky shot ended it by striking Don Hugo de Moncada. According to a gentleman from Salamanca, taken prisoner a few minutes later, " a small shot of musket pierced both his eyes." First into her was William Coxe, of the 50 ton pinnace *Delight,* who had already distinguished himself off Portland.

" Within one half hour," wrote Thomson, " it pleased God, by killing the captain with a musket shot, to give us victory above all hope or expectation; for the soldiers leaped overboard by heaps on the other side, and fled with the shore, swimming and wading. Some escaped with being wet; some, and that very many, were drowned."

" The loss amounted to about 50 English and a similar number of Spaniards and slaves, who made a terrible outcry," wrote the anonymous Spanish witness. " While the rest sought safety in flight, the English to the number of 200 entered, robbing what they could lay hands upon and carry." Amyas Preston, Howard's lieutenant, was one of the casualties, severely wounded in the open pinnace. " The few soldiers remaining in the galleass," wrote Thomson, " seeing our English boats under her sides and more of ours coming rowing towards her, some with 10 and some with 8 men in them, for all the smallest shipping were the nearest to the shore, put up two handkerchiefs upon two rapiers, signifying that they desired truce. Hereupon we entered, with much difficulty, by reason of her height over us, and possessed us of her, by the space of an hour and a half as I judge; each man seeking his benefit of pillage until the flood came, that we might haul her off the ground and bring her away." According to Ubaldino, they "looted 22,000 golden écus which were there, belonging to the King, and 14 chests of very noble spoil, belonging to the Duke of Medina Sidonia, together with other monies and spoils and several prisoners, among them Don Roderigo de Mendoza and Don Giovanni Gonsalez de Solorzano, the true captain of the galleass."

The English had lost heavily in this encounter, their open boats being raked by Spanish fire, and they were in a savage temper. Many of their friends were lying huddled on the floorboards of the longboats, and the planks were wet with blood. They were in no mood for French courtesy from the good townsfolk of Calais, their hereditary enemies, who had been spectators at the battle and now sought to interfere, legitimately, for the galleass was in French waters commanded by the guns of the town. "During our fight to get her," sneered Thomson, "the men of Calais stood in multitudes upon the shore hard by us and beholding all things, showing themselves at that instant indifferent lookers-on; but so soon as they saw us possessed of so princely a vessel, the very glory and stay of the Spanish army, a thing of very great value and strength, as was well known to them; then, I say, Monsieur Gourdan, seeing us thus possessed, sent aboard to us that were in her, in which boat came his kinsman and another captain, desiring to parle with us." No other Englishman there either spoke or even understood French, except Thomson, so he stepped forward to question them.

"I asked them from whom they came. They answered: From Monsieur Gourdan, the Governor of Calais. I demanded to know what his pleasure was." Then came the politeness. "They answered that he had stood and beheld our fight and rejoiced of our victory, saying that for our prowess and manhood showed therein we had well deserved the spoil and pillage of the galleass, as a thing due unto us by our desert; and that he willingly consented that we should have the pillage of her." Then came the catch. "He further required and commanded of us not to offer to carry away either the ship or ordnance, for that she was on ground under the commandment of his castles and town, and therefore did of right appertain to him."

Thomson was sarcastic. "I answered unto them that, for our parts, we thanked Monsieur Gourdan for granting the pillage to the mariners and soldiers that had fought for the same; acknowledging that without his leave and good will we could not carry away anything of that we had gotten, considering it lay on ground hard under his bulwarks." And he added a hint of threat. "As concerning the ship and ordnance, we prayed it would please him to send a pinnace aboard my Lord Admiral, who was here in person hard by, from whom he should have an honourable and friendly answer which we all are to obey and give place unto." Howard's presence had accomplished something, for the moment at any rate, for Thomson noted: "With this answer, to my seeming they departed well satisfied." But the English were not to get the great prize after all, which had already cost so much.

The high-born French envoys, one a relative of Gourdan, had hardly moved away out of Thomson's sight, before the blood-drunk, loot-mad English began to jostle them. "Some of our rude men, who make no account of friend or foe, fell to spoiling the Frenchmen, taking away their rings and jewels as from enemies," he recorded. "Whereupon, going ashore and complaining, they were the cause that all the bulwarks and ports were bent against us, and shot so vehemently that we received sundry shot very dangerously through us. They shot our ship twice through. And the like powder and shot did Monsieur Gourdan bestow upon sundry of our countrymen, and make us relinquish the galleass, which otherwise we had brought away, being masters of her above two hours, and gotten by hard assault, to the great credit of our country, if Monsieur Gourdan had not seemed by force to wrest from us that which we had gotten with bloody heads." According to Ubaldino, the English now lost "about 20 more in the sea, on account of the hurry in which they regained their boats." About half the English losses in the entire Armada campaign seem to have occurred in this abortive and wasteful assault on the stranded *San Lorenzo*. No doubt those who came away safe from her, with écu-lined pockets, took a different view, although Thomson blandly reported " very little or no treasure " in her, which was true enough after the English sailors and soldiers had finished with de Moncada's flagship.

The English were pleased with their high-ranking prisoners, who could be ransomed; but all unaware, failed narrowly to put a Prince " in the bag " also; but they can hardly have expected to find the natural son of the King of Spain wandering about in a pinnace in the rear of the English fleet. As they were streaming away from Calais Bar, with the French guns thundering after them, they saw the lone enemy pinnace and chased it. " I had decided to follow in the wake of the fleets," wrote Ascoli, " but I was so hotly pressed by the boats which had attacked and defeated the galleass flagship that not a sailor could be induced to stir." The Prince was completely cut off, and never rejoined the Armada; later, he got into Dunkirk, where he found Parma supervising the loading of the invasion barges as a gesture to show that he had been ready all the time.

The Armada, however, was in no state then to think of invasion; Medina Sidonia's only concern was to save as many of the ships as he could from the rout.

CHAPTER SEVENTEEN

An Italian Ship all Full of Blood

The Battle of Dunkirk—Monday, 29 July

All that day we had with them a long and great fight, wherein there was great valour showed generally of our company. In this battle there was spent very much of our powder and shot; and there was some hurt done among the Spaniards.

John Hawkyns to Walsyngham

THE BUSINESS-LIKE Hawkyns was almost startled into eloquence by the events of that Monday off Dunkirk, but recollected himself in time, made one passing reference to " a great ship of the galleons of Portugal, her rudder spoiled, so that the fleet left her in the sea," and hastily concluded: "I doubt not but all these things are written more at large to your Lordship than I can do; but this is the substance and material matter that hath passed." He was quite right. A score of witnesses on each side penned accounts which have survived; and there must have been many more not preserved. The ship casualties on the Spanish side were not known, even approximately, for days afterwards, as news came in of this ship seen to sink by so-and-so, of that one last seen out of control and drifting shorewards, now definitely reported taken by the Dutch. Even now, the full losses cannot accurately be stated, for the Armada was going to a place where many accounts would be closed, many witnesses silenced forever, and no complete reckoning ever made. On the English side, however, there were no ship losses at all; not even any very severe damage to the Queen's ships, which were all minutely inspected by the dockyards afterwards. And two things were certain. Howard had thrown away the chance of a much greater victory; and God, by changing the wind at the critical moment, had saved the Spaniards.

The battle was, of course, confused; all battles are, from the point of view of the participants. So much going on, simultaneously, in every direction of the compass, that the brain of no one man could possibly take it all in, let alone remember the detail or record the exact sequence; and so much going on, out of sight, hidden by the great clouds of powder smoke, lit by the lightning flashes of the artillery. But the purposes of the contestants were plain enough. Seymour's report makes distressingly clear that tin-pot manoeuvring, so dearly beloved of some students of the sailing navy, had no place in the Elizabethan concept of battle at sea. "Sir Francis Drake gave the first charge upon the Spanish Admiral," wrote Seymour in unmistakable cavalry terms, while "myself charged upon the tail." The English object was to overwhelm the best and most powerful units among the scattered Spanish fleet; to defeat in detail the enemy's strongest ships, an application of orthodox military principles. The elements of sea and wind, however, having a powerful effect on sailing machines, must also have been considered. From the English side there is no hint of this; presumably, they were careful to preserve "the secrets of the services intended." But the Spaniards had no doubt about the English aims. Even the anonymous Spanish witness of the fight for the *San Lorenzo* saw it: "The Spanish fleet is very powerful, but with bad weather it may be driven onto the banks, which is the English plan."

"At seven o'clock in the morning," wrote Calderon, "the enemy opened a heavy artillery fire on the Duke's flagship, which continued for nine hours. So tremendous was the fire that over 200 balls struck the sails and hull on the starboard side, killing and wounding many men, disabling and dismounting three guns, and destroying much rigging. The holes made in the hull between wind and water caused so great a leakage that two divers had as much as they could do to stop them up with tow and lead plates, working all day. The crew were much exhausted by nightfall, with their heavy labours at the guns, without food."

"The wind was blowing strong, from the north-west, nearly straight onto the coast," recorded Medina Sidonia. "The enemy's fleet, wherein were 136 ships, came on suddenly with wind and tide in their favour, so as the Duke, who was in the rear, seeing that if he bare room with his fleet, it would be to their destruction, for that it was already very near the banks of Dunkirk, as he was assured by his Flemish pilots, chose rather to save it by abiding the enemy's fleet. And so he cast about to meet them, discharging his ordnance, and sending off pinnaces to order all

7*

the ships to keep a close luff, as otherwise they would drive onto the banks of Dunkirk. The enemy's flagship, with the greater part of their fleet, assaulted my flagship, with great shooting of ordnance, approaching within musket-shot, or even harquebus-shot; but my flagship did not bare room until the Armada was clear of the shoals."

"The Duke kept luffing up continually upon the enemy's fleet, transfigured and shrouded in the smoke of his guns, which he ordered to be fired with the greatest rapidity and diligence," wrote another Spanish witness. "In truth, if he had not held on upon that tack so long, it was not possible but that the greater part of our Armada must have run ashore and been the end of all."

"It was the greatest war and confusion that there has been in the world, in respect of the great amount of fire and smoke and of there being ships on the shores of Flanders," wrote Friar Gongora in the *San Martin*. "There were many ships which went on fighting in eight cubits of water. And all this day we have been holding ourselves with the bowlines hauled against the weather so as not to run around on the banks, and thus our ships could not ply their artillery as they wished. Some of the people died in our ship, but none of quality, and it was a miracle that the Duke escaped."

It was touch and go, whether or not the Armada could be run aground in a battle of total annihilation. Therefore, Drake did not allow himself to be delayed by the *San Martin,* which was supported only by the *San Marcos* at that moment, although the Castillian galleon *San Juan* and the Portuguese galleon *San Mateo* were making their way back towards her. He fired his bow guns into the Armada flagship, altered course, poured in a broadside, and hurried on down after the bulk of the Armada, re-loading as he did so; and after him, likewise, his squadron and that of Hawkyns, firing a hail of ball into the luckless flagship as they passed her ravaged sides. Only Frobisher stayed to fight, bitterly critical of Drake. "He came bragging up at the first indeed, and gave them his prow and his broadside; and then kept his luff, and was gone again, like a cowardly knave or traitor," snarled Frobisher afterwards.

The remainder of the Drake battle group struck the centre

of the milling mass of Spaniards, who were beginning to shake themselves out into some sort of order again and in danger of grounding in the shallows meanwhile; trying to force the lumbering enemy vessels into fatally shoal water. Hawkyns and his squadron, which included Fenton's *Mary Rose*, old George Beeston's *Dreadnought*, and Richard Hawkyns in the *Swallow*, as well as John Hawkyns in the *Victory*, " bare with the midst of the Spanish army, and there continued a hot assault all that forenoon," according to Howard's report. The *Mary Rose*, going east, passed close alongside a galleon headed in the opposite direction, to help the Duke, and put such a broadside through her that Howard thought it worthy of remark. At such short range, it seems that some of the English high velocity guns were piercing the enemy hulls through and through. "As soon as we that pursued the Spanish fleet were come within musket shot of them, the fight began very hotly," wrote Henry Whyte, the evicted captain of the burnt *Bark Talbot*. " Myself was now aboard the *Mary Rose*, of the Queen's with Captain Fenton, whose value for that day's service deserved praise."

" That day," reported a contemporary writer, " Sir Francis Drake's ship was riddled with every kind of shot, and was letting fly everyway from both her broadsides, so that she seemed to repeat her fire as rapidly as any harquebusier." That was the way the new-type galleons were meant to be fought; for it took many minutes to re-load the guns in a battery, and it was foolish to stay in range while doing it. They bore down, fired one broadside, passed on, turned, came back and fired the other broadside. Consequently, they were in gunshot of the Spaniards only for a minute or so each time; and on the second run in there would probably be no reply from the empty Spanish guns. Or, as another contemporary writer expressed it: " The English ships using their prerogative of nimble steerage, whereby they could turn and wield themselves with the wind which way they listed, came often times very near upon the Spaniards, and charged them sore, that now and then they were but a pike's length asunder; so continually giving them one broadside on another."

It was method as much as courage which counted, stressed Ubaldino, " the judgement and military skill and naval seacraft of the English leaders, who made good use of the most reliable quality of their excellent and speedy ships, not crowded out with useless soldiers, but with decks clear for the use of artillery, so that they could safely play it at any hour to harm the enemy, at any moment which suited them best to do." And he condemned " all the news spread by the press and by people who go about singing their praises and ineptly flattering them."*

There was nothing wrong with Spanish bravery; or Italian, for that matter, as they fought back desperately to prevent themselves being driven to ruin in the shallows. " Since the ships were so scattered and could not help one another," wrote a priest, Geronimo de la Torre, " the enemy's galleons came together and charged us in such numbers that they gave us no time to draw breath." Some Dutch mariners, who deserted from the Armada next day, reported: " In the fleet we did see, through the port holes, an Italian ship all full of blood, which yet maintained the fight in her rank three hours after." Spanish and Portuguese prisoners, taken later, spoke of: " three great Venetian ships which were in danger of sinking, being sore beaten and shot through in many places, but were for the time being holpen by the carpenters." According to Medina Sidonia, this battle in the centre was waged principally by three great Italian carracks, Don Alonso de Leyva's *Rata Encoronada*, Martin de Bertendona's *La Reganzona*, and the *San Juan de Sicilia* of Don Diego Tellez Enriquez, the Camp Master; as well as by two strong galleons of Castile, the flagship *San Christobal* and the *San Juan*, commanded by Don Pedro's successor, Don Diego Enriquez, son of the Viceroy of Peru.

" Fighting in eight cubits of water," they gave ground eastwards, towards Dunkirk, and, hard as the English tried, they could not push them ashore; they were too tightly bunched together, for the squadrons of Drake and Hawkyns alone to deal with. " There were made several very hot charges," wrote Sir Horatio Palavicino, the Genoese banker now serving as a volunteer with the English fleet. "A great quantity of ordnance was fired on one side and on the other. Our fleet had the wind

* This sounds like a first-hand comment from Drake or Hawkins. Nothing is more infuriating to the skilled technician than the thoughtless, sentimental insinuation that it was all done by brute force and ignorance.

throughout, and gave occasion to the enemy to open out to fight; but they chose rather to be followed and bear away, as well from Calais as from Dunkirk, than to open out and permit the fight to become general. So as it was not convenient to attack them thus together and in close order, for that our ships, being of smaller size, would have had much disadvantage; but in the continued assaults which they gave on them without entering, they made them to feel our ordnance; and if any ship was beaten out of their fleet, she was surrounded and suddenly separated from the rest."

Then, three hours late, long after the presence of his powerful squadron could have had maximum effect, Howard crashed into the fight with the *Ark Royal, White Bear, Golden Lion,* and the rest. " This fight continued hotly," he reported, " and then came the Lord Admiral, the Lord Thomas Howard, the Lord Sheffield, near the place where the *Victory* had been before, where these noblemen did very valiantly." The arrival of these fresh reinforcements, which had spent half the morning watching the fight for the *San Lorenzo,* hit the Spaniards hard; but the decisive moment was gone. " We had not fought above three hours," reported Whyte, who, in the *Mary Rose,* was accompanying Hawkyns' *Victory,* " but my Lord Admiral with the rest of the fleet came up, and gave a very fresh onset, which continued amongst us some six hours more; and truly, sir, if we had shot and powder sufficient to have given them two such heats more, we had utterly distressed them."

All these Spanish ships in the centre, as well as the group of galleons which had come to the support of his flagship to windward of them, reported Medina Sidonia, " sustained the assault of the enemy as stoutly as possible, so as all these ships were very much spoiled, and almost unable to make further resistance, and the greater part of them without shot for their ordnance."

Meanwhile, a third and quite separate battle had been going on downwind in the rear, where Seymour and Wynter, passing the struggling Spanish flagship, which was being hammered by Frobisher, and leaving the central group to Hawkyns, and possibly to Drake also, had charged what Wynter described as the " starboard wing " of the Spaniards, which included some of the galleasses; that is, the most easterly of the groups which were re-forming, but still separated from each other. " My fortune was to make choice to charge their starboard wing without shooting of any ordnance until we came within six score paces of them," wrote Wynter, " and some of our ships did follow me. The said wing found themselves, as it did appear, to be so charged, as by making haste to run into the body of their fleet, four of them did entangle themselves one aboard the other. One of them recovered himself, and so shrouded himself among the fleet; the rest, how they were beaten, I will leave it to the report of some of the Spaniards that leapt into the seas and were taken up, and are now in the custody of some of our fleet."

Describing the same action, Howard wrote: "Astern of the Lord Admiral was a great galleon assailed by the Earl of Cumberland and Mr. George Raymond in the *Bonaventure* most worthily, and being also beaten with the Lord Henry Seymour in the *Rainbow,* and Sir William Wynter in the *Vanguard,* yet she recovered into the fleet. Notwithstanding, that night she departed from the army and was sunk."

The " great galleon which recovered into the fleet " after a battering from two English flagships and the ship of the pirate Admiral, the Earl of Cumberland, was the powerful war galleon of Portugal, the *San Felipe,* commanded by the Camp Master Don Francisco de Toledo, who put up a brave and desperate defence. " He fought neither more nor less than most valiantly," wrote Padre de la Torre, " placing himself in the hottest of the fight and fighting with twelve or fifteen galleons, without help except from God, and moreover close enough to use his muskets. My own vessel was received with such a hail of balls that it was cut to pieces alow and aloft. Yea, in the end I saw myself that day in such sore straits that it was a miracle of God we escaped."

" The *San Felipe* was surrounded by 17 of the enemy's ships," wrote Calderon. " They directed against her a heavy fire on both sides and on her stern. They approached so close that the muskets and harquebusses of the galleon were brought into service, killing a large number of men on the enemy's ships. They did not dare, however, to come to close quarters, but kept up a hot artillery fire from a distance, disabling the rudder, breaking the foremast, and killing over 200 men on the galleon."

Two hundred dead meant many more wounded, cruelly torn by the whining wooden slivers that flew from the planks like hail under the thunderous impact of the cannon balls; the dead were down in heaps, the decks slippery underfoot with blood and the squirming remnants of men, their screams and moans a keening accompaniment to the roar of battle and the defiant popping of musketry all along the battered Spanish bulwarks, where the soldiers of the tercio of *Entre Douro y Minho* were trading musket balls for cannon shot. This was the spirit which had made the Spanish infantry invincible in Europe, which had enabled a few hundred men to carve out an empire in the New World. They died, jeering at the English, for their lack of courage in not coming to close quarters. The few dazed prisoners, weaker spirits who had leapt overboard, gasped out to their English captors that they had fought at Lepanto, that great battle of the galley fleets long ago, and that this unendurable cannonade was twenty times worse. And as the great galleon rolled idly in the swell, her foremast down and her sails and rigging trailing in the water, a consort came to her aid—another Portuguese warship, the *San Mateo*, commanded by another of the Camp Masters, Don Diego de Pimental.

The ships of Seymour and Wynter closed on her too, firing into her on both sides simultaneously, the Spaniard towering above them. She fought, said Padre de la Torre, until " she was a thing of pity to see, riddled with shot like a sieve; and had it not been that the Duke afterwards sent his divers to her to get the water out of her, she must have gone to the bottom with all hands. All her sails and rigging were torn and sorely destroyed; of her sailors many perished, and of her soldiers few were left." But the battle madness had infected the English also. As one of the English ships raced down her side, only a few feet of heaving sea between, the cannon bellowing and shaking the timbers underfoot and the musketry banging away, an Englishman, crazy with excitement, leapt clean onto the *San Mateo* in a lone attempt to board. But no one followed his example, and, as Calderon wrote, " our men cut him to bits instantly."

Around her consort, the smashed *San Felipe*, the English were circling in the cold fury of victory, closing to within earshot before they fired their battery guns, and yells and jeers

echoed across the water between them and the shattered Spaniard.
" She had five of her starboard guns dismounted," said Calderon,
" and a Italian gunner, who was afterwards killed, spiked another
of her great guns. In view of this, and that his upper deck was
destroyed, both his pumps broken, his rigging in shreds, and
his ship almost a wreck, Don Francisco de Toledo ordered the
grappling hooks to be got out, and shouted to the enemy to come
to close quarters. They replied, summing him to surrender
in fair fight. And one Englishman, standing in the maintop with
his sword and buckler, called out: ' Good soldiers that ye are,
surrender to the fair terms we offer ye.' But the only answer
he got was a gunshot, which brought him down in sight of
everyone, and the Maestre de Campo then ordered the muskets
and harquebusses to be brought into action. Thereupon the
enemy retired, while our men shouted out to them that they
were cowards, with foul words reproached them for their want
of spirit, calling them Lutheran hens, and daring them to return
to the fight."

The *San Martin* was now wallowing far astern, with the
divers at work on her hull trying without success to stop the
leaks. The English had left her, in order to bring their whole
weight to bear in the centre and so smash the Spanish movement
to reform, because if even half the Armada could assume some
sort of order, it would be almost impossible to break; they had
not enough powder and shot left to do it. And because other
ships were coming to the rescue of the two battered Portuguese
galleons, the conflict began to revolve around them, as ships
of both sides were sucked into the battle. In place of three
separate battles—four, counting the fight for the *San Lorenzo*,
which had occupied Howard for half the morning—there was
now one great whirlpool of conflict. Even the battered Armada
flagship came limping towards it eventually. According to Medina
Sidonia, he actually climbed the mast to see what was happening
over there.

" Whenas the Duke heard the harquebus-fire and the musketry
in the rear, but by reason of the smoke was unable to see from
the top what it was," he wrote, " except that two of our ships
were surrounded by the enemy, and that their whole fleet, having
quitted my flagship, were assailing them, he gave order to cast

about to succour them, although the flagship was sorely distressed by great shot between wind and water, so as by no means could the leak be stopped, and her rigging was much spoiled." Actually, there was nothing else he could do, unless he was prepared to face being cut off from the main body of his fleet. But before he got there, two other groups had come to the rescue of the *San Felipe* and the *San Mateo*.

The first consisted of Recalde's flagship, the *San Juan* of Oporto, and the ship Calderon was in, the *San Salvador*, vice-flagship of the hulks. They were shortly supported by Don Alonso de Luzon, Camp Master of the tercio of Naples, in *La Trinidad Valencera*, an 1,100 ton Italian carrack; another Italian ship, the *San Juan de Sicilia*, under Don Diego Tellez Enriquez; and Garibay's *Nuestra Senora de Begona*, of the Armada of Castile. The *San Martin* eventually broke through the battle smoke, followed by the *San Marcos*, which accompanied her all day, and in which Pedro Estrade was serving.

Then, said Calderon, his ship, the *San Salvador*, " with the Duke's flagship engaged an Admiral's and a commodore's flagships of the enemy, her bows, side, and half her poop being exposed for four hours to the enemy's fire, during which time she received no aid." If Calderon is correct, then he was probably helping to fight Seymour's 500 ton *Rainbow* and Wynter's 500 ton *Vanguard*, two warships of the latest type. " The *San Salvador* had a number of men killed and wounded, and her hull, sails, and rigging so much damaged that she was obliged to change her mainsail. She leaked greatly through the shot holes, and finally the *Rata* came to her assistance, distinguishing herself greatly. On board the *Rata* there fell, killed by a shot, Don Pedro de Mendoza, son of the Commander of Castelnuovo, Naples; and other persons. The Duke's flagship lost 40 soldiers; and others. The *San Juan de Sicilia*, which carried Diego Tellez Enriquez, suffered to such an extent that every one of her sails had to be replaced; Don Pedro Enriquez, who was also on board, had a hand shot away. The galleon *San Juan* also suffered very severely, as did the *San Marcos;* Don Felipe de Cordoba, son of Don Diego, his Majesty's Master of the Horse, had his head shot off." The casualty lists were almost a roll-call of the nobility of Spain.

Estrade witnessed the death of Don Felipe. " This day was

slain Don Felipe de Cordoba," he wrote, "with a bullet that struck off his head and splashed with his brains the greatest friend that he had there, and 24 men that were with us trimming our foresail. And where I was with four other men, there came a bullet that struck off the shoe of one of them, without doing any other harm, for they came and plied us so very well with shot. And, as I was below in the afternoon, discharging my artillery, there was a mariner that had his leg struck all in pieces and died presently. The *San Juan de Sicilia*, and the ship of Pedro de Ugarte (the *Maria Juan* of Biscay), and one hulk, remained this day among more than twenty galleons and ships; but they were not boarded but with bullets, and so they cleared themselves and cast about towards us, but very evil entreated."

"Yet the English would not board our ships in any wise," wrote Estrade, "although we did amain and tarried for them and suffered all their shot of good artillery. And the ship of Pedro de Ugarte remained much spoiled and we left her, for we had not time to take in all the people. So we bare out of the north and north-east with great disorder, some investing one with another, others separating; and the English in the wind of us discharging their cannons marvellously well, and fired not one piece but it was well employed, by reason we were so nigh one another and they a good space asunder one from the other."

From the opposite side, Captain Thomas Fenner of the *Nonpareil*, one of Drake's ships, made the same point, more brutally: "A thing greatly to be regarded, that the Almighty hath stricken them with a wonderful fear; in that I have hardly seen any of their companies succoured of their extremities which befell them after their fights, but left at utter ruin, without regard, bearing as much sail as possible they might, holding the rest of their army together."

Sir William Wynter, whose ships had been helping to pound Estrade, wrote: "The fight continued from 9 of the clock until six of the clock at night, in which time the Spanish army bare away NNE and N. by E., as much as they could keeping company one with another, I assure your honour in very good order. Great was the spoil and harm that was done unto them, no doubt. I deliver it under your honour upon the credit of a poor gentleman, that out of my ship there was shot 500 shot of demi-cannon, culverin, and demi-culverin; and when I was furthest off in discharging any of the pieces, I was not out of the shot of their harquebus, and most times within speech one of another. And surely every man did well; and, as I have said, no doubt the slaughter and hurt they received was great, as time will discover it; and when every man was weary of labour, and our cartridges spent, and munitions wasted—I think in some of our ships altogether— we ceased and followed the enemy, he bearing hence still in the course as I have said before." Wynter was bone-weary and bruised when he wrote that, for he had hurt his hip during the fight by the recoil of a demi-cannon.

The battle had indeed been more terrible than Lepanto, in the nerve shock of the gun-fight, the howling battle storm of missiles, to which the Spaniards were unaccustomed. But the casualties were nothing like as great, even in the worst-hurt Spanish ships, for the new and fearful weapons were actually merciful, hurling their rain of destruction at hulls and men alike. They could not rage with sword and dagger into every nook and cranny of them as a blood-maddened surge of boarders could. Their main effect was on the manoeuvrability of the ships, and upon morale; the Spaniards were " appalled," wrote Drake.

When he sat down that night to write a report for Walsyngham, he made it brief, for the letter was to go by hand, and the bearer had been present at the battle. " God hath given us so good a day in forcing the enemy so far to leeward as I hope in God the Prince of Parma and the Duke of Sidonia shall not shake hands this few days; and whensoever they shall meet, I believe neither of them will greatly rejoice at this day's service. Business commands me to end. God bless her Majesty, our gracious Sovereign, and give us all grace to live in his fear. I assure your Honour this day's service hath much appalled the enemy." After the signature " Fra Drake," he added a P.S.: " There must be great care taken to send us munition and victual whithersoever the enemy goeth." Walsyngham must have had this sort of postscript by heart, for no English Admiral, throughout the campaign, ever wrote him a letter without adding something to that effect.

Various grimly comic tales went round the fleet, as to the colander appearance of the *Revenge* at that moment. " Sir

France's Drake's ship was pierced with shot aboue forty times, and his very cabben was twice shot thorow, and about the conclusion of the fight, the bed of a certain gentleman lying weary thereupon, was taken quite from under him with the force of a bullet," wrote the Dutch historian, Meteren. Ubaldino testified to the truth of that widely told story, and added that: " Shortly afterwards the Earl of Northumberland and Sir Charles Blount were resting on the same bed in the same place when it was again hit by a ball of a demi-culverin which passed through without doing any harm other than scrape the foot, taking off the toes of one who was there with them."* But Drake himself, unlike Howard, whose account is mainly personal experience narrative, would talk only of tactics, not of what he and his squadron had done. Except for Seymour's brief statement, we know little of his part in the victory; but it is enough. We know that he led the English fleet into action; and we know what the result of the battle was; and that the Spaniards, at any rate, were not laughing.

The news came into Calais that the two fleets had been seen, still cannonading each other, off Zeeland; the fisherman who brought it reported: " He saw some ships broken into bits, others without masts or sails, from which they were throwing overboard artillery, trunks, and many other things, whilst men were striving to save themselves by escaping in boats, with such lamentation as may be imagined." In Calais, they must have wondered: whose ships? What the fisherman had seen must in fact have been the end of Toledo's *San Felipe*, Pimental's *San Mateo*, Pedro Ugarte's *Maria Juan*, of Biscay, and possibly also the patache *San Antonio de Padua*, and an unknown ship which sank next day. For, including the flag galleass *San Lorenzo*, the Armada lost at least six ships as a result of the battle off Dunkirk. This was what Hawkyns meant, when he claimed, judiciously, " there was some hurt done among the Spaniards."

By sunset, the three big ships were drifting slowly, out of control, the water pouring in below; and the sea was getting up. Furthest away was the shattered *Maria Juan*, 665 tons, of Recalde's Armada of Biscay; her decks were almost awash and

---

*Compare with Estrade's narrative. Incidents such as these, not necessarily much exaggerated, are fairly typical " battle stories."

the remnants of her crew of 92 seamen and 183 soldiers were perched like black crows high up on the spars and rigging. The mizzenmast was over the side, with canvas and ropes trailing in the water; her rudder had been shot away. She was done for, and signalling desperately for assistance. "The Duke sent the aid requested," said Calderon, " but it was possible to save only one boatload of men, for she sank, to the great sorrow of everyone."

At about 7 o'clock, the *San Felipe*, 800 tons, had begun to fire slow cannon shots, as a signal for aid also. The galleass *Zuniga* and a Seville galleon circled her protectively, while the hulk *Doncella*, which had been battered off the Isle of Wight and had suffered more damage this day off Dunkirk, closed in to take off the men from the foundering Portuguese galleon. "She found the galleon sinking," wrote Calderon, "and took on board 300 of her men." They included the Camp Master, Francisco Toledo, and the captain of the *San Felipe*, Juan Posa de Santiso. " Then," recorded Medina Sidonia, " they heard a cry that the hulk *Doncella* was herself sinking." Toledo's reaction to this news, according to Calderon, showed a wry spirit. " When Captain Juan Posa said that the hulk was going down, the Maestre de Campo replied that, if that were the case, they had better be drowned in a galleon than in a hulk; and they both went back to the *San Felipe*." " This was a great misfortune," wrote the Duke, " for it was not true that the hulk was sinking, and Don Francisco was carried in the *San Felipe* towards Zealand."

A similar determination, to stay with his ship, was shown by the other Camp Master, Don Diego Pimental, of the 750 ton *San Mateo*, rolling in the swell nearby, her pumps hard at work, but unable to stem the inrush of water. "The Duke ordered boats to go to bring away the people from the *San Mateo* also," recorded Medina Sidonia. " But Don Diego Pimental would not leave the ship, and sent Don Rodrigo de Vivero and Don Luis Vanegas to me, to ask if it were not possible to save her; whereon I sent a pilot and a diver from this galleon, though there was much peril in remaining without him, my flagship having suffered from great shot, whereby she was in danger of being lost. But because it was now late, and the sea grown very heavy, they could not reach the *San Mateo,* beyond seeing her afar off, going towards Zealand."

The determination of the youthful Pimental, who was 29, contrasted strongly with the indecision in the flagship; he and Toledo represented the best spirit of Spain. There were many in the Armada, at that moment, whose comments on the inoffensive Duke, and the real commander of the fleet, Diego Flores, who was with him all the time, were unprintable. Uncomfortably aware of this, Medina Sidonia tried to protect himself by concluding that day's entry in the War Diary: " This day the Duke wished to turn on the enemy with the whole Armada, so as he would not leave the Channel; but the pilots told him that it was unpossible because with the sea and wind, setting straight on the coast, they must by force go into the North Sea, or else the whole Armada would be driven on to the banks. Thus in no way could they avoid leaving the Channel; nearly all the ships being spoiled and unable to resist longer, as well as from the damage they had received as from not having shot for their ordnance."

Whichever way one looked at it, it was defeat. The Armada running away from Dunkirk, sailing further and further with every hour from the waiting invasion barges; and with stricken ships falling astern, to sink, or to drift helplessly ashore into the hands of the furious Dutch. Mixed emotions of sadness, rage, and terror filled the minds of the men who were part of that great, ruined enterprise. Sadness at the loss of friends, rage at the humbling of Spain, terror of the night and the spume-covered sandbanks to shoreward of them, and the deadly English ships riding easily somewhere in the darkness to seaward. " Hardly a man slept that night," wrote de la Torre. " We went along all wondering when we should strike one of those banks."

CHAPTER EIGHTEEN

Ask Diego Flores

The Pursuit—Tuesday, 30 July

> Our ships, God be thanked, have received little hurt, and are of great force to accompany them, and of such advantage that with some continuance of the seas, and sufficiently provided of shot and powder, we shall be able, with God's favour, to weary them out of the sea and confound them.
>
> *John Hawkyns to Walsyngham*

NEXT MORNING, the wreck of the enterprise was plain. The great *capitana* of the Armada, Medina Sidonia's *San Martin,* was driving helplessly onto the banks beyond Dunkirk, lagging behind, with one of her anchors down for sounding purposes. "There appeared to be no hope for her; either she must fall into the hands of the enemy or run on the banks," wrote Calderon. Oquendo's flagship came nosing up alongside, and the Duke cried out desperately to his Admiral: "Senor Oquendo, what shall we do? We are lost!"

"Ask Diego Flores!" came the unfeeling reply.

Which, being translated, meant: "Run aground, and be damned to the pair of you!" To rub it in, Oquendo shouted: "As for me, I am going to fight, and die like a man. Send me a supply of shot."

Astern, left to her fate, another great Spanish ship was wallowing out of control. One of Recalde's men, taken later, thought she was Castilian, but that is all we know of her identity, for her end was very sudden. The Queen's ship *Hope,* 600 tons, Captain Robert Crosse, had barely run alongside her, in view of both fleets, when she foundered. Howard reported briefly: "One of the enemy's great ships was espied to be in great distress by the captain of her Majesty's ship called the *Hope;* who being in speech of yielding unto the said captain, before they could agree on certain conditions, sank presently before their eyes." In all, reported Howard, "we sank three of

their ships, and made four to go room with the shore so leak
as they were not able to live at sea." Four certainly were ashore
that morning, but we know nothing of the third ship which
Howard claimed sunk. He, however, was sure of it; he referred
to it in three separate documents, one of which included the
delightful phrase: " whereof there is three of them a-fishing on
the bottom of the sea."

In all, Howard claimed nine enemy ships sunk, stranded, or
surrendered in the fighting since Plymouth: Don Pedro's *Rosario*,
Oquendo's vice-flag *San Salvador*, de Moncada's *San Lorenzo*,
Toledo's *San Felipe*, Pimental's *San Mateo*, the pinnace *San
Antonio de Padua*, and three sent to the bottom, the *Maria Juan*,
a possible Castile ship, and one unknown. Eight great ships and
a pinnace. Both Seymour and Fenner made the same claim,
independently, Seymour listing eight " great ships " and Fenner
eight " of the best sorts of shipping." And all this for no ships
sunk, or even badly damaged, on the English side, and " the
least losses " of men, for the English decks were bare, except
for mariners and gunners; there was no massed human target
for the Spanish cannon to play on. Indeed, it was the necessary
presence of such a target which made the Spanish losses so
exceptionally heavy. History in future was to show such fights
as surprisingly economical in life (the British losses at Trafalgar
were only 1,158 killed), and the actual sinking of a ship as very
much the exception to the rule (only one at Trafalgar, and she
caught fire). But, by then, both sides had reverted to boarding,
following bombardment, because there was no such tremendous
disparity in numbers between one side and the other as that
which had made the Armada campaign unique. The English
had done well; but felt that, with a little luck and plentiful
ammunition, they could have done very much better. The
Armada, with its mixture of nationalities, began to fray at the
edges; and first to go were the Dutch, who were being carried
past and away from the shores of their own country in a defeated
and probably doomed expedition.

They saw the ruined ships simply abandoned to their fate,
and a group of Dutch mariners, 14 in all, who were serving in
one of the Armada vessels, read that as a lesson that there was
no hope except for he who helps himself. This day, therefore,

probably in the early hours of the morning, they had recourse to a desperate expedient, for their Dutch interrogator reported: " Having made sails for their cockboat with their shirts, they are now fled away from the Spanish fleet." They reported that three ships had been sunk in the recent battle, which is some confirmation of Howard's claim, and that " one of her Majesty's ships valiantly passed through them to charge the Admiral, who fled away, and—as they say—doth seem to be wonderfully dismayed and discouraged." A Spaniard taken later from Recalde's ship said much the same thing: " The English fleet pursued the Spanish fleet in such sort as if they had offered to board the Spanish fleet, he saw their admiral so fearful, he thinketh they had all yielded." Oquendo's jeered advice to his commander-in-chief was representative of much feeling in the Armada as a whole.

Meanwhile, in Dunkirk haven that morning, the Duke of Parma and Don Jorge Manrique almost came to blows. Juan Manrique wrote to Juan de Idiaquez, the King's Secretary: " Don Jorge Manrique is here, and it is quite pitiable to see how he goes on." Ships of the Armada were drifting ashore all along the coast, and the dull boom of cannon showed that the Dutch were furiously assailing them. Cruising off Dunkirk, where the waves seethed whitely over the banks, were forty Dutch ships under Count Justinus of Nassau, riding in plain view of the Spaniards; the Armada was gone from sight, harried by the English. The quays of Dunkirk and the other invasion ports were crowded with armed and armoured Spanish soldiery— 16,000 of them—and at last Don Jorge Manrique saw the pitiable craft in which they were supposed to cross the Channel, mostly flat-bottomed barges, mere empty scows. The King knew it, for Parma had told him often enough. The English knew it, for Seymour had reported to Walsyngham on 20 July: " They be no boats to be hazarded to the seas, no more than wherries or cockboats." But Don Jorge Manrique, the Inspector-General of the Armada, did not know it. No one in the Armada flagship apparently knew it, for the Duke had for days been showering Parma with begging letters, asking him to come out with his fleet to help the Armada. But, even when Don Jorge Manrique saw what that fleet actually consisted of, he persisted in giving

the Duke's message, and angrily tried to insist that Parma ought
to comply.

At 10.30 that morning, he tracked Parma down on the
quayside at Dunkirk, having missed him the previous day, for
Parma had just left his main H.Q. at Bruges to visit the soldiers
embarking at Nieuport; and there he presented to him Medina
Sidonia's incredible demands. " The Duke requests that we here
should go and help him obtain a port, and especially to capture
the Isle of Wight," complained Parma to the King. " This is the
request brought to me by Don Jorge Manrique. Or else, that I
should join him to engage the enemy . . ." Exasperated, Parma
called in the Marquis de Renti and other experts, and questioned
them in front of Don Jorge Manrique, so that the latter might be
satisfied that he was not fabricating difficulties and that, in
particular, these unseaworthy scows were not capable of a sea
voyage of seven or eight days, which would be the time required
to carry out the Duke's favourite plan, not yet abandoned, of
capturing the Isle of Wight. Baffled by seamen's science, Don
Jorge and some other officers from the Armada who had brought
messages during the previous week, furiously pointed out that
the scows had no guns, that they had seen no troops embarked
in them, and that it appeared no real preparations had been
made.

Parma patiently explained that his boats were troop transports, invasion barges; not fighting ships. The Armada was
supposed to provide the fighting ships. " The most we could
hope from these boats," he said, " would be, in fine, settled
weather, and with the Channel clear of enemies, to ferry our men
across, as had been arranged." As for the boats not being loaded,
surely they did not expect the men to be herded into them like
cattle for days at a time? They could all be loaded very quickly,
when required, almost simultaneously, in the great network of
rivers and canals behind Nieuport and Dunkirk. Three days was
his estimate. Parma had detected long ago the flaw in the
whole enterprise—the lack of a port in which the Armada could
make a safe junction with the invasion craft and safely escort
them out, granted that they had previously beaten the English
fleet, and driven off the Dutch. That is, if the Armada seriously
intended a full-scale landing in the Thames estuary, and was

not just a gigantic bluff to influence the English peace commissioners (who were still at Ostend). One may suspect that Parma's ostentatious embarkation at Nieuport the previous day was a bluff, too, for only the most reckless commander would send out his soldiers in such craft across the Channel when it was obvious from the hysterical messages of Medina Sidonia that he was quite unable to cope with the English fleet at sea.

Into this heated discussion, however, strode Philip's bastard son, the Duke of Ascoli, whose pinnace had just got into Dunkirk after its narrow escape from the English; and also, in other small boats, two men with even more up-to-the-minute news, Captain Marolin de Juan, the Armada's navigator, and Major Gallinaro. Their news abruptly terminated the debate. Invasion had become an academic exercise. Parma summed up their reports: " The Duke is running to the north, his full losses unknown, and the English continue to follow him with very swift vessels, manned by good and experienced sailors." Ascoli begged to be allowed to rejoin the Armada, but Parma, taking pity on him, absolutely forbade it.

Meanwhile the Armada, or part of it, hemmed in on the banks by a north-west wind and the English fleet, hovering with silent guns to seaward of them, was still in danger. Calderon's narrative implies that it was only the flagship which was in deadly peril, but Medina Sidonia wrote that it was the whole fleet. " The Duke shot off two pieces to collect his Armada, and sent a pinnace with a pilot to order them to keep a close luff, because they were very near to the banks of Zealand. For which cause the enemy remained aloof, seeing that our Armada must be lost; for the pilots on board the flagship—men of experience of that coast—told the Duke at this time that it was not possible to save a single ship of the Armada; for that with the wind as it was, in the NW, they must all needs go on the banks of Zealand; that God alone could prevent it. Being in this peril, without any sort of remedy, God was pleased to change the wind to WSW, whereby the fleet stood towards the North without hurt to any ship, the Duke sending order to every ship to follow the flagship, for that otherwise they would go on the banks of Zealand." Possibly there is some exaggeration here, for the Duke also wrote that he was in this plight because he and some other ships had remained in the rear and defied the English, " in the hope of returning to the Channel "; which was very far from being their intention. This was the crushing moment of defeat, the season for excuses; and the War Diary was duly written up to this effect, Medina Sidonia inserting a paragraph at this point to show where the blame really lay.

" In regard to the fighting, and the turning to relieve and assist his ships, and the abiding of the coming of the enemy, the Duke took counsel with the Camp Master Don Francisco de Bobadilla; but in regard to the conduct of the fleet, and such matters as related to the sea, the Duke had the council of the general Diego Flores, whom he also ordered to move into the flagship, because he was one of the oldest and most experienced in sea affairs." Quite clearly, the Armada's calculated policy of desertion of all its damaged ships, from Don Pedro's *Rosario* off Plymouth to the last unfortunate ship which went down that day, her survivors being picked up by the English, not the Spanish, had aroused outspoken resentment; as it was bound to do. It was just about the worst possible blow that any leader could deliver to morale and to his own authority; in effect, an abdication of leadership. Hence the well-calculated stress, written into the War Diary, of the brave part played in the actual fighting by the *San Martin*, the ship of the headquarters trio—Medina Sidonia, Bobadilla, and Diego Flores de Valdes.

There is no word, from the English side, of any attempt to put the Armada ashore, off the Isle of Wight, off Dunkirk, or on this day. But then, except for an occasional hint from Howard, the English leaders are resolutely silent about their battle aims, even in official correspondence. In the public accounts of the campaign, written shortly afterwards, there was naturally no highlighting of the dreadful fact that the whole Spanish fleet was running away from empty guns, for that reflected just as badly on the efficiency of the English Government as it did on the nerve and resolution of the Armada leadership. But we do know that there were outbursts of rage among the English; for, clearly, this was the moment to tear into them, hammer the defeated, damaged, demoralised enemy, and sink, cripple or ground many more of his ships. We know, from the statement of Fray Bernado de Gongora, that the previous day " many of the ships went on fighting in eight cubits of water, and as the enemy knew the danger we were in, they harried us so much that we were almost lost." And we know, from Estrade's narrative, that at that time the Armada was in "great disorder." To drive their worst-beaten opponents onto the banks was an obvious gambit which the English would not have overlooked; but the victory could not be made final and crushing, neither on the Monday nor on the Tuesday, because there was not enough powder and shot left in the English ships with which to do it. That they knew what opportunity was missed, is very clear. Howard was to tell Walsyngham so, on 7 August; and Henry Whyte was to write in the same terms on the day following: " By this simple relation, your Honour may see how our parsimony at home hath bereaved us of the famousest victory that ever our navy might have had at sea." It would have been as great, or greater than, Trafalgar, the future " finest hour " of the British navy.

As it was, on this day, Tuesday, 30 July, the shot-torn Armada presented to the English an unhappy spectacle. "At this instant," wrote Tomson, " we are as far to the eastward as the Isle of Walcheren, wherein Flushing doth stand, and about 12 leagues off the shore; and the wind hanging westerly, we drive our enemies apace to the eastward, much marvelling, if the wind continue, in what port they will direct themselves. There is want of powder, shot and victual amongst us, which causeth that we cannot so daily assail them as we would, but I trust her Majesty may, by God's help, little fear any invasion by these ships; their power being, by battle, mortality, and other accidents, so decayed, and those that are left alive so weak and hurtless, that they could be well content to lose all charges to be at home, both rich and poor."

It was imperative, in both fleets, that urgent decisions be made; and both Howard and Medina Sidonia called to council in their flagships. We know that the Spaniards asked for ammunition states, damage reports, and casualty returns, or, as Gongora put it in the more dramatic language of the day: " Finally it was decided that a count should be taken, with all the ships, of how it had gone with them, and how many people were dead; and it was found that the ships which were from the fight, all no longer had any cannon balls, and they came to the flagship to ask for them." That is, the strongest and most important ships, which had borne the brunt of battle, were reduced to musket and harquebus fire in future, unless the weaker ships could be milked of some of their ammunition. The English must have reported, informally, under similar headings; and we know from a dozen or more witnesses that they were almost out of shot, like the Spaniards, and lacked in addition powder and victual. But damage and casualties had been relatively light. "Received little hurt" was the phrase used by Hawkyns; "the least losses that ever hath been heard of; I verily believe there is not three score men lost of her Majesty's forces," reported Fenner. The position in the Armada was very different, according to the Duke: "The ships were spoiled and unable, that hitherto had resisted the enemy," another reference to the decimation of the most powerful units.

Ironically, neither side knew that the other was out of ammunition. Armada ships had been cannonading until late the previous day, and although the guns of some ships had fallen silent, so that the only reply from them was musketry, these few were in a shot-torn and sinking condition, with masts gone by the board and guns dismounted, blood running from the gun-ports in their holed and splintered sides; that firing aboard them ‚virtually ceased, was only to be expected. All the English estimates of Spanish weakness after the battle speak of the shot-damage, the inevitably terrible battle casualties among the close-packed men aboard, the equally inevitable sickness casualties, the loss of sailing power, anchors, and boats. Similarly, and this throughout the whole series of Channel battles, no one in the Armada guessed at the continual English ammunition short-ages; when the English broke off each action, the Spaniards flattered themselves that they had "beaten off" the enemy.

The simultaneous shortage of ammunition in both fleets, however, did not leave them equal. Far from it. The offensive power of the English fleet lay solely in its guns; when its artillery fell silent, it was impotent. The Armada, on the other hand, still had teeth—the remnants of the 19,000 fighting soldiers originally embarked. According to the Dutch deserters, 10,000 of these were highly-trained fighting men, virtually without equal in Europe, the rest being "vine-growers, shepherds, and the like." Except for the unfavourable wind, and the ruined condition of some of the ships, there was now nothing whatever to stop Medina Sidonia returning to the Channel, or even landing this still formidable force of troops on the shores of the Thames estuary. The Duke had a real card left to play; Howard had nothing up his sleeve. Consequently it was with some trepidation, and the thought of a kingdom at stake, that he regarded the great hulls of the retreating Spanish ships that afternoon. If they decided to beat back to the Channel, as some of the Spanish leaders were even then urging, there was nothing he could do to prevent it.

Howard must have been excessively conscious of the empty threat his guns now presented, for his assessment of the Armada at this point is strikingly different to that of every other English seaman who put his views on paper. " Their force is wonderful great and strong," he wrote on the evening of the battle, " and yet we pluck their feathers by little and little." " Some made little account of the Spanish force by sea," he wrote a week later, " but I do warrant you, all the world never saw such a force as theirs was." And the day after, he told Walsyngham, " It is very likely they will return; for, in my thinking, they dare not go back with this dishonour and shame; for we have marvellously plucked them." Of course, the Spanish force was " wonderful great and strong " compared to a fleet without an army aboard, and with no powder and shot for its guns. Possibly he was over-painting the picture a little, in his reports to the authorities in London, in the belief that only a dramatically presented threat would stir them into further action. Hawkyns, cold, accurate, business-like as usual, ended his own favourable assessment of the situation with the sharp reminder, " Yet I gather certainly, there are amongst them 50 forcible and invincible ships . . ." These he listed, as a pertinent hint that his demand for powder and shot was no idle request.

Fenner thought the Armada was done for; Wynter was confident, too. "And in my conscience, I speak it to your Honour, I think the Duke would give his dukedom to be in Spain again. But the worst is to be reckoned of . . ." and he at once went on to demand " victual, powder, shot, match, lead, and canvas to make cartridges." Drake was worried only about Parma's force, for, unlike Wynter and Seymour, who had been watching it for months, he did not know how weak it was, and perhaps feared a sudden descent on the English coast on a calm day. " We have the army of Spain before us," he wrote on 31 July, " and mind, with the grace of God, to wrestle a pull with him. There was never anything pleased me better than to see the enemy flying with a southerly wind to the northwards. God grant you have a good eye to the Duke of Parma; for with the grace of God, if we live, I doubt it not ere it be long so to handle the matter with the Duke of Sidonia as he shall wish himself at St. Mary Port among his orange trees."*

Whatever Howard wrote, his actions belied his words; for the decision of the council, held on the afternoon of 30 July, off Walcheren, was to detach two squadrons from his force that night to guard the approaches to London. In short, he intended to weaken his force by nearly a third, and with the remainder to " set on a brag countenance, and give them chase, as though we wanted for nothing, until we had cleared our own coast and some part of Scotland of them." Wynter did not receive the bad news in person, and so was unable to argue. " I was not able to go aboard, by the reason of a hurt that I had received in my hip, by the reversing of one of our demi-cannons in the fight. But after the Council was ended, my Lord Admiral sent aboard me a gentleman of his, both to see how I did, and also to tell me that my Lord Seymour had order to repair back again, to guard the Thames mouth from any attempt that might be made by the Duke of Parma; and that I was to attend upon him, and so were all the rest that were of his former charge; and that we should bear away in the twilight, as the enemy might not see our departing. And so, obeying the commandment, I did about 8 of the clock in the night, bear back again through our fleet."

* On 23 August, Drake put his expert finger on the fatal flaws in the Spanish plan, which was Philip's. It demanded, he pointed out, an impossible combination of a high spring tide, a flat calm sea, a wind favourable for England, a lightning embarkation within 24 hours, and an unimpeded assembly. " My judgement is that the Duke of Sidonia, his fleet, needs jump with fair weather, the highest of a spring, with good wind, and the Duke of Parma embarking all in one day. This were very meet for them; for if any one of these fail them, they shall never perform as much as they have promised to the King, their master. Now, for the Duke of Sidonia, his fleet, there is no harbour for them upon that coast, so that to stir it requireth fair weather; which, when it happen that we should find them there, he is like, God willing, to have unquiet rest."

ABOVE: Plymouth Sound from the Hoe, with an American warship passing Drake's Island. The Armada first came into sight on the horizon beyond this island, towards Looe. BELOW: Carisbrook Castle, in the Isle of Wight, where Sir George Carey had his headquarters. The troops were probably camped in the fields outside

Statue of Sir Francis Drake on Plymouth
Hoe, alongside the Naval War Memorial

But Seymour was present, and Seymour was furious. He complained about it officially, not only to Walsyngham, but to the Queen. Although "his Lordship was altogether desirous at the first to have me strengthen him, so having done the uttermost of my good will (to the venture of my life) in prosecuting the distressing of the Spaniards, I find my Lord jealous and loth to have me take part of the honour of the rest that is to win, using his authority to command me to look to our English coasts, that have been long threatened by the Duke of Parma. I therein have obeyed his Lordship much against my will, expecting your Majesty's further pleasure. I pray God my Lord Admiral do not find the lack of the *Rainbow* and that company; for I protest before God, and have witness for the same, I vowed I would be as near or nearer with my little ship to encounter our enemies, as any of the greatest ships in both armies; which I have performed to the distress of one of their greatest ships sunk, if I have my due." But this was mere eagerness for battle, for he told Walsyngham: "I presume the Spaniards are much distressed for victuals, which I hope will be the cause to make them yield to her Majesty's mercy." And so, in the darkness off Lowestoft that night, the Narrows fleet set course for Harwich.

The council held the same day in the *San Martin* confirmed exactly the assessments of the majority of the English leaders. There were 3,000 sick already, and victuals left for less than a month, the way home round Scotland and out into the Atlantic being long and arduous. For the record—and for the record only—an undefeated note was inserted in the War Diary. "The Council was wholly of the opinion that they should go back to the Channel if the weather would permit it; but if not, that then, constrained by the weather, they should return by the North Sea to Spain . . ." But in a letter to the King, written at sea nearly two weeks later, when all pretence had gone, Medina Sidonia confessed: "This Armada was so completely crippled and scattered that my first duty to your Majesty seemed to save it, even at the risk which we are running in undertaking this voyage, which is so long and in such high latitudes. Ammunition and the best of our vessels were lacking, and experience had shown how little we could depend upon the ships that remained, the Queen's fleet being so superior to ours in this sort of fighting,

8

in consequence of the strength of their artillery and the fast sailing of their ships." Fray Bernado de Gongora, also in the flagship, was slightly more explicit. " The enemy did not dare to come alongside because he knew the advantage we had The Duke offered him battle many times and he never wanted it, but only to fire on us, like a man who had better artillery with longer range." The King's own prediction of the English tactics, made so many months before, echoed in defeat. And Medina Sidonia's warning, too. " If you send me, depend upon it, I shall have a bad account to render of my trust."

But for Howard, there was no exultant sense of triumph. He had been promised that powder and shot would be sent after him, but it had not arrived. It never did arrive. On 9 August, Sir Thomas Heneage, Vice-Chamberlain of the Household, was told by the Earl of Cumberland that " Her Majesty's navy has not received a corn of all that was set down in paper by my Lord Treasurer, which I take to be above 30 last, and sent by us . . ." The Armada flew from an enemy not capable of fighting even half a battle, and the pursuing English were unable to complete their hard-fought victory of Dunkirk. Howard summed up: " If we had had that which had been sent, England and her Majesty had had the most honour that ever any nation had. But God be thanked; it is well."

And Seymour echoed him. " I can say no more, but God doth show his mighty hand for protecting this little island, for His glory and to the honour of our country."

CHAPTER NINETEEN

It will be to Their Great Ruin

Conjecture and Rumour, August

THE ARMADA was abreast of Lowestoft, when Seymour and Wynter turned back for Harwich on the evening of 30 July; next day, it was well on its way to Newcastle. Very soon now, the sea astern of the Spanish ships was to be horrible with a trail of drowning horses and mules, thrown overboard to save water. "We threw them into the sea because there was nothing to drink," wrote the shamefaced Friar Gongora. "May God put it right." But astern of the Armada, more than a hundred miles astern on Wednesday, 31 July, Don Diego Pimental's abandoned galleon *San Mateo* was still resisting, fighting on into the afternoon against an encircling ring of Dutch ships. She had fought against heavy odds all day on the 29th, "until she was a thing of pity to see, riddled with shot like a sieve"; she had been hopelessly aground on the banks to seaward of Blankenberg all day on the 30th, moving sluggishly in the waves, a stranded wreck, with 350 shot holes in her hull; and on Wednesday, 31 July, the Dutch had come down to get her. Sir Pieter van der Does, Vice-Admiral of Holland, led the attack, and in one of his ships went an English liaison official, William Borlas. He expected a swift surrender from the riddled thing, but from her ruined sides Pimental's seasoned infantry sent out volley after defiant volley at the savagely determined Dutch. "They fought it out until they saw no remedy," was the report that reached the Earl of Leicester at Tilbury camp a few days later. But the actual battle had little chivalry; it was grim and, with the fall of the first Dutchman, waged without quarter.

William Borlas penned a brief description to Walsyngham, from Flushing. "The last of July my Lord Governor was advertised by a small boat that came from the sea that there was one great ship of the Spaniards lying between Ostend and the Sluys. Whereupon my Lord sent out presently three men-of-war that lie here before the town, and I myself went out in them; so that the same day about one of the clock we came where he was, having been beaten and dispersed from the fleet by her Majesty's ships; yet he fought with us two hours, and hurt divers of our men; but at the last yielded himself. The commander in her was Don de Pimental, the son and heir of the Marquis de Tavara. There was another marquis's son in her, and divers particular gentlemen of good account. I was the means that the best sort were saved; and the rest were cast overboard and slain at the entry. There was slain in her two Englishmen; the one was a brother of my Lord Montagu's as your Honour shall see by a letter that I found in the ship." When the States of Zealand reported on this to Queen Elizabeth, they wrote: " The Spanish prisoners do hold it for a miracle that amongst the slain, as well by the English ordnance as our own, for the little it did, hath always struck down the principal traitors, and amongst others hath slain the banished English lords."

The same day, another group of Dutch ships closed in on the equally battered galleon *San Felipe,* aground between Nieuport and Ostend, in full view of Parma's forces. As most of her crew had transferred to the hulk *Doncella* on the evening of the battle, she put up small resistance, and Don Francisco de Toledo, who had gone back into her, remarking that if he had to die, he had rather do it in a galleon than in a hulk, escaped to Nieuport with some of his companions in boats sent out by the Duke of Parma. Pimental of the *San Mateo* was also alive, but a prisoner at Flushing. The Dutch had also spared the lives of two youths, Frantz Muelenpeert, of Herenthals, 17 years old, who had been for the last nine years in Spain and forgotten almost all his Flemish; and William Olychers, of Luxembourg, 20 years old, who had been in Spain a similar time. Truly, the Armada was an international force, whereas the English fleet was manned entirely by Englishmen—if we exclude one Genoese banker known to be aboard. In fact, so distrustful of foreigners were they, that they chose, at this turn of the crisis, not to rely in any way even on their allies, the Dutch.

Howard had contemptuously reported, after the battle off Dunkirk, " There is not one Flushinger or Hollander at the seas," which was probably a contributory factor, their lack of victuals was the other, for sending Seymour and Wynter back to guard the Straits. But the Dutch fleet, as it had just shown, was ready to pounce on any Spaniard; and if Parma's unarmed barges came wallowing out, they were in favour of letting them get out, right out into the middle of the Channel first. It would be a long way to swim, in breastplate and helmet. But the English Government was worried. Indeed, they wrote, on the day the *San Mateo* was taken, a warning letter to Howard, to inform him " that some Englishmen, and Spaniards also that are taken, do say that the intent of the Spanish navy is to draw along the English navy from the coast of Flanders, that the sea being clear, the Duke of Parma might come out with his forces to invade the realm." Only the Dutch knew what complete mastery they had in their own waters, and, although the States of Zealand wrote to the English Queen to assure her of it, the English continued to believe in the possibility of a sudden descent on their coasts by Parma, and the arrival of the Spanish Army even in the Thames.

In the end, the Dutch lost both their Spanish prizes, for the *San Felipe* and the *San Mateo* had been so shattered that they sank, reported the States: " One in the haven of Flushing, and the other athwart of Rammekens. The third sank between Ostend and Blankenberg, without anything being saved." The third ship was presumably the 75 ton pinnace *San Antonio de Padua,* whose loss off Ostend was reported by Parma. News of the captures, however, embittered some of the English. Seymour wrote: " These Hollanders have lighted upon these argosies which *we* did distress; and they have received great spoil thereof." Rights of pillage were then highly regarded; and legitimate.

Together with their well-meant warning about Parma, the Council sent that day to Howard a lengthy questionnaire calculated to delight the heart of any accountant with a few weeks to spare. " What number of ships are in service, and of what burden? How many are the Queen's own ships? how many of them are ships of good bulk? how many are pinnaces, and how many of the country's charge?" Three questions simply begged for a NIL Return. " How are the Queen's ships victualled?" " How are the other ships victualled?" " What powder and shot every ship hath?" Then, understandably, " How much powder and shot doth the navy use to spend in the fights with the enemies upon one day?" And so on endlessly. " What losses of men and ships hath been on the Spanish side? and where were the losses? and where are the prisoners? And what powder, munition and any treasure hath been taken upon them? What losses hath happened to the Queen's army of ships and men? What causes are there why the Spanish navy hath not been boarded by the Queen's ships? And though some of the ships of Spain may be thought too huge to be boarded by the English, yet some of the Queen's ships are thought very able to have boarded divers of the meaner ships of the Spanish navy." That was the sting in the tail, from the bureaucrats at sea in their offices in St. James's.

Oddly enough, only the previous day, Calderon had reported a contrary rumour current in the Armada: " We learnt that the enemy had orders from the Queen, that, on pain of death, no ship of theirs was to come to close quarters with any of ours." And on Thursday, 1 August, he drew an equally fallacious conclusion from observed facts. " The enemy's fleet now numbered only 90 vessels, which continued to follow us. It is to be concluded from this that their ships had suffered much, and had been obliged to put into port to refit." Then came a startling observation. " On this day the Duke ordered Don Cristobal de Avila, captain of the hulk *Santa Barbara,* to be hanged; and condemned to the galleys other ship captains, as well as reducing some army officers. It is said that this was because on the day of the battle they allowed themselves to drift out of the fight." One of the captains condemned to death was Francisco Cuellar of the Castilian galleon *San Pedro.* His narrative is rather different, and probably more accurate, giving a plausible reason for this outburst of savagery on the part of the Duke, whose neighbour in Spain Don Christobal de Avila was.

The order now enforced was that promulgated by the Duke on 22 July, after the rout of his rear wings off Plymouth, that " the sergeant majors should range the fleet, giving to each ship captain in writing his place in the fleet, and that if any ship left her appointed place, they should without further stay hang the captain of the said ship." With them had gone the hangmen, ready to carry out the order. This erratic vengeance, not invoked at any time during the fighting, now fell when the entire Armada, led by the Duke, was hot-footing it homeward, hustled on towards Spain by an English fleet with empty guns. And, moreover, leaving behind them, still fighting, better men than they in the two stranded galleons of Portugal. If the craven leadership of the Armada had had one-half the spirit shown by Pimental and Toledo, the English Government might have rued their administrative shortcomings. Nothing, certainly not the weather, " constrained " the Armada from returning to the Channel, except the anxiety of Medina Sidonia, Diego Flores, and Bobadilla not again to face the English. And the immediate cause of their fury was that Don Christobal and Cuellar had gone ahead of the fleeing flagship, in order to lie-to for a while and repair damage sustained in action. It was the reaction of a man who, after a bad day at the office, expends his temper on his own family.

Don Christobal must have been overwhelmed by the sudden irrationality of the order, for in a short time he was writhing by the neck from the yardarm of a pinnace, which displayed his kicking body throughout the fleet. Cuellar was made of sterner stuff. First, he shouted at the executioners, quoting the casualty list of his ship. Then he asked for a copy of their orders. Then he insisted that his crew should be questioned, to prove that this ship at least had never shirked her duty. " If any of them should blame me, you can cut me into four quarters! " he roared. " But they would not listen to me," he afterwards wrote, " nor to many gentlemen who interceded for me, answering that the Duke at that time kept his cabin and was very unhappy and did not want anybody to speak to him. For besides the ill-success he always had with the enemy, on the day of my tribulation he had been told that the two galleons, *San Mateo* and *San Felipe,* had been destroyed and sunk, and almost all hands drowned. For this reason the Duke kept himself in his cabin, and his Councillors did acts of injustice right and left in order to correct his neglect, disregarding the lives and honours of those that were not to blame, and that is so public that everybody knows it." The news must have been brought by a pinnace, so that it was obvious to everyone that Don Diego de Pimental had gone down fighting, alone, forty-eight hours after the Great Armada had given up the fight and fled north for Spain. No one, not even the premier nobleman of Spain, could ever outlive that disgrace.

Medina Sidonia was a thing that no one cared to look upon at that moment; and forever afterwards. As for Diego Flores, no fighting man in the Armada would ever take another order from him. Oquendo had not even bothered to attend the Council held after the battle; or had not been invited, because his insults would be unendurable. The man now in charge of the retreat was Don Francisco de Bobadilla, the Camp Master; and that was fitting, for according to Medina Sidonia, it had been at his promptings that the Armada had always abandoned its cripples. Cuellar, who " had thought to burst into a passion " when he first heard his sentence, was carried to the flagship and brought before Bobadilla. He must have argued equally forcefully there, for Bobadilla washed his hands of the matter and ordered Cuellar to be given into the custody of the Judge Advocate, Martin de Aranda, whose ship was one of the Levant squadron. Aranda made brief enquiries, and reported to the flagship that there were no grounds for an execution and that he refused to carry out the sentence unless he received a written order from the Duke in person. "And the Duke sent answer to the Judge Advocate that he should not execute the sentence upon me, but upon Don Christobal, whom they hanged with great cruelty and insult, considering that he was a gentleman and known to many." But Cuellar was not given back his command; he remained under open arrest in the Levanter in the custody of the Judge Advocate, as the Armada continued its homeward voyage. And at noon on Friday, 2 August, the Spaniards saw the English fleet, those familiar ships which had dogged them at the heels since Plymouth, wear round and dwindle rapidly to the south. They were alone.

Howard had expected the Spaniards to put into the Firth of Forth, and had based his plans on that. " Verily thinking that they would put into the Firth, his Lordship had devised strata-gems to make an end of them," he wrote. But the Armada had had enough, and it was Howard who set course for the Firth of Forth. A Queen's pinnace, the *Advice*, and a caravel of Drake's, were left to shadow the Spanish fleet " from afar off, until they were shot beyond the Isles of Orkney and Shetland," wrote

Fenner. If for any reason, the Spaniards turned back, the pinnaces were to report it. " Therefore the 2nd of August, about 12 of the clock at noon, we hauled west, the better to recover our coast to attain the Firth, the enemy going away North-West and by North, as they did before. The third of August in the morning, about ten of the clock, the wind came up at North-West. Counsel therefore taken—it was thought meet to take the benefit thereof for our reliefs of powder, shot, and victual, so as to bear with all possible speed to the North Foreland; and as if the enemy should return, we might be beforehand furnished of some of our wants, the readier thereby to offend them." In this report, written on 4 August from the *Nonpareil*, Captain Fenner made his prophetic estimate.

" I verily believe great extremity shall force them if they see England again. By all that I can gather they are weakened of eight of their best sorts of shipping, which contained many men; as also many wasted in sickness and slaughter. Their masts and sails much spoiled; their pinnaces and boats many cast off and wasted; wherein they shall find great wants when they come to land and water, which they must shortly do or die; and where or how, my knowledge cannot imagine. As the wind serveth, no place but between the Foreland and Hull. If the wind by change suffer them, I verily believe they will pass about Scotland and Ireland to draw themselves home; wherein, the season of the year considered, with the long course they have to run and their sundry distresses, and—of necessity—the spending of time by watering, winter will so come on as it will be to their great ruin."

Barely had Fenner finished the letter, when the wind, favourable for the return of the Armada, if to return was their intention, changed once again. " Within two hours after the writing of this letter the wind came up at South West, so as thereby the enemy was able neither to seize England, Ireland, Scotland, Flanders, and hardly the out isles of Scotland. This 4th day and 5th, especially at night, continued very great storm at South-West, we being forced to ride out in the sea the extremity thereof. Which storm hath, in mine opinion, touched the enemy very near. Mine opinion is they are by this time so distressed, being so far thrust off, as many of them will never see Spain again."

231

8*

Scattered by the storm, the English fleet put into this port and that in small groups. Howard wrote: " My Lord of Cumberland bare with a pinnace into Harwich; I bare with some of the ships into Margate road; where the rest are gone I do not know, for we had a most violent storm as ever was seen at this time of the year, that put us asunder athwart of Norfolk, amongst many ill-favoured sands. I know not what you think at Court, but I do think, and so doth all here, that there cannot be too great forces maintained yet for five or six weeks, on the seas." The chickens of ill-preparation, which had prevented crushing victory, were coming home to roost.

By 8 August, most of the ships were safely in, and the English Admirals had time to write to Walsyngham. " Whether the Duke mind to return or not, I know not," said Drake, " but my opinion to your Honour is that I think he neither mindeth nor is in case to do so." But he added, in a letter to the Queen: " My poor opinion is that I dare not advise her Majesty to hazard a Kingdom with the saving of a little charge." And, again to Walsyngham: " The Prince of Parma I take him to be as a bear robbed of her whelps; and no doubt but, being so great a soldier as he is, that he will presently, if he may, undertake some great matter." And Howard conjectured that the Armada might after all go to the Orkneys, or to Norway, or to Denmark, to rest, repair damage, and re-victual, before coming south again, " for I think they dare not return to Spain with this dishonour and shame to their king, and overthrow of their Pope's credit."

With a sheaf of doubtful letters on his desk, Walsyngham complained to the Lord Treasurer: " It is hard now to resolve what advice to give her Majesty for disarming, until it shall be known what is become of the Spanish fleet." And to the Lord Chancellor, he wrote: " I am sorry the Lord Admiral was forced to leave the prosecution of the enemy through the wants he sustained. Our half-doings breed dishonour and leaveth the disease uncured."

Disease was present in the most literal sense, for the wooden ships were insanitary and the food, stored and prepared under appalling conditions, probably semi-poisonous. On 10 August, Howard wrote to Burghley from Margate: " My good Lord,— Sickness and mortality begins wonderfully to grow amongst us;

and it is a most pitiful sight to see, here at Margate, how the men, having no place to receive them into here, die in the streets. I am driven myself, of force, to come a-land, to see them bestowed in some lodging; and the best I can get is barns and such outhouses; and the relief is small that I can provide for them here. It would grieve any man's heart to see them that have served so valiantly to die so miserably." An infinitely terrible epitaph, compared to that spoken in a like and later crisis: " never have so many owed so much to so few."

Not only were the men dying, but they were dying unpaid, wretchedly, in poverty, begging for a place to lie, for a bite of food. Howard was so furious at the Lord Treasurer's neglect, that he raided Don Pedro's golden hoard, kept safe aboard Drake's *Revenge* until now, and pawned his own plate. He explained to Walsyngham exactly what he had done. " Sir, I send you here enclosed a note of the money Sir Francis Drake had aboard Don Pedro. I did take now, at my coming down, 3,000 pistolets, as I told you I would; for, by Jesus, I had not £3 besides in the world, and had not anything could get money in London; and I do assure you my plate was gone before. But I will repay it within 10 days after my coming home. And by the Lord God of Heaven, I had not one crown more; and had it not been mere necessity, I would not have touched one; but if I had not some to have bestowed upon some poor and miserable men, I should have wished myself out of this world."

The only thing Howard kept for himself were the banners from the captured *Rosario;* anticipating a later commander-in-chief who, having obtained an enemy's written surrender at Luneburg Heath, retained the document for his own personal files. On 25 August, however, Howard was prepared to loan the standards to the Government for a victory celebration, telling Walsyngham: " I have sent a good many ancients (ensigns) and banners by this bearer, Thomas Cely; but Sir, they must be returned when they have been used; they may be kept till I do come home." Cely, who seems to have been present at the capture of the *Rosario,* had a job after his own heart now. After so many years spent " in the King of Spain's most filthy galleys " he was to convey the fallen standards to London for the great thanksgiving service to be held at St. Paul's Cross on

8 September. Nor did he waste his time in London; there is a note of jewelry and valuables he took off Spanish prisoners incarcerated in the Bridewell. For him, history had come full circle.

The reason for planning a victory celebration was the arrival of two confirmatory reports, one from a merchant ship coming into Southampton on 22 August, the other from one of the pinnaces which reached Dover on 24 August. Sir George Carey, the Isle of Wight Garrison commander, wrote on the 22nd: "This morning there arrived here divers mariners of this island, which came in a bark of Hampton from Shetland; who upon oath affirm that on this day fortnight, being the 8th of this present, they being 12 leagues from Shetland, where they had been fishing, they descried a very great fleet of monstrous great ships, to their seeming about 100 in number, lying just west, with both sheets aftward, whereby their course was to run betwixt Orkneys and Fair Isle." Edward Wynter reported from Dover two days later: "Young Norreys, that was sent after the enemy's fleet to discover which way they meant to take their course, brings certain news that he left them to the westwards of the Islands of Orkney, which is their course directly for Spain." That same day, he reported that he had spoken aboard the *Ark Royal,* in Howard's cabin, to a spy who had been in Dunkirk a few hours earlier. Parma had gone to Brussels, the victuals had been unshipped from the landing barges, and the sails stripped from their yards. The Armada campaign—and the invasion crisis —were over. Let the bells ring.

But the Spaniards did not know it. No one in Europe knew it. Only one authentic report reached Philip, and, although its source was England, security precautions had rendered it vague. Dated Calais, 21 August, it ran: "The messenger I sent to England has returned hither. He brings no letters, as no one dares to write letters nor he to carry them. He reports that the Lord Admiral has arrived with part of the fleet, and to Court on 8th instant. Drake arrived with the rest on the 14th. Both of them were compelled to return in consequence of shortness of victuals, leaving the Spanish Armada beyond Newcastle in Scotland. They say, however, that the principal reason for their return was lack of powder, as they had not enough for one day's fighting. They do not say much about the losses of the Spanish Armada, except of the six ships that were lost on these coasts (i.e., Calais-Ostend), nor do they boast much of their victory. They do not dwell yet upon their own losses, Their ships have arrived in very bad case. They report that the horses had to be thrown overboard from the Spanish Armada near Newcastle, in consequence of lack of water. They are speaking rather ill of the Lord Admiral, who they say did not do his duty. All the credit is given to Drake. They still have an army of 8,000 men between Sandwich and Dover, under the command of a brother of Norris, the Camp-Master being Thomas Scott. Neither of them knows much. There is another army in Essex under Leicester. The Queen was at Dartford and crossed the river to visit that army. They have seven armies under arms but they have no money, and if the affair lasts many of the men will desert."

Apart from a few minor inaccuracies (Newcastle is in England, not Scotland) and a naturally too optimistic tone, it was a reasonable enough summary of affairs in England during the first three weeks of August. Hitler would have given his eyebrows to get anything half as good out of England during the summer of 1940. But the unfortunate spy was not believed, for news of great Spanish victories in the Channel and in the North Sea had been echoing through Europe for weeks.

On 3 August, an otherwise accurate report from Rouen was followed by a hurriedly scribbled postscript, describing a full fleet engagement in which " the Spaniards captured Drake with many ships, sinking others, and disabling 15 which took refuge at Harwich; the Lord Admiral was in as bad case as Drake." The cautious Philip was wary, writing to his ambassador in Paris, Bernadino de Mendoza: "As you consider the news to be true, I am hopeful that it will prove to be so; particularly as the author claims to have been an eye witness. I am looking anxiously for the confirmation, this report having been the first intelligence I have had of the event." The King also wrote, ironically, to Medina Sidonia, requesting confirmation. " This news is asserted in France to be true, and witnesses of the engagement are said to be in Havre de Grace and Dieppe. I hope to God it may be so, and that you have known how to follow up the victory. . . ."

On 10 August, Mendoza had confirmation of a previous rumour about a Spanish victory in the Channel. " You will see that, in their description of the engagement between the Armada and the English off the Isle of Wight, the Breton sailors did not lie, for the English lost seven ships, and amongst them three of the largest the Queen possessed. As the London people were so alarmed, Don Pedro de Valdez and the rest of those who were captured, owing to their ship being disabled, had been taken in carts to London, so that the people might see that some prisoners had been captured; the rumour being spread that the whole Armada had been dispersed." This part of Mendoza's report was perfectly accurate, but he concluded with a vague statement: " Letters from Rouen, dated 9th, say that there is a man there who left London on the 2nd, who asserts that the English lost heavily in the engagement, and they were very sad, as it was said that Drake had been wounded in the legs by a cannon ball."

On 11 August a Spanish spy in London, Antonio de Vega, sent a long and fairly authentic account of the whole series of Channel battles, including a description of how the " bonfires were lit all over the city, and the bells rung " when the news of the taking of the *Rosario* and the *San Salvador* reached London. He was obviously an eye-witness, and well informed otherwise, reporting accurately that 40 prisoners had been lodged in the Bridewell prison for examination and that Don Pedro and his friends " were afterwards carried to the house of Richard Drake, 16 miles from here, where they are well treated." Of the Calais-Dunkirk battle, he reported that some Portuguese deserters had swum to the English ships one night, telling their captors that " the Armada would be ruined in a very short time "; and that the English Admirals had, at one point, " looked upon the Armada as lost, as it was surrounded by sand banks." All this seems to be authentic, adding detail to our knowledge. He reported the Armada as last seen heading for Norway, and added that the English were claiming three ships sunk, in addition to those lost in other ways, 6,000 Spaniards killed or captured, and their own loss as less than 300. But, he wrote, " it is really over 1,500, and it is secretly stated that they have lost 12 ships, although they deny it."

Thus it was still possible to believe the stream of rumours which continued to come in, describing a Spanish victory in the North Sea. On 14 August, an Advice from Antwerp had news of this engagement and the capture of " about 30 English ships." Four shiploads of killed and wounded had arrived at Dover. On the same day, an Advice from Bruges confirmed it, with the crews of two of Parma's pinnaces quoted for authority, and giving Newcastle as the site of the Spanish victory.

The " Battle of Newcastle " was again referred to in Advices from Dunkirk via Lille on 20 August. " It was asserted in England as a positive fact that the English have lost 40 ships of their fleet, the flagship, the vice-flagship, the *Elizabeth,* and the *Virgin* having been sunk. The great sailor, John Hawkyns, has also gone to the bottom, not a soul having been saved from his ship. Drake escaped in a boat, wounded in the cheek." As late as 25 August, these rumours were still being forwarded to Spain. On that day, on the authority of some fishermen, it was reported that : " M. de Gourdan advises that Drake's death is confirmed from Holland. The Lord Admiral has returned to England with 36 ships in very bad case, no person being allowed to land. The Catholics were disturbed." And on the same day, not uninfluenced by the news that Drake had been wounded in the legs/cheek and was now dead/captured/escaped, the King thought it would be well to remind his Captain General of the Ocean of his main task : " It occurs to me to instruct you that if the Duke of Parma should consider that the presence of the Armada would be of use to him . . . and the Armada be strong enough . . . you will endeavour to follow his instructions."

It might be thought that poor communications were responsible for the spread of these rumours, but that is not so. On the first day of World War Two, the British press had the Polish army advancing victoriously into Germany, as a glance at the files will show; indeed, for many years, the start of every victorious German offensive was reported as an Allied victory by the Ministry of Information. Modern communications meant that their untruths were exposed more rapidly, that was all. Not that Mendoza and his spies were lying; they merely desired victory too much. Perhaps they really thought the Armada invincible and could expect nothing less. There was plenty of cold fact mentioned in the agents' reports, pointing to an English victory, but if the spies themselves chose to disregard it, one can hardly blame Mendoza too much. Any authentic news from England was instantly and furiously suppressed, as Mendoza reported: "The English ambassador here has had some fancy news printed, stating that the English had been victorious; but the people of Paris would not allow it to be sold, as they say it is all lies. One of the ambassador's secretaries began to read in the palace a relation which he said had been sent from England, but the people were so enraged that he was obliged to fly for his life."

But, whether in victory or defeat, men die; and, for the relatives, waiting anxiously in Spain for news of the great enterprise in which sons, fathers, and husbands were engaged, this was a time of long trial. For nearly two months they heard nothing, except rumours of great battles, with no word as to the dead and wounded, except for the names of a few senior officers in the great ships taken between Plymouth and Ostend. Then reports began to come in from a different quarter. Ireland.

CHAPTER TWENTY

The Grave of the Son of the King of Spain

The Armada Wrecks—Cork, Kerry, and Clare

The course that shall be held in the return of this army into Spain. The course that is first to be held is to the NNE until you be found under 61½ degrees; and then to take great heed lest you fall upon the island of Ireland, for fear of the harm that may happen unto you upon that coast. . . .

(*Captured Spanish document in State Papers, Ireland*)

" FRIDAY THE 2nd of August the English left us and went towards the shore, and we followed our voyage with evil and contrary winds until we came to 61 degrees, leaving every day behind us ships that were spoiled," wrote Estrade in the *San Marcos.* " On the 3rd and until the 8th, we experienced squalls, rain, and fogs, with heavy sea, and it was impossible to distinguish one ship from another," noted Calderon in the *San Salvador.* " We climbed to 62 degrees, where it is not warm," recorded Friar Gongora in the *San Martin.* " I am cold, because I left my cloak behind when, by a miracle, I came out of Don Pedro de Valdes' ship. But now the Duke himself has given me a cloak of his which for me is cape and bed for the preaching of the Gospel. The Lord may He receive it as a penance for our great sins." The fair weather sailors of Spain, Portugal, and the Levant were going north to the endless, icy seas, with Norway on their right hand and Orkney and Shetland on their left. Even Seymour, 700 miles to the south, was then complaining about his " summer ship," the *Rainbow.* " Our men fall sick," he wrote, " by reason of the cold nights and cold mornings we find; and I fear me they will drop away far faster than they did last year, which was thick enough."

It is possible to be cold at sea in the middle of an August heatwave; the wind, blowing across hundreds of miles of water, picks up some of the chill of the ocean depths, so that men shiver under a blazing sun. But this was a wild and bitter August, and as the Armada turned west onto the second leg of its course for home and ran between Orkney and Shetland, for the safety of the open Atlantic, it entered onto a desolate and tossing waste of water, inhabited by the mammals of the northern seas, the whale and the seal. The great waves, riding free for 3,000 miles, came punching down on the shot-battered hulls of the salt-caked ships; icy water swept across their decks and streamed below through the cracks in the planking; hissing sheets of rain stormed at and blinded them, carried by a howling wind that roared in the rigging and bellied the torn canvas of their sails. There was no way to get warm, no way to stay dry; and just when they needed hot food, their ration of rotting victuals had to be reduced, for their way home was long and tortuous, straight out into the Atlantic for the high latitudes, well clear of Ireland, before turning southward for the last, long run to the Groyne or Ferrol in sunny Galicia. There was, too, very little water; in some of the ships, hardly any was left. Therefore the horses and the mules had to be abandoned, forced over the side, to stream away astern, a strange and dreadful trail of flotsam in the wake of the defeated fleet. A German ship captain, who saw horses' heads rearing out of the waves, miles out at sea, out of sight of land, carried his weird tale to England.

On the damp and heaving decks, shivering and cold, the wounded and the sick lay wrapped in sodden blankets in their own private and personal hells. For them, the fate of the Armada no longer had any meaning, pain and weakness engulfed them; helpless, they were carried on into an eternity of suffering. On his own initiative, Calderon had the hospital stores carried in his ship distributed among the vessels nearest to the *San Salvador*; rice for the sick, and the delicacies to supplement the ordinary rations. Originally, these had been earmarked for the use of the artillerymen in a land campaign, but there was no use husbanding them any more, if they could save lives now. " On 9 August," he wrote, " the Armada again collected, and we found ourselves near the galleon *San Marcos*, the Duke's flagship, and thirteen other vessels. I supplied Juan Martinez de Recalde with a quantity of delicacies, and tried to do the same for the *San Marcos*, but was prevented by the rough sea." The mainsails and topsails of the *San Marcos* were torn to ribbons, according to Estrade, but otherwise she was better off than most, having had only 20 killed in battle and no other fatal casualties. Recalde's *San Juan* of Oporto, however, the vice-flagship of the whole Armada, was losing four or five men dead every day, from thirst, hunger, and sickness combined, according to the statement of one of her crew, Emanuel Fremoso, a Portuguese. And she, he said, was by no means the worst off. Five Scottish fishing vessels had been captured off the Shetlands, but their catch, such as it was, would not suffice to feed the whole Armada. Some of the ships would have to put into an Irish port, or risk the death of their crews by thirst and starvation.

By mid-August, the Armada was visibly no longer a fleet; it consisted of scattered groups of refugee ships. The largest group, those following the flagship, continued to steer out into the Atlantic, to avoid the danger of turning south while still too near the coast of Ireland. Others, badly damaged, were no longer able to keep on course as long as the wind stayed at south-west, and drifted slowly towards Iceland. Others again, began to work back for the west of Ireland. If the wind changed to north-west, they would be in deadly peril. Calderon's diary depicts best what happened. On 9 October, when a break in the weather brought better visibility, many ships were missing. "We looked anxiously for the *San Juan de Sicilia,* on board of which was Don Diego Tellez Enriquez, son of the Grand Commander of Alcantara, who had fought so bravely. She had been so much damaged that not a span of her sails was servicable; and as we could not find her, it is feared she may be lost." We know from Cuellar's narrative that she, and two other ships of the Levant squadron, one of which was the *Lavia,* the vice flagship, and the other probably the *Juliana,* were unable to hold the course set and drifted into Sligo Bay, where they took shelter. They were quite unable to work out, against the wind, round the great westward projecting bulge of County Mayo, and they had lost their heaviest anchors off Calais, under fireship attack. If any great storm blew up, they were doomed.

"The weather being very heavy on the night of 9 August," wrote Calderon, "we lost sight of Juan Martinez de Recalde and all the ships that followed him; so we continued our voyage alone, through squalls and fogs. "On the 14th the Duke asked me whether I had heard anything of Don Alonso de Luzon (in

La Trinidad Valencera), as he had not seen him for 13 days, although he had sent the despatch boats to seek him. I replied that I had not, nor of the galleon *San Marcos* and the other 13 vessels from which I had parted company two days before, under the command of Juan Martinez de Recalde, who was dreadfully in need of everything, and his ship in a very injured state. From the 14th to the 26th August, we sailed without knowing whither, through constant storms, fogs, and squalls, but on the 26th discovered the main body of the Armada again. 13 ships with Recalde were still missing, and on this day, as we ourselves were drifting to leeward of the Armada, we saw the ship " Villafranca " of Oquendo and another ship fall away towards the Faroes and Iceland." The former was Martin Villafranca's command, the *Santa Maria de la Rosa,* also known as the *Nuestra Senora de la Rosa,* vice-flagship of Oquendo's Armada of Guipuzcoa.

From then until the end of August, Calderon's ship was alone, " always working to windward, breaking our tackle and making a great deal of water." On 1 September, they saw, across the tossing wave-crests, the distant sails of a group of unknown ships, but could not close them. Then they saw land, a large and unknown island, obviously part of Ireland, " the sea running strongly towards the land, to the great danger of the hulk. I ordered her to tack to the north-west, which took her 30 leagues distant, and it is believed that the rest of the Armada will have done the same. If not, they will certainly have lost some of the ships, as the coast is rough, the sea heavy, and the winds strong from seaward." The *San Salvador* did not sight Ireland again, but ran out to safety on an S.S.W. course.

By then, the galleass *Zuniga* was also alone. On the 24th she broke her rudder in the heavy seas—the rudder was a weak point of the design—and was told by the Duke that he could do nothing for her. On 29 August she sighted Recalde's group of 13 ships, and spoke them. For a full week after that, she was struggling southwards along the Irish coast, using her twin banks of 28 oars in lieu of a rudder when necessary, but was trapped on 5 September. " We saw we were in great danger, and in order not to be driven ashore in the strong wind we followed the creek and, by God's grace, found shelter in an uninhabited place. Here we cast anchor, not far from a tower held by the enemy, where we remained for eight days, until the 13th, when we went out with a wind astern." The tower was Liscannor Castle. The *Zuniga* then passed out of the Irish story, but her troubles were not yet over; far from it. A trail of Armada wrecks was soon to be reported, from as far north as Fair Isle, between Shetland and Orkney, right down the Irish coast, inside the Hebrides, in the west of England, and on the north coast of France. Already, the guns were thundering again in the Channel, as the English went in to violate neutral waters in an attempt to finish off an Armada cripple at Le Havre.

From the first week of September onwards, the commanders of the English garrisons in Ireland were receiving reports of Spanish ships sighted off the coast—there were no fewer than 59 sightings, many of them naturally of the same ships; and of unknown ships ashore and splintered in the shallows, and of unknown men drowned or slaughtered as they staggered up out of the sea. "A ship lost off Cape Clear, from which 60 men were drowned or killed," read one of the early, laconic reports. " In the Bay of Tralee 25 men surrendered, amongst them some servants of the Duke." No one knows to this day what ships these were. There were no survivors. Lady Denny, wife of the local English commander, parleyed with the men, who said they were "all of Castille and Biscay," and then hanged them, because "there was no safe keeping for them." When this news reached the Spanish spy group in London, on 1 October, they speculated on " the special hatred which Captain Denny bore against the Spaniards," because he had once had an important Spanish prisoner who had escaped through the intriguings of Bernadino de Mendoza, then Spanish ambassador in London. They heard that " The Council has sent order for everyone to be hanged, as they do not want to feed them, and Spain will not ransom them. I cannot believe they will do it." But they did.

Occasionally, they held their prisoners for a short time, for interrogation, so that some of the reports are detailed and accurate. "Admiral Juan Martinez de Recalde has entered an Irish port with another ship of 900 tons and a barque, and is still there. His ship is in a very bad state, having had 14 or 15 cannon-shot through her, and her mainmast damaged so much that she could not carry sail. He has but few sailors, mostly very ill. They are dying daily in great numbers and being thrown into the sea." Recalde had sent watering parties ashore, and some of the men had been captured, including the Portuguese, Emanuel Fremoso, and three others whose interrogations survive. One, a Fleming, reported: "They have bread sufficient; their beef is corrupt; water they want; many of them are sick." Fremoso testified: "There is left but 25 pipes of wine, and very little bread; and no water, but what they brought out of Spain, which stinketh marvellously; and their flesh meat they cannot eat, their drouth is so great. It is a common bruit among the soldiers, that if they may once get home again, they will not meddle again with the English."

Of Recalde's thirteen ships, only these three were still together, he said, although, as they had neared the Blaskets, he had seen " one great hulk of 400 ton, which was so spoiled as she cast towards the shore about 20 leagues from Dingle-i-couch." It may have been the great ship *Trinidad* of the Castilian squadron. It was in any case distinct from the wreck for which Lady Denny organised her hanging party, for it was separately reported by the English as: "Another large ship was lost off Tralee, in which there were 30 gentlemen, with a bishop, a friar, and 69 men who surrendered to William Bourke of Ardnerie; the rest of them were drowned or killed. Of those who got ashore, a single Irish gallowglass killed 80." According to a later account, the gallowglass who knocked 80 bedraggled Spaniards on the head was McLaughlan MacCabe, a Scottish mercenary soldier, of whom there were many in Ireland. In due course, this English report was laid on the desk of Philip of Spain, who annotated it: " Perhaps they called Don Martin de Carrion a bishop. No bishop went." He knew all the details, for the Armada was peculiarly his enterprise; but from now on, he had news only of its sorrowful end. Including the supposed death of his own son, and the reported capture of the Duke of Medina Sidonia.

The Fleming taken from Recalde's longboat had told the English, accurately enough, " There is a bastard son of King Philip, called the Prince of Ascoli, in ship with the Duke. This Prince passed from them in a pinnace about Calais." But before the saga of Blasket Sound was over, the English had another prisoner from another ship—the sole survivor—who told them that the Prince of Ascoli had been aboard her. His name was Antonio Meneses and his ship was the *Nuestra Senora de la Rosa*.

Recalde was a dying man when he brought the great *San Juan* of Oporto through the difficult entrance into Blasket Sound, not far from Dingle. But he knew that coast well. With him came a 40 ton pinnace, and a galleon of Castile, the 750 ton *San Juan Bautista,* a vice-flagship, aboard which was Marcos de Aramburu, paymaster of the Castilian squadron. They had already seen the *Trinidad* drifting away out of control towards Tralee, and they had a few breathless moments as they followed the 1,050 ton *San Juan* of Oporto through a rocky channel about as wide as their ship was long. But, said Aramburu, one of the Scotsmen taken from the fishing boats off Shetland was in Recalde's ship, and he conned her through safely some time on 5 September. A longboat with eight men was sent away on reconnaissance at once, and never returned; this was the boat containing Emanuel Fremoso and the other men taken prisoners and interrogated at Dingle. On the 7th, wrote Aramburu, " Juan Martinez sent a large boat with fifty arqubusiers to look for a landing place, to collect information, and to treat with the Irish for a supply of water and meat. They found nothing but steep cliffs on which the sea broke; and on the land, some 100 arquebusiers were seen, waving a white flag with a red cross on it. It is supposed that they were English, and that the eight men sent in the long boat had been taken prisoners by them, or perished in the sea."

Notwithstanding this, the Spaniards spent the next three days taking in water; though much reduced from their paper strength of about 800 men, they still considerably outnumbered the English troops, and their ships could of course beat off any attack. On the morning of 11 September, a great westerly gale began to blow, sending tremendous seas surging through the anchorage. Recalde's *San Juan* began to drift down on Aramburu's *San Juan*, and bumped against her stern, smashing the lantern and the tackle of the mizzenmast. At midday, two more Spanish ships were seen approaching the anchorage. From the nearest, which was the vice-flagship of Oquendo's squadron, Martin Villafranca's 945 ton *Nuestra Senora de la Rosa,* came a puff of smoke and the dull boom of a gun, a signal for help. " She had all her sails torn to ribbons, except the foresail," noted Aramburu. " She anchored with a single anchor, as she had no more. And as the tide, which was coming in from the south-east, beat against her stern, she held on until 2 o'clock, when it began to ebb. And at the turn, she started drifting, about two splices of cable from us, and we with her; and in an instant we saw she was going to the bottom, with not a soul escaping—a most extraordinary and terrible occurrence. And we were drifting down on her to our peridition."

As they came down with the tide onto the wreck, a spare anchor, which Aramburu had borrowed from Recalde and repaired, was dropped; and the *San Juan Bautista* brought to. When they raised the anchor which had failed to hold them, they found that it was broken and the cable itself nearly cut through by chafing on the rocks. The ship which had come in with the *Nuestra Senora de la Rosa* was still afloat; she was commanded by Miquel de Aranivar. Then, at 4 in the afternoon, yet another derelict came drifting into the anchorage; and she was yet another *San Juan,* the vessel commanded by Fernando Horra. With one mast gone, she presented a strangely gap-toothed appearance; and to complete the picture of distress, as she swung round to anchor, rolling and pitching on the gale-lashed water, her foresail blew to shreds, dissolving before their eyes as if someone had worked a conjuring trick. Nothing could be done that day, as the seas were too wild for any boat to be lowered, but on the 12th, her longboat put over to Recalde to inform him that she would not float much longer. His decision was to distribute her men among the remaining ships, get the guns out of her, and burn her. Removing the guns proved to be quite impossible, in that sea, and with so many weakened by sickness; in Recalde's ship alone, 200 men had died. So the *San Juan* went to the bottom of the Sound, with all her artillery on board, to join the silent guns and drowned men of the *Nuestra Senora de la Rosa,* black fathoms down in the swirling tide.

Then first, the *San Juan* of Aramburu, and later, the other ships and pinnaces put out to sea for the stormy voyage home to Spain. As Recalde's flagship at last left that anchorage of dread, she carried sail only on the mainmast and mizzen; the foremast was bare, weakened by Drake's guns off Plymouth and only hastily repaired. The English ashore were glad to see them go. Mr. James Trant, their agent for the Dingle district, responsible to Sir Edward Denny in Tralee, had found them too much of a handful to attempt anything, and was unable to prevent them watering. He could only nibble at the edges, and one of the prisoners he took was the sole survivor from the *Nuestra Senora de la Rosa*. Unseen in the confusion of impending disaster, this youth had drifted ashore on some wreckage. He was, he said, the pilot's son; Don Antonia Meneses was his name, according to the English report which eventually reached Philip of Spain, but the Irish papers give it as Antonio de Monana. This frightened boy, pressed by his interrogators for the names of the great nobles in the ship stammered out a great many, including the Prince of Ascoli, went on to describe the rich treasure in her, including 50,000 ducats in gold, 50,000 ducats in silver, and masses of gold and silver plate off which the grandees were served. Her armament, he said, included " 50 great pieces, all cannons of the field " (i.e., stored for use of the army); " 25 pieces of brass and cast-iron belonging to the ship; and 50 tuns of sack." The 25 brass and iron guns seems reasonable for a vice-flagship; at that moment Burghley was snarling over a report that, after the people of Dorset had whipped the best pieces out of the blown-up *San Salvador,* there was left, " to wit, eight pieces of brass, four old iron minions, and two old fowlers." In short, a collection of old junk, an apt commentary on the artillery deficiencies of the Armada. The treasure seems inflated, and, of course, the Prince of Ascoli was not dead. But these stories were believed, and when the grotesquely swollen corpses rose from the bottom of the Sound and bobbed horribly to shore, their place of burial was named *Uaig Mhic Ri Na Spáinne,* the Grave of the Son of the King of Spain.

One other group of ships, seven in all, put into an Irish port, and mostly got out again; this was Scattery roads, in the Shannon, to the north of Tralee. Here, too, one of them was so shattered that she had to be burnt, the men being distributed among the remaining ships. She is sometimes supposed to be the *San Marcos,* but Estrade, who was in that ship, makes no mention of changing house. Off County Clare, north of the Shannon, near where the *Zuniga* lay at anchor in Liscannor Bay, two unknown ships were driven helplessly on shore, with their few fit men, their wounded, their sick, their dying. At Doonbeg, from a wreck which may have been the *San Esteban,* sixty men struggled ashore through the surf, leaving 200 dead behind them in the sea. From another great ship which went down on a reef inside Mutton Island, four men only escaped, giving to that bare rock a new name— Spanish Point. All along the coast where they struck, headlands and reefs acquired these names—*Port na Spáinneach, Carraig na Spáinneach.* Their graveyards and burial grounds similarly— *Reilg na Spáinneach, Tuama na Spáinneach.* And another, even more sinister. As in the case of the survivors from the wreck at Doonbeg, who were marched to the castle of Boetius Clancy, the Queen's Sheriff of County Clare, and taken to a place, still called after what happened to them there, *Cnoc na Crochaire.* Gallows Hill.

CHAPTER TWENTY-ONE

The Rags that Yet Remain

The Armada Wrecks—Galway, Mayo, Sligo, Ulster

After the Spanish fleet had doubled Scotland, and were in their course homewards, they were by contrary weather driven upon the several parts of this province and wrecked, as it were by even portions, three ships in every of the four counties bordering upon the sea coasts—namely, in Sligo, Mayo, Galway, and Thomond—on the rocks and sands by the shore side, and some three or four besides to seaboard of the out isles, which presently sunk, both men and ships, in the night time. And so can I say, by good estimation, that 6,000 or 7,000 men have been cast away on these coasts, save some 1,000 which escaped to land in several places where their ships fell, which since were all put to the sword.

Sir Richard Bingham, Governor of Connaught to the Queen's Secretary, 1 October, 1588

BINGHAM WAS speaking for Connaught only, the area for which he held responsibility under the Lord Deputy of Ireland, Sir William Fytzwylliam; for Sligo, Mayo, Galway, and Clare (which was known then as Thomond); not for Cork or Kerry in the south, nor for Donegal, Derry, and Antrim in the north. But he knew of them, for he added: " Other great wrecks they had both in Munster (the south) and Ulster (the north), which being out of my charge I have not so good notice of, but the same (I doubt not) is fully made known unto your honour." These included five known wrecks in Munster—the unknown vessel at Cape Clear, the two known ships in Blasket Sound, the two unknown ships near Tralee. In Ulster there were seven more, three with names, four unknown. Some twenty-five ships in all, in the three provinces of Munster, Connaught, and Ulster. But from the north, Ulster, the English reports were as yet vague. Munster and Connaught they held, with a force of 2,000 men; but the north was a focus of resistance, which they could penetrate but not firmly control. With their comparatively tiny force of occupation troops—for the experienced soldiers were at the front, in the Netherlands—they could not line the coasts with men; they had to move outward from central

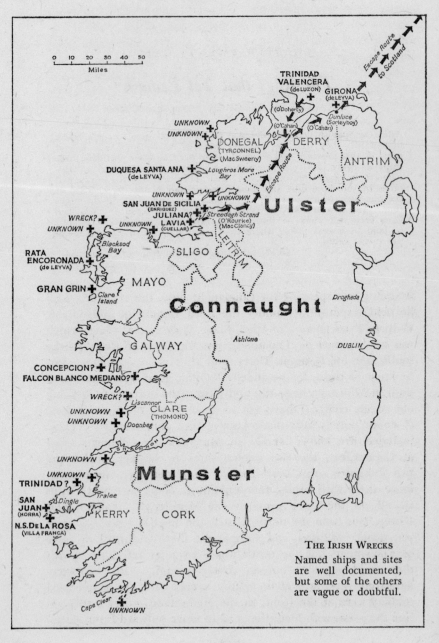

THE IRISH WRECKS

Named ships and sites
are well documented,
but some of the others
are vague or doubtful.

250

points when Spaniards were reported ashore; and the foul
weather of that summer had brought floods which made movement difficult and slow. And it was faulty news which made
Bingham pass on a rumour which soon reached Spain. " The
Duke himself was upon the coast of Erris in Mayo," he wrote,
" and there received into his ship Don Alonso de Leyva, with
a 600 men that had been cast ashore out of the *Rata,* Horatio
Palavicino his ship, which ship lies there all split to pieces."

The wreck he had seen was certainly all that remained of
the proud *Rata Encoronada,* headquarters ship of the Land
Forces commander, Don Alonso de Leyva, who had indeed been
taken off by another ship. But the captain of the *Rata* was
Horatio Donago, not Palavicino (who was serving with Howard),
and the Duke was far away. Nevertheless, the story, embellished,
was in London by 25 September, where it was picked up by the
Spanish spy ring, of which Marco Antonio Messia (a friend of
Palavicino's) was a leading figure. And it was transmitted to
Spain, together with a new rumour from the continent, which
chimed exactly with all the previous tales from that source,
of a crushing Spanish victory. " Reports come from Rouen that
the Spanish Armada has arrived at Lisbon with various prizes,
but here (in London) quite the opposite is asserted; namely,
that after it had almost reached Spanish waters it was caught
in a great storm and driven back to Ireland. Trustworthy news
has been received from there, saying that 15 ships have been
wrecked on the coast, amongst them the galleon *San Martin*
with the Duke of Medina Sidonia on board, the Duke himself
having been taken. It has since been asserted, however, that
he had left the galleon and gone on board the *Rata,* of which
ship nothing has been heard." In effect, Bingham's story, the
other way round, a week before Bingham penned his report
on Connaught. The Spanish spy caught up with it, before it had
even arrived, for he wrote a postscript to his own report a
few days later. " Since I wrote the above I was told on Change
this morning, by a person who was with the Secretary for an
hour last night, that two squadrons were seen off the Irish
coast, one being that of the Duke of Medina, who sailed away
again. The other squadron was caught in a storm, and 18 ships
were lost. They say that what with these drowned, killed by

steel, and taken prisoners, 6,000 men have been lost." The fate
of the Armada was the topic of the town, right up until
December, for Spanish wrecks were occurring even at the end
of October; and the English were afraid of what might happen
if large numbers of Spanish soldiers got ashore from them and
established themselves. " The news spread hourly here keeps
one in suspense," complained a Spanish agent, to whom Palavicino reported in confidence (possibly with tongue in cheek) that
the Spanish losses now totalled more than thirty. Which in fact
they did, although not all occurred in Ireland.

In Thomond, which is present-day Clare, the most southerly
county for which Bingham was responsible, his three reported
wrecks have documentation but no names. In Galway, immediately to the north, there are only two known wrecks within
the present borders of the county; one, almost certainly the
Falcon Blanco Mediano, in Galway Bay, possibly at Barna, and
the other, perhaps the *Concepcion,* near Ards Castle, at a place
now called *Duirling na Spáinneach.* The " common sort "
among the prisoners were put to death, to the number of
about 300, and the " better sort," to the number of about 50,
were held by Bingham in the hope of ransom. But when Fytzwylliam heard the news, he was not pleased by this clemency.
Off the borders of Galway and Mayo is Clare Island, and here
a third wreck occurred, which Bingham may have included in
his list of three for Galway. If so, it would make his arithmetic
—three in each county—absolutely exact. This last ship was
the 1,160 ton *Grangrin,* vice-flagship of Recalde's Armada of
Biscay. She made Clew Bay in a sinking condition, and about
a hundred men out of her, under Pedro de Mendoza, landed on
Clare Island; they were attacked by the local Irish, under
Dubhdara Rua O'Malley, and slaughtered for their valuables,
" saving one poor Spaniard and an Irishman of the County of
Wexford." The *Grangrin* then drifted away, to sink finally at
a place not properly identified but known then as " Fynglase."
Sixteen survivors " wearing chains of gold " got ashore, and were
handed over by the Irish to the English.

In Mayo proper, there were two certain wrecks. Bingham
himself saw the *Rata,* " all split to pieces " in Blacksod Bay.
A second vessel came ashore at Inver, in Broadhaven, with

not a single stick left; she is remembered as " an long maol," the
bare ship. There is tradition, but no documentation, for a third
ship supposed to have sunk off the savage cliffs near Kid Island.
Perhaps she was one of those reported " sunk to seaboard of the
out isles, in the night time," of which, naturally, there would
be little trace. To complicate matters, the wreck identified by
the gallowglass McLaughlan MacCabe who killed 80 sick,
starving, half-drowned Spaniards for his master, William Bourke
(or Burke), which was placed by the English report at Tralee,
far to the south, is connected with Mayo by a recent Irish author,
who maintains that the place meant must be " Tyrawley,"
between Killala and Belderg. On the other hand, he says that
" the exact place is not given, nor is it remembered in tradition,"
as one would expect it to be, had it occurred there.

Bingham's three reported wrecks in Sligo, however, are not
in dispute; for they came ashore, simultaneously, side-by-side, on
Streedagh Strand, and one of them was the *Lavia*, vice-flagship
of the Levanters, in which Cuellar was being held under open
arrest by the Judge Advocate, Martin de Aranda. For Bingham
and Fytzwylliam, however, there was plenty of confusion, for
these events were occurring nearly simultaneously, tending to
interlock, and tending to move north into Ulster, their most
sensitive point. Don Alonso de Leyva was their first worry, for
he was a fine general and he brought his force ashore from the
wrecked *Rata* virtually intact, with arms, armour, money, and
plate. Then he fortified himself in the castles of Ballycroy and
Doolough. Shortly afterwards, he marched his men over to
Tiraum Castle, near Elly Bay, and was joined there by the
survivors from the Broadhaven wreck, " an long maol," the
bare ship which had lost her masts. When two Spanish ships
appeared off the coast, he embarked himself and most of his
men in one of them, the 900 ton hulk *Duquesa Santa Ana* of
the Andalusian squadron; was promptly blown to the north
by a gale, and wrecked again, this time in Ulster, at Loughros
Bay, County Donegal, just across the water from Streedagh
Strand in Sligo. There were four other wrecks in Ulster, from
which some survivors came to shore, and one very large wreck
from which a large, armed force landed and established itself
under Don Alonso de Luzon. If the two main forces of Don

Alonso de Leyva and Don Alonso de Luzon could join together, and rally also the scattered survivors from the other ships in Ulster, and perhaps also some of the men saved at Streedagh Strand, on the borders of Ulster, the Spaniards would have an armed force in Ireland of a strength at least equal to that of the total English garrison of only 2,000 men. And it would be concentrated in the north, the potential centre for Irish revolt, which was in a ferment anyway. Fytzwylliam and Bingham moved out savagely against them, to try to mop them up at once, before the Spaniards could establish themselves.

Streedagh Strand was the first place they reached, and there they saw a sight to gladden any English commander's heart. The beach was strewn with wreckage, described by Fytzwylliam as: " Timber enough to build five of the greatest ships that ever I saw, besides mighty great boats, cables, and other cordage, and some such masts for bigness and length, as I never saw any two could make the like." Five miles of wreckage and more than a thousand corpses, drowned or slain, estimated Secretary Fenton. The first English horseman had reached the scene soon after the disaster. From hiding, Cuellar had watched them go thundering down on to the sand, where his friend, Martin de Aranda, and Don Diego Tellez Enriquez, the hunchback Camp Master of the *San Juan de Sicilia,* lay dead at the edge of the tide.

They were the victims of the English guns, partly, which crippled their ships, and partly of the great bay formed by the counties of Mayo, Sligo, and Donegal. Once in, with the prevailing winds, such unwieldy ships could never get out. " The ship I sailed in was from the Levant," wrote Cuellar, " to which were attached two others, very large. On account of the severe storm which rose upon the bow, we were forced to make for land and anchor, where we remained four days." The third ship was probably the *Juliana,* another Levanter, known to have been lost in this area. All were of about 800 tons. Then, " on the fifth day there sprang up so great a storm on our beam, with sea up to the heavens, so that the cables could not hold nor the sails serve us, and we were driven ashore with all three ships upon a beach, covered with fine sand, shut in on one side and the other by great rocks. Such a thing was never seen: for within an hour all three ships were broken in pieces, so that there did not escape 300 men, and more than one thousand were drowned."

The scene was the more terrible for Cuellar, for he could not swim. Nor could many other Spaniards. Standing there in the howling, screaming wind, with the great breakers building up from seawards, and racing down to beat upon the stranded, shifting hulls of the ships, many took to desperate expedients. On the deck of the *San Juan de Sicilia* was a large, decked boat. Don Diego Enriquez, the Camp Master, two Portuguese gentlemen, and the son of the Count of Villafranca, got into it, with 16,000 ducats' worth of jewels and crowns, and had the hatchway fastened down over them and caulked. Immediately it had been launched, wrote Cuellar, "seventy men who were still alive threw themselves from the ship onto the tender, and while that was struggling to make its way to shore, a great wave came over it, which sunk it and washed off all who were on it. The tender went tossing with the waves hither and thither, until it reached the beach, where it stuck fast upside down, and the gentlemen who had got under the little deck perished inside. After it had been aground a day and a half, some savages came and rolled it over, and breaking the deck took out the dead men. Don Diego Enriquez breathed his last in their hands. They stripped him and took the jewels and money, letting the bodies lie there without burial."

If the foaming sea was of awe-inspiring strength, the prospect which visibly awaited them on that desolate beach was equally horrifying. "I placed myself on the poop, and gazed at the terrible spectacle. Many were drowning inside the ships, others were throwing themselves into the water, vanishing from sight; others were clinging to rafts and barrels, and gentlemen on pieces of timber; others cried aloud from the decks, calling upon God; captains cast their chains and crown pieces into the sea; and the waves swept others overboard. The waves and storm were very great, on the one hand; but, on the other, the land and shore were full of enemies, who went about jumping and dancing with delight at our misfortunes; and when any one of our people reached the beach, two hundred savages and other enemies fell upon him and stripped him of what he had on until he was left in his naked skin. Such they maltreated and wounded

9

without pity, all of which was clearly visible from the battered ships. So I went up to the Judge Advocate—may God have mercy on him—he was very sad and downcast, and I bade him try to do something that might help save his life before the ship should break up completely, as it could not last more than ten minutes; and in fact it did not."

Don Martin de Aranda had sewed gold coins in his doublet and hose, which was bound to destroy his buoyancy, so they looked around for some rough life raft, and eventually found "a scuttle-board as large as a table." Over the side it went, and they jumped after it. "I sank six fathoms under water and swallowed so much of it that I was almost drowned," wrote Cuellar feelingly. Of course, he went nothing like as deep as that, but, to a non-swimmer, it was a terrifying experience to be deep down in the choking depths of the sand-stained sea. Both of them reached the scuttle-board and hung on, until an enormous breaker reared up under them, the board rolled over with the crest, and Martin de Aranda was plucked away instantly. Hampered by the heavy weight of the coins, he struggled convulsively, the waves going completely over his head, his mouth open, breathing water in his last agony for life. His head came up once, and Cuellar heard him scream, "calling upon God." Then he was gone.

"Four waves came, one after the other, and without my knowing how to nor being able to swim, they carried me ashore, where I landed; but I could not stand up, for I was all bruised and bleeding, from a log of wood which almost broke my legs when I was in the water. The enemy and the savages who were on the beach stripping all those who had succeeded in swimming ashore, seeing my plight, legs, hands, and linen all covered in blood, did not touch me, nor did they come near me; so I crawled along, little by little, as best I could." The survivors, from their immersion in the water, the cutting wind on the beach, and the fact that many were now completely naked, were shaking uncontrollably with cold. Cuellar crawled off the beach into a field, where a boy, who had been stripped naked, joined him; the youth was so chilled and terrified, that he could not utter a word, even to say his name. It was then about 9 o'clock in the evening, the light dim, the wind dying away, and the sea calmer,

although the waves still roared all along the curve of the bay.
In this ghostly light, Cuellar saw two black shapes approaching
from inland, coming towards the beach; two men, both armed,
one with a great iron axe. The strangers walked up to the two
shivering Spaniards, and looked down on them silently; then
without a word, they began to cut rushes and grasses, which
they piled over Cuellar and the youth, before they went down
to the beach, still without saying anything.

In pain, but now better protected from the cold, Cuellar
drifted off to sleep. He was awakened at about one o'clock in
the morning by the thunder of hooves, as a great troop of
horsemen, about two hundred in number, went galloping down
to the beach. Turning to see how his companion was, Cuellar
found that the youth was lifeless. "I learned afterward that he
was a gentleman of quality," wrote Cuellar. "But there he lay,
with more than six hundred other dead bodies which the sea
had cast up. The crows and the wolves fed upon them, and there
was nobody to bury any of them, not even poor Don Diego
Enriquez."

It was clear that he ought to get away from the beach, so
Cuellar set off for a little monastery which, when daylight came,
he could see inland; hoping to receive food and help from the
monks. But the English had been there before him. The place
was a wreck, smoke-blackened, with the holy images destroyed;
and in the window apertures, black against the sun, their heads
turned at a dreadful slant, their toes sweeping the floor, were
the suspended bodies of twelve hanged men; survivors from the
wrecks. "As I found nobody in that monastery except the
Spaniards dangling from the iron grates in the church windows,
I went out very quick and took a path that led through a wood,"
said Cuellar, with considerable understatement.

Limping along as quickly as he could, he came on an old
crone, driving before her a herd of cows, to hide them from
the English. "Thou Spain? Thou Spain?" she mouthed at him,
telling him by signs not to go on, as the English were there,
and beginning to sob at his wretched state. She gestured for
him to go in the direction of the beach, and he did so, keeping
in cover as far as he was able, and avoiding the obvious
danger spots, where people with carts were milling around

among the wreckage, loading up the spoils that had come from the sea. Seeing, but not being seen, he stepped out of hiding when two moaning, naked men appeared, staggering inland, their wounds still bloody. "They told me of the cruel deaths and tortures that the English had inflicted upon more than a hundred Spaniards whom they had captured." But death from starvation awaited them if they did not get food soon, so the three distressed men went down again to the scene of their disaster. "We saw dead bodies—for the sea was still throwing them up. We recognised some of them, among others, poor Don Diego Enriquez, and in spite of my forlorn condition, I could not bear to pass him by without burying him, and so we dug a hole in the sand by the water's edge, and there we laid him with another much honoured captain, a dear friend of mine." Then their luck changed. They found food on the beach, mainly biscuits, and when four Irish rushed up to tear the blood-stained linen from Cuellar's back, a man who was obviously a chief stopped this, then showed the Spaniards to a road leading inland. They were to go along that road, he said, and would find a village, where they would get help. Limping, the tattered trio set out on a stony path, knowing nothing of the land to which they had come, nor what to expect from its people. They were " on the run," with death for penalty if the English caught them.

Where the Spaniards landed in force, there was no plundering by the poverty-stricken inhabitants of the country. In the extreme north of Ulster, near Lough Foyle, Don Alonso de Luzon's great Levanter, the 1,100 ton *Trinidad Valencera* of Venice, limped to land in a sinking condition on 4 September. Her pumps had been working continuously for two days and she had crammed into her half the 200 man crew of the 600 ton *Barca de Amburg* (the bark of Hamburg), which had gone down out at sea, north of Ireland. The other 100 men had been taken off by the *Gran Grifon*, flagship of the hulks, shortly to be wrecked in her turn on Fair Isle. One of her crew, Juan de Nova, a Galician, testified that: "All the soldiers (except 40 who remained in the ship and were drowned when she afterwards foundered) were put on shore, with their arms, in a little boat." Their commander, Don Alonso de Luzon, stated: " We landed by shipwreck as many of us as could in a broken boat of our own, some swam to the shore, and the rest were landed in a boat of O'Doherty's country, for the use of which we gave in money and apparel 200 ducats. I and five more of the best of my company landed first, only with rapiers in our hands, where we found 4 or 5 savage people, who bade us welcome. We were about two days landing our men, and had very ill entertainment, finding no other relief of victual in the country than of certain horses, which we bought of poor men for money, which we killed and did eat."

This large armed force worried the English, but they had so many wrecks to deal with—there were four more within fifty miles of the *Valencera*—that they could only spare 400 men to head them off, but having some advantage as half these were cavalry and the Spaniards facing them had many sick and weak. They marched up, banners flying, horsemen, harquebusiers, and bowmen, and the Spanish column came to a halt, both sides facing each other, and beating the drums for a parley. " Who are you?" was the first question. " Spanish soldiers wrecked on this island, who wish to hire a ship in which to return home." " That cannot be," was the reply, " you must surrender as prisoners of war." " If that is the alternative, we would rather die fighting, as befits Spaniards," was the retort

The two bodies of armed men remained camped opposite each other, in a rising tension, for 36 hours; then the English launched a night attack. Next morning, they again beat their drums for parley, and as food was short, de Luzon went down to talk to them in a chastened mood. " I and my whole company yielded ourselves, within 6 or 7 days after our landing, to the captains that carried the Queen's ensigns, O'Donnell and his wife being present, upon condition that our lives should be saved until we came to the Viceroy; whereupon we laid down 350 muskets and calivers and some few pikes to her Majesty's use, all which were seized on by John Kelly, whom they term sergeant-major, and Captain Richard Hovenden's lieutenant; after which one promise was not kept with us, for the soldiers and savage people were allowed to spoil us of all we had." Then began the march into captivity, by a line of nearly naked men, hemmed in by the armed English soldiers. They had been promised that they would be housed and re-clothed in a castle that night, but the English commander rode up later to say, that as the road was bad, they would bivouac in the open instead. Silently, they were marched off the road into a field; then, with shouted orders, the men were separated from the officers, who were forced inside a square of armed men, together with the Spanish chaplain-general, the vicar of the shoeless Carmelites of Lisbon, and two other friars.

Next morning, seeing that some of the Spanish officers were still with their men, the English came to get them, leaving only the soldiers and seamen. These were then driven into a field, wondering helplessly what was about to happen. They saw the English forming up their soldiers, a troop of cavalry on one side, a line of harquebusiers on the other. There was a harsh command. The muzzles of the fire-arms came down to cover them, the horsemen broke into a trot, then a gallop; then, with a flash of steel and the crackling of musketry, the massacre was on. "The harquebusiers came at us from one side, the cavalry from the other," wrote Juan de Nova. "With lance and bullet, they killed over 300 of us." The men fell in heaps, groaning and screaming, as the English fired into them, then rode them down, lances thrust viciously at the fleeing, naked men. It was not a tidy affair. One hundred and fifty Spaniards escaped, among them de Nova, running desperately through a bog and turning and twisting like snipe to avoid their assailants.

But, unlike Cuellar, they had been ashore long enough to know that there was a strong resistance movement among the Irish in Ulster, although the motions of "collaboration" were gone through; and they knew where to contact it, at the castle of bishop Cornelius. He passed them on to a chief named O'Cahan, who kept them for a few days, then passed them on in turn to his brother 12 miles distant. The plan was to get them to Sorleyboy McDonnell, lord of Dunluce, who would get them out of the country and into Scotland. An underground escape route came suddenly into being; Cuellar was drawn into it later, after fantastic adventures, was hidden by O'Cahan, and passed north to Dunluce the following year. But the master of the *Valencera* was in London by 3 December, reporting to the Spanish spy ring.

Meanwhile, Don Alonso de Luzon and the other officers were marched along the stony roads to Drogheda for questioning. It was the road to the Lord Deputy of Ireland, Sir William Fytzwylliam, and for most of them it was the last road they would ever take. When Don Alonso was brought in for interrogation, he was faced by, had he but known it, an old shipmate of the Armada, who had sailed with the great enterprise from Lisbon, but never seen England from a Spanish ship. It was David Gywnn, galley-slave in the *Diana*, who had escaped the wreck, got to La Rochelle, and crossed over to England with the aid of some English merchants there and a tale of the important information that had come into his possession. If contemporary Dutch historians are to be believed, he was also claiming to have freed the slaves and captured the galley on the high seas, instead of being a fugitive from its wreck. There is no mention of that in the English records, merely a brief heading to the list of set questions to be put. " Instructions for the Lord Primate, and Sir Henry Wallop, knight, and David Gywnn, gent., or any two of them, to be dealt in with the Spanish prisoners at Drogheda." But David Gywnn, gent., did not last. On 16 October, a Mr. Eustace Harte deposed to the Lord Deputy that he had met Gywnn at Rochelle and that the wretched man, " being in necessity and want, did make report that a Spanish secretary had showed him a letter which had come from Mr. Secretary Walsyngham, that he was wholly for them, and would deliver her Majesty's person into their hands. Moreover, he did take forth a paper out of his pocket, wherein were written certain verses by him of her Majesty, concerning the estate of England, and did name her Majesty by the name of Bess." There had been a demand " to get that lewd, prating fellow punished," but he had said nothing upon it at the time, because he thought the English authorities would deal with him. Shortly after Mr. Harte's deposition before the Lord Deputy, David Gywnn, gent., became David Gywnn, captive, once again.

By 3 December, the number of Spaniards " put to the sword " in Ireland by the English totalled 1,100, according to Bingham. Amongst them were " divers gentlemen of quality and service, as captains, masters of ships, lieutenants, ensign-bearers, other inferior officers and young gentlemen, to the number of some fifty, whose names I have for the most part set down in a list." They included that Ensign Juan Gil, who, under the Duke's orders had gone off to capture the English fishing boat near Plymouth. Bingham had hoped to receive ransom money for them, but "I had special direction from the Lord Deputy to see them executed, reserving alive only Don Luis de Cordova, and a young gentleman, his nephew, until your Highness's pleasure be known," he wrote to the Queen. "My brother George had two Spanish gentlemen, and some five or six boys, who coming after the fury and heat of justice was past, by entreaty I spared them, in respect they were pressed into the fleet against their wills. But the Lord Deputy caused both these two Spaniards to be executed, and the Dutchmen and boys that were spared before, reserving none but Don Luis and his nephew." Bingham summed up his news: "I, your poor and faithful soldier, present your highness with these humble and few lines, as a thanksgiving to Almighty God for these his daily preservations of your sacred person, and the continual deliverance of us, your Majesty's subjects, from the cruel and bloody hands of your Majesty's enemies . . ."

Bingham was an old soldier; he had fought at Lepanto, long ago, on the side of the men he had been slaughtering that month. He knew Spaniards; and he had given them as much mercy as they would have given him: none at all. The unfortunate Dutch boys had been a different matter; but in none of the English reports is there a sign of regret; on the contrary, they were extremely satisfied. Sir John Popham, another of the commanders in Ireland, wrote: "The people in these parts are for the most part dangerously affected towards the Spaniards, but thanks be to God that their power, by her Majesty's good means, is shorter than it hath been." The tone was set by Fytzwylliam, who after looking at the shambles on Streedagh Strand, wrote religiously to the Queen: "Since it hath pleased God by His hand upon the rocks to drown the greater and the better sort of them, I will, with His favour, be His soldier for the despatching of those rags which yet remain." And the gentlewoman, Lady Denny, marching out to hang up by the neck

25 shipwrecked men, is clear sign that he was not alone in this attitude.

Of course, it was very embarrassing for Ubaldino when he came to write the history of the campaign for contemporaries; he was an Italian, and could not share these sentiments. Indeed, he had to find excuses for them. Admitting that the Lord Deputy had been " sour and severe," he felt in duty bound to point out that " in every nation there are to be found men of every kind "; not all the English were like that. Against these acts, "leaving a lasting record of their shame for all those who read," he quoted an opposite case, that of Christopher Carleill. Carleill was Governor in Ulster. He had taken 14 wretched men who had stumbled ashore from some unknown wreck, and was told by Fytzwylliam " to put them to death in any manner "; which meant on the gallows, slow death by strangulation, kicking and struggling, tongues protruding, eyes sticking out of their heads. Instead, he paid a Scottish boatman to get them overseas before the Lord Deputy could " make a progress " into Ulster. And it was in Ulster, too, that the final act of the tragedy took place; which ensured that Don Alonso de Leyva and the young nobleman cadets who were with him should never fall into the hands of the English, to die in such a fashion. This was the man the English were really worried about, the man who might, with force enough, shake their hold upon the whole of Ireland.

Having been wrecked in the *Rata* at Blacksod Bay, but ferried all his men ashore with their weapons, he had embarked them in the *Duquesa Santa Ana* and been wrecked in her, further north, at Loughros Bay in Donegal, shortly after. In this wreck he was seriously injured. According to one of the crew, James Machary of the Cross, captured later, " there fell a great storm which broke in sunder all our cables, and struck us upon the ground; and Don Alonso was hurt in the leg by the capstan of the ship in such sort as he was able neither to go nor ride." But de Leyva was not finished yet. He heard of yet another Spanish ship, at anchor further up the coast, which was not damaged beyond repair. Four men carried him in a chair the nineteen miles to Killibegs, where they found that the report was true. The galleass *Girona* lay at anchor with a broken rudder, as her compatriot the *Zuniga* had off Liscannor.

Cuellar had heard of her, too—and he set off with twenty companions from O'Rourke's country, where the Irish had been hiding them, but they were too late. The *Girona* had gone, with Don Alonso de Leyva and the crews of the *Rata* and the *Duquesa Santa Ana* packed into her—1,300 men in all. She was dreadfully overcrowded, and with not enough food even to consider making Spain; and so she sailed to the northwards, round Ulster, to bring the wheel full circle, and perished in sight of Dunluce Castle, the fortress of Sorleyboy McDonnell, the most influential man in the whole hurriedly improvised escape organisation.

When Juan de Nova was passed on to Dunluce by the Irish underground, with his friend Francisco de Borja, he found the survivors of the *Girona* already there, and talked to one of them, a sailor. He gave them the story in detail, explaining that de Leyva had intended to make for Scotland originally, but that the wind had come up fair for a quick passage to the south, and their pilot had promised them that they would make Spain in five days. But the wind had swung round and blown a full gale off the north coast of Ulster. " We ran upon a submerged rock and the galleass went to pieces, more than 1,300 being drowned," the sailor told them. " There were only nine men saved." The flower of Spanish chivalry perished with the splintered galleass, rolled under by the tides that washed at the foot of Dunluce, a grim castle on a great cliff overhanging the never-ending thunder of the sea.

Captain Merriman reported to Fytzwylliam on 28 October : " With regard of my most humble duty, I thought good to acquaint your Honour with the occurents here, that the Spanish ship which arrived in Tyrconnel with the McSweeny was on Friday the 18th of this present descried over against Dunluce, and by rough weather was perished, so that there was driven to the land, being drowned, the number of 260 persons, with certain butts of wine, which Sorley Boy hath taken up for his use."

It was not until the following year, 1589, that Cuellar came at last to Dunluce. " I went travelling by the mountains and desolate places, enduring much hardship," he wrote, " and at the end of my journey, I got to the place where Alonso de Leyva was lost, with many others. I went to the huts of some savages who were there, who told me of the great misfortunes of our people who were drowned, and who showed me many jewels and valuables of theirs, which distressed me greatly." He was still not out of danger, and it was only in October, 1589, that the man who had been condemned to death by the Duke of Medina Sidonia, and survived not only that but many perils much greater, could sit down in the city of Antwerp to explain why it was that he was no longer under open arrest for cowardice; and, incidentally, to give a vivid picture, probably the most detailed in existence, of conditions in Ireland at that time.

He had certainly shown more initiative than eight other Spanish soldiers, survivors from the *Valencera,* from the *Lavia,* his own ship, and from the *Juliana,* probably the third ship destroyed at Streedagh Strand. For when Captain Cobos, a Spanish liaison officer to the Irish underground, came over to Ulster on November, 1596, eight years after the defeat of the Armada, they were still there, serving the Irish chiefs as soldiers. They asked to see Spain once more, and if Cobos would not allow it, because of their value to any Spanish invading force, then at least, please, could they have their back pay?

CHAPTER TWENTY-TWO

Take, Burn, or Sink

The Battle of Le Havre

DURING SEPTEMBER and October, 1588, Armada ships were coming
to grief in the most surprising places; the most northerly wreck
was separated from the most southerly by a distance of over 1,200
miles, and there was just under a thousand miles distance between
the most westerly and the most easterly, which we know about.
Some ships may have sunk, unreported, out in the Atlantic,
which would place the wrecks within a box 1,200 miles square.
There could be no better illustration of the complete defeat
and scattering of the great Enterprise of England. The last ship
of all to sink was one of the vessels taken off Plymouth, which
went to the bottom with some of her prize crew while en route
to Portsmouth on 15 November. The English were cock-a hoop,
now, at the humbling of so mighty a force, a combination of the
power of half Europe, which the tiny island had first defied,
and then defeated, entirely alone (for they never counted on
their allies, the Dutch, but made their dispositions without
regard for any help from that quarter).

For the Spaniards, the news of their defeat, and the first
hint of their terrible roll of casualties, came in slowly and hap-
hazardly; in reports from their spies in London, which were not
believed, and, more surely, from the French port of Le Havre,
at the mouth of Seine, which eventually became a funnel
for the escape route from Ireland. By the end of the year,
ragged survivors of the wrecks in Ireland brought testimony
that could not be disbelieved. One ship, which actually got
back to Spain in the end, came direct to Le Havre from the west
coast of Ireland, and was holed up in that French port, in
continual danger of English attack, for a whole year. In so
doing, she had made a more than complete circumnavigation of
the British Isles.

This was the galleass *Zuniga*, which had anchored off Liscannor Castle, to repair a broken rudder pivot, her crew and galley slaves half dead of hunger. " The inhabitants were rustic savages devoted to England, with a few officials amongst them," recorded Juan de Saavedra, a captain in the Neapolitan Regiment. " We were in such dire need of food that nearly 80 of our soldiers and convicts died of hunger and thirst, the inhabitants refusing to allow us to obtain water; nor would they sell us food. By necessity, we took up arms and obtained supplies by force." According to the collated diaries of several of her crew, the galleass went out of Liscannor Bay with a wind astern on 13 September. " On the 18th we were driven by a furious gale into the English Channel. Next day, two guns were thrown overboard, we were in great trouble for want of food, and the ship was leaking very badly, both fore and aft. On the 22nd, with the same wind, we entered the roadstead of Havre de Gráce." And there, under Havre Castle, they saw the stranded wreck of another Armada ship, with splintered sides and shot-torn masts.

The wreck was the 768 ton *Santa Ana*, flagship of Recalde's Armada of Biscay. Her purser, Pedro de Igueldo, watched the disordered galleass limp in. " I found that the galleass *Zuniga*, storm beaten, with the rudder and spars broken, and the ship in a sinking state, had brought up at the anchorage before the town. As she was in great danger, we got her into the port, not without much trouble and risk, as she grounded at the entrance of the harbour and was within an ace of being lost. She arrived without a bit of food, or drop of water; a day later, and they would all have perished of famine. I have brought bread, cider, and other necessities, and am distributing the ordinary rations. They need it badly enough, so emaciated are they; pitiably broken and miserable." The galley slaves, a motley collection of condemned men, including Spaniards and Frenchmen, had had enough. No sooner was she in, than they took the first opportunity to make an attempt at freedom. " The convicts tried to escape at the entrance to the town, and those who were Frenchmen succeeded, with some others. The rest were detained with great trouble, and are under strong guard," reported the harassed Iqueldo. The poor purser had been forced to take charge of the men from the *Santa Ana*, as her commander, Camp Master Nicholas de Isla, had been mortally wounded at the battle of Le Havre, three weeks before, when Captain George Raymond had led in an English force to get her. Now he had the helpless survivors of the *Zuniga* on his hands as well, and the galleass little better than a wreck.

His own ship, the *Santa Ana*, was the former flagship of Recalde's squadron, but not Recalde's own ship. She proved unseaworthy, being dispersed from the Armada in that same storm which had sent the galleys running for port, on 17 July. Nevertheless, the old soldier, Nicholas de Isla, did not want to be out of the fight; and so the *Santa Ana* crept from French port to French port on her way to the rendezvous with Parma. First, she put into Conquest, in Brittany, then to La Hogue. Parma advised: " The Channel being so full of enemies, it will be highly imprudent for them to go in search of his Majesty's Armada." But Nicholas de Isla would not turn back, and when he got her into Le Havre, Mendoza remarked with relief: " They are now, thank God, out of peril." He had heard, however, that the Governor of Le Havre was pro-English, and reported: " M. de Montpensier has sent word to the coast of England for them to come and capture the galleon."

Le Havre was almost directly opposite the English naval base of Portsmouth, and from there the Earl of Sussex reported on 30 August that the *Elizabeth Bonaventure,* Captain George Raymond, the *Aid,* Captain William Fenner, the *Foresight,* Captain Christopher Baker, and the *Charles,* Captain John Roberts, had ammunitioned, " So as, upon Tuesday, about two of the clock after midnight, they set sail for the coast of France. Hoping very shortly to hear some good news of their happy success in this their enterprise." In the 70-ton pinnace *Charles* sailed William Monson, then a young officer volunteer.

" On the afternoon of 30 August," reported Iqueldo, " we were informed that three great English ships, one of 500 tons, the others of 200 tons each, with a patache, had appeared in sight, and it was feared they were coming to attack us. The Maistre de Campo and I went on board at once, and at dawn yesterday morning the three ships and the patache bore down on us, and the patache opened fire. We replied, and meanwhile the Governor of the port sent off a boat to them requesting that they would not break the peace in neutral waters, as he would resent it with all the means in his power. They replied that they came at the command of their Queen, and would not retire for anybody until they had taken, sunk, or burnt the *Santa Ana*." It was Mers-el-Kebir—the Battle of Oran—in miniature, 352 years earlier. The English intended to let no Armada ship escape, if they could help it; and any Frenchman, friend, foe, or neutral, who stood in the way, was going to be unlucky.

Le Havre echoed and re-echoed to the thunder of their gun-fire; the main yard-arm of the *Santa Ana* came down almost at once, crushing and pinning underneath it the gallant Nicholas de Isla, but leaving unscathed Purser Iqueldo, who was standing by his side. Another shot severed the mooring cables, and the Spanish flagship went drifting away with the tide, bumping on the ground two or three times, and heeling over under the press of water almost to the point of capsize. But the rising flood lifted her free each time, carrying her nearer and nearer to the town and fortifications of Le Havre. " The townspeople helped us all they could, firing at the English from the fort, and dragging out two guns onto the shore, which inflicted much damage on the enemy. The English then fired on the people ashore, as well as us. I had the ship moved by the port pilots, and taken to another place; and that was the salvation of all. I had the Maestre de Campo put on shore, where he now is in grave danger, unable to speak, his head and chest badly crushed. The enemy was in sight, cruising near us, all that night, but they did not attack us." Isla died of his injuries a few days later, and the *Santa Ana* broke free from her moorings in a gale, going aground near the castle, where she was looted by the French and finally lost.

The *Zuniga* was repaired during the winter, and in April, 1589, made one of several unsuccessful attempts to get home, under the command of Captain Marolin de Juan, nearly going ashore on the English coast. Masts, booms, and yards were carried away, the decks opened; 12 guns, their ammunition, the anchors, cables, and barrels of provisions were jettisoned to save her, and in the last extremity, more than half her oars as well, 30 of them, " which the convicts were ready enough to throw overboard." And back she went to Le Havre, with all to do again, and promptly ran aground once more. In the end, she made Spain; but the galleass design was abandoned, as too weak for ocean work.

On 16 December (which was the day after Christmas by the New Style European calendar used by the Spaniards), a number of Scottish vessels put into Le Havre, bringing 32 soldier survivors from Don Alonso de Luzon's *La Trinidad Valencera* of Venice and a number of sailors, including some from the *Girona*. They brought certain news of the extermination of most of de Luzon's men and of the death of de Leyva. During their stay in Scotland, which had become the mid-point staging post for the return of shipwrecked men from Ireland to the Spanish Netherlands and neutral France, they had heard of the fate of other ships also. After questioning them, Captain Marolin de Juan, former Pilot-General of the Armada, reported: " The ship *San Juan Bautista*, of Ragusa, of 800 tons, was burnt in a Scottish port, with Don Diego Manrique on board. They say that the only persons who escaped were 15 who were on shore at the time." The story of the " Tobermory Galleon " had begun. Even then, there were conflicting stories concerning her identity, for on the same day that Marolin de Juan made his report, on 17 December (Old Style), Bernadino de Mendoza, the Spanish ambassador in Paris, separately reported to the King what he had been told by a " person who has just come from Scotland."

"A Spaniard of rank was in the Scottish islands; he frequently went from one island to another, and he carried with him 400 or 500 harquebusiers, who guarded him well day and night. These islands must be the Hebrides because, according to another advice, there is a Spanish galleass amongst these islands, and the Queen of England had sent three ships to try to capture it." Mendoza's unlikely story was in fact more or less correct, but he was confused because he thought there was only one Spanish ship in the area, whereas there were two. Both ships had been unable to get round Ireland at all, presumably because their sailing gear was so badly damaged that they could only go with the wind; consequently, they drifted backwards and forwards between Ireland and Scotland. " The Spaniard of rank " was Admiral Juan Gomez de Medina in the *Gran Grifon*, flagship of the squadron of hulks, which piled up on the Fair

Isle, between Orkney and Shetland, but got ashore with most of his men, and was taken off eventually by a fishing vessel bound for Scotland. The *San Juan Bautista,* " burnt in a Scottish port " while some of the men were ashore, was the other ship, but not a galleass, for which the English were hunting. She put into Mull, in the Hebrides, and was destroyed by internal explosion, just as the *San Salvador* had been off Plymouth; this, too, was sabotage, this time by one of Walsyngham's agents.

Thus began one of the most extraordinary mysteries of the sea ever to be recorded, still unsolved, and probably never now to be solved. There were so many San Juans and San Juan Bautistas that she could be several different ships—but not a " Treasure Ship." But it is precisely a treasure ship that she has become, and not just a treasure ship, but the only one in the Armada—the " Greate Treasure Shippe of Spaine." Of course, everyone who looks at the records, both Spanish and English, knows where the treasure was, and how much it was; and what happened to it. Indeed, it is not even necessary to consult a single contemporary document to tell where it was; ordinary military and naval practice gives the answer. The money was with the paymasters, and the paymasters were in the headquarters ships, the flagships and vice-flagships. And they are all accounted for. The " Tobermory Galleon " was not a treasure ship in any sense of the word; or if she was, then so is any old packet boat to the Isle of Wight. No one in his right mind would dream of diving to the Tobermory galleon, except out of archaeological interest; and that will be of little value, for the rabid treasure seekers have smashed her up. What little she had—the purser's official chest, the captain's personal plate, and above all, the immensely valuable guns, may have been lifted long ago, by diving bell.

For several centuries she was the *Florida,* according to local tradition; then the scholars got to work, and found no ship of that name in any Armada list. So they decided she must be the *Florencia,* actually Gaspar de Sosa's *San Francesco,* the galleon of the Duke of Florence, which figures several times, quite prominently, in Medina Sidonia's accounts of the fighting. She ended her career, smashed to matchwood by the English guns, and was scrapped immediately after the Armada campaign. In

due course, some other scholars caught up with the previous
results of scholarship, and turned her into the *San Juan de
Sicilia* of Don Diego Tellez Enriquez, whom Cuellar buried at
Streedagh Strand, a stone's throw from the wreck of his command.

The Tobermory Galleon has been dived on since certainly
1607, twenty years after the sinking, but these first divers kept very
quiet. The standard method of dealing with a ship from a
diving bell was to raise the items from the upper deck first, then
tear the deck clear off in order to get at the deck below. The
diver was equipped with a number of fearsome instruments, in
the rough shape of tongs, bills, baskets, and hooks for recovering
guns and "goodies"; and there was apparently some method
of coaxing guns out of gunports, which may have required the
diver to leave the bell.

The Government of Elizabeth had a great many Spanish
wrecks on their hands, and they were particularly interested in
the guns, a practical and valuable salvage proposition. To put
the matter of the treasure in perspective, the average amount
carried in an Armada flagship was about 50,000 ducats; and the
cost of the anchors and cables lost at Calais, according to what
Friar Gongora heard, was 100,000 ducats. The value of the
guns in a single ship was immensely greater. Consequently, when
Sir George Carew, Master of the Ordnance, went over to Ireland
during the summer following the Armada, he found himself in
the undersea salvage business. Indeed, he was away so frequently,
that in some light-hearted official correspondence it was suggested
that his wife might become a "diving widow." "Repair to that
part of Thomond upon the sea," Fytzwylliam directed him,
"where some of the Spanish fleet perished, and where there are
certain pieces of ordnance meet to be recovered, carrying with
you artificers and setting forth boats and other necessaries."
Soon afterwards, Carew was able to report: "Already we have
weighed three pieces of artillery of brass, and yesterday we
fastened our haullsers to a canon of battery or Basalyke, as we
suppose by the length, for they lie in four fathoms and a half
of water, which was so huge that it brake our cables. Our diver
was nearly drowned, but Irish aqua vitae hath such virtue as
I hope of his recovery. If the diver of Dublin with his instru-

ments were here, I would not doubt to bring good store of artillery from thence, for if I be not deceived, out of our boats we did plainly see four pieces more. As yet I cannot find any small pieces of brass or iron. I think the inhabitants of this country have gotten them."

After that, he was sent to Ulster, " her Majesty's gallyon, called *The Popingay*," being ordered to assist him; and there, too, someone had been before him. He was told by Mr. Auncyent Dallawaye that " there are two Spaniards and a Scottish captain come over to weigh the ordnance in the Routt; and it is reported that there is great store of gold and silver there . . " Sir Henry Bagnall wrote: " I long to hear of the safe arrival of your last comfort (i.e. Carew's wife.) If she be come, let her know that there is no artillery left at Dunluce to draw you from her. The King of Scots, as I hear say, sent for the same, and at first they did weigh two great pieces. I am sure they have all, and are gone . . ."

The Government of Elizabeth was eventually presented with an Armada wreck right on their own doorstep, not far from Plymouth; but the loot was depressingly poor. Two San Pedros re-entered the Channel, going round and round the British Isles in a great circle. The first, the hulk *San Pedro el Menor* (Saint Peter the Lesser), anchored off Morvien, on the Brittany coast. This was the vessel which had reached the Lizard in June, with the other storeships, and had been in action then; her master and pilot had subsequently deserted off Calais, just before the fireship attack. On 10 October, her captain, Don Juan de Monsalve, reported: " Our persistent evil fortune has just decreed that the cruel weather we have experienced should break our cables and drift the hulk ashore this morning. She is now half full of water, and I am taking out the powder and other things I can rescue." Meanwhile, the *San Pedro el Mayor* (Saint Peter the Greater) was not far behind; she was one of the two hospital ships attached to the Armada, and serving in her was Rodrigo de Calderon, comptroller of the hospital, brother of Pedro Coco Calderon, Auditor-General of the Armada, who was in the *San Salvador,* vice-flagship of the same squadron. On 28 October she ran out of sea in Hope Cove, near Salcombe, Devon, and well and truly piled herself up on rocks owned by Sir

William Courteney of Ilton, to the great annoyance of the English.

Late again, George Cary of Cockington galloped down to the shore side, to find that, as in the case of the *Rosario* at Torbay, the locals had been there before him. " Having understanding of the great pilfering and spoils that the country people made, I rode thither. She is a hulk, in burden, as they say, 550 tons, but I think not so much. The ship is not to be recovered; she lieth on a rock, and full of water to her upper decks. She will prove of no great value; the ordnance is all iron, and no brass, their ground tackle all spent. There hath been some plate and certain ducats rifled and spoiled at their first landing, and such drugs and pothecary stuff as came to 6,000 ducats." The report which reached Spain, that the Council had ordered the execution of her whole crew, was apparently correct; for Anthony Ashley learned on 12 November of " your Lordships' pleasure for the deferring of the execution of the Spaniards." He also reported on the international nature of her crew, which included Spanish soldiers and mariners; Portuguese soldiers; and French, Italian and Dutch mariners. But murdering the crew of a hospital ship, on home ground, was apparently just a little too much for the Council, and they relented. One of the prisoners, Gonzalo Gonzales de Castilla, of Granada, did not get out of England until 1592, by which time the Armada was distant history, a golden tale of the past. The puzzle of why she piled up there at all is answered by the statement of her crew: " We were pursued by continual tempests; the ship was unseaworthy; and we were in want of food." They were, quite literally, dying of starvation.*

The last report on the sinking of an Armada ship was made by John Thoms, an official of Portsmouth Dockyard, on 15 November: "And may it please your Lordship to be advertised of the great Spaniard; she was lost at Studland, but, God be

---

* All that remains of the wreck was fleetingly seen in 1960 by George Tessyman of Dartmouth, who, finding himself under-weighted while aqualunging in Hope Cove, stuck his knife into a wooden post to keep himself on the bottom. Only as he was returning to the surface, did he notice that there were many similar posts sticking out of the sand—the ribs of a big wooden ship. He never saw them again, for the tides had exposed them only momentarily, but Spanish coins of the Armada period are sometimes picked up on the beach after a gale.

praised, there is saved 34 of our best men. By good hap there came out of Studland a small man-of-war and saved these men. And there was lost 23 men, whereof 6 of them was Flemings and Frenchmen that came in the same ship out of Spain." She was the gutted *San Salvador* of Oquendo, being sailed to Portsmouth Harbour for final disposal. The man who sank her, alleged John Thoms, was Mr. Nicholas Jones of Portland Castle, recommended to him by George Trenchard as a sailmaker who would supply him with the canvas necessary to move her that short distance. " Pray send for it, you shall have it, and a dozen of oars," Jones had promised him.

" But it was the least part of his meaning, for the next day the said Jones rode away to London, and left no order to deliver the same sail; neither none could be had. And please your Lordship, I charged him before Mr. Trenchard, that the ship or men should miscarry, that he should answer for it. There be of his neighbours that are saved, and others of the company, that will venture their lives whenever they meet with him; for all those that are saved will depose that he was the casting away of the ship and the death of the men."

A garland of ropes and shrouds, trailed from bobbing masts and yards, drifted slowly on the cold winter sea, marking only for a brief space that very silent grave where English mariners and the last men of the Armada lay at peace together. Seventeen Englishmen, four Germans, two Frenchmen. They lie there still, with no treasure seekers to tear apart their tomb. And the unknown woman, whose husband—or was it father?—lay deep in the English sea; where was she then, and how much did she grieve? No one knows.

CHAPTER TWENTY-THREE

The Year of the Eights

The Homecoming of the Armada—September, 1588

I pray that God in His mercy will grant us fine weather, so that the Armada may soon enter port; for we are so short of provisions that if for our sins we are long delayed, all will be irretrievably lost. There are now a great number of sick, and many die. Pray consider the distress of this Armada after so terrible a voyage, and the urgent need for prompt measures of relief.

Medina Sidonia to the King, 25 August

ON 11 August, when still far north in the Atlantic, Medina Sidonia had sent Don Baltasar de Zuniga in a fast pinnace for Spain, carrying the war diary of the Armada and a desperate plea for help to be available on the quayside when the surviving ships came home. " Crippled . . . scattered . . . no ammunition . . . provisions scanty . . . rations reduced . . . half a pound of biscuit a day . . . 3,000 sick . . . without counting the wounded . . . who are numerous . . ." On 25 August, he sent another letter on ahead, reporting that he was with some of the ships in the Bay of Biscay, again stressing " the urgent need for prompt measures of relief." Philip had been warned what to expect, but what he had not anticipated was that the plight of the ships would be so terrible that they would attempt to struggle into the first Spanish port they saw, instead of putting into the naval dockyards in the north-west, where an organisation existed which could take care of them. Even so, the first sight of the leading ships of the Armada must have horrified the watchers on the shore.

The waves were still thundering on the rocks of Santander, in the aftermath of gale, when the weather-stained, shot-battered hulk of a great galleon was seen, drifting with limp sails towards the rocks in the shore-setting current; and alongside her, a little caravel, equally weather beaten. Puffs of smoke leapt out from the galleon's sides, hazing her outline in the still air. Again and again, she fired; distress gun after distress gun. The fishermen put out hurriedly to take her in tow; and found that she was a reeking charnel house inside. Hardly a man on board could keep his feet, so many were sick. 180 of her crew, dead of typhus and other diseases, had been thrown overboard; and many more corpses from those killed in action. The wounded and ill lay feverish and untended on filthy decks. There was only one pilot left alive among four. Out of the retinue of the great admiral aboard, 60 were dead or incapable, and only two of his staff remained on their feet. The admiral himself, his eyes deep sunken in his face, gave the impression of being, not merely a sick, but a broken man. He did not wait to see his flagship brought safely into Santander, but scrambled into a boat and, head bowed, hurried ashore, as if he could not too quickly put a great distance behind him that abode of evil memories. The galleon rolling helplessly off the rocks was the great, gilt-adorned *San Martin,* flagship of the Great Armada and of Spain's Captain General of the Ocean. The Duke of Medina Sidonia had come home.

In a short while, many more of these floating wrecks came drifting in. Eight into Santander, but not the *San Martin,* for a fresh wind made her uncontrollable and she was blown down the coast to Laredo. Soon, 21 great-ships were anchored there, in Laredo, with their cargoes of agony, together with the three galleys which had never seen England, and the *Patrona,* the only surviving galleass of those which had. The Levant squadron was gone, almost wiped out; but Oquendo was off shore with five or six ships, running for the Biscay ports, a dying man. Still far out at sea was Recalde, staggering home on two masts in the great *San Juan* of Oporto, never leaving his bunk, and like Oquendo, dying. Calderon, on 11 September, the day the Duke came home, was still out to sea, but within sight of land; not a drop of fresh water was left in the *San Salvador,* and the pumps had been groaning day and night, for days, to keep the water in the holds from gaining. Nothing they could do could force it out; it was a question of whether they would get to the shore before the sea pulled them down. They saw four ships steering confidently for Brittany; white canvas, painted hulls, healthy, purposeful ships, which had never been to England. But the water-logged hulk did not signal for help; on the contrary, "we wished to avoid them," said Calderon. They needed to be alone with the dishonour and shame of their defeat.

Only another Armada ship would know what they had gone through, and understand; and you could easily tell an Armada ship, just by looking at her. "On the 12th, in the afternoon, we sighted a dismasted ship, which fired a gun," he wrote. The *San Salvador* made no reply; she was beyond giving help to anyone. "At nightfall she came to reconnoitre us. It was the *Nuestra Senora de Juncal* of Don Pedro de Valdes's squadron; one of the best ships in the Armada, with three captains of infantry on board. She reported that she was much damaged, with many sick, and entirely without food; and did not know her position. On the morning of 13 September, we sighted another hulk, which followed in our wake with the other ship. We entered Santander that night, and there I found the Duke had already arrived, but was very ill, though delighted at my arrival, as he had quite given me up for lost."

On the following day, Bernadino de Mendoza, Spanish ambassador in Paris, wrote his usual letter to the King. Philip had grown slightly impatient with the stream of rumours about the total ruin of the English fleet, the death of Drake, and the downfall of the Lord Admiral. Mendoza had just received a stiff letter from him, in which he had said, in effect: "I am not satisfied with your spies. Get some better ones." Mendoza was hurt, explaining that he was only passing on reports received from the crews of fishing vessels. And he promptly passed on the two latest. From Hamburg, that a vessel "had met your Majesty's Armada, 115 to 120 sail, in the Northern Sea, sailing in good order and fine weather." And, from "a man who left Edinburgh on 24 September," that the Armada had captured the entire Scottish and English fishing fleets and "had nearly 300 sail, and the weather was so fine that it would very soon arrive in Spain." Even on 19 September, he was still at it, confirming the news; and, just to stress its authenticity, he passed on a revealing story from "a trustworthy source."

When "a Flemish heretic (i.e., a Protestant) complained at court of the little courage displayed by the queen of England, the Queen said that your Majesty had undertaken an enterprise which she and others believed you never would undertake. She had been much injured by your Majesty's Armada, even under the shelter of England. She had lost 4,000 men, and over 12 ships, two of them the finest she possessed, and she hoped to God she should now have peace with the king of Spain, with whom she was sorry she had gone to war." But, by now, the King had had enough of Armadas sailing victoriously home with captured fishing fleets, and he scrawled on Mendoza's letter the words: "Nothing of the sort, and it will be well to tell him so."

The English were, in fact, counting their losses. A complete inspection of the fleet was undertaken at this time, towards the end of September. It makes tedious reading; there is very little battle damage, mostly hard wear, although the *Revenge* "is to have a new mainmast, being decayed and punished with shot as otherwise." There had been a serious loss of boats. *Triumph* —"The long boat lost at sea." *Elizabeth Jonas*—"The grete botte lost at sea." *White Bear*—"The great boate with all her furniture lost, with the saile." *Victory*—"Item, the longe boate, with a shever of iron in the hed & one other in the daffid." *Golden Lion*—"The longe boate not servicable, with a shyver of iron in the hedd and one in the davith. Flags of St. George, two, old." *Elizabeth Bonaventure*—"Flags of St. George, two, and 'a bluddeye flagge'. Ensigns of silk, one, spoiled with shot and given to the captain." (A little souvenir of the campaign for George Raymond.) Boats were vulnerable items in battle, particularly when towed astern, which presumably explains these losses.

They were much less particular about the human element. But the figure of around 100 killed in action is frequently mentioned; and too many witnesses exclaimed with delight on "the least losses that ever hath been heard of" to doubt that battle casualties were remarkably light. Equally, it is impossible to doubt that sickness casualties were very heavy; although no exact figure is given.

The English were also trying to work out the Spanish losses. Eight great-ships lost in the Channel battles, plus the pinnace; about 4,000 men. Eighteen to their knowledge already lost in Ireland, probably not less than 10,000 men. Cuellar, who was only in the north, had heard of twenty, and the real figure was higher. Indeed, the full toll of Spanish losses, being so wide-spread, was never accurately determined. But ships were still being destroyed, even as they reached home. The hulk *Doncella* went down off Santander, and the flagship of the Armada of Guipuzcoa, another *Santa Ana,* was accidently burnt inside San Sebastian. And there was the *San Juan Bautista* (of Tobermory), the *Gran Grifon,* the two *San Pedros, mayor* and *menor;* and the shambles at Le Havre. Including David Gywnn's late ship, the galley *Diana,* and the *Barca de Amburg,* which foundered out at sea, the total could not have been less than 45, and may well have been more. And most of them were great-ships. It was a staggering loss. But the toll in human life and suffering was far worse. Probably half the men in the expedition perished: by battle, shipwreck, murder, or typhus.

The unfortunate man who had to sort it out, almost single-handed, with no organisation behind him, was Garcia de Villejo, who took over from the Duke at Santander. He reported, on the last day of September, to Andres de Prada, Secretary of the Council of War: " The Duke left today, saying that he had no instructions to give me. He leaves affairs in such a condition that I feel it my duty to say what I think about it." And he did. At this port alone there were over 1,000 sick already, and the list must lengthen if they continued to " sleep in ships full of stench and wretchedness." So many ships were missing, presumed lost, and those which had returned were so shattered, that the Armada could be considered no longer in existence. " If you cannot come here at once, yourself, I shall look upon the Armada as in abeyance until the year '90." he wrote bitterly. " I am bound to think that the year of the eights, so ardently looked forward to, will turn out to be 1800."

What Europe thought of it was made gallingly clear to Bernadino de Mendoza, ambassador in Paris, at the court of a captive king, a satellite of Spanish power. The news had produced a change in this wretched man, and Mendoza was forced to report on 3 October: "This King in conversation with some of his favourites, greatly praised the valour, spirit, and prudence of the queen of England, aided, as she was, by marvel-ous good fortune. He said that what she had done lately would compare with the greatest feats of the most illustrious men of past times, for she had ventured, alone and unaided, to await the attack of so puissant a force as Spain, and to fight it whilst preventing the passage of the Duke of Parma's fleet, which was as powerful as the Spanish. He said that it had taken your Majesty four years to gather these great fleets, which had been the wonder of the world, and yet it might be said that the queen of England had triumphed over them all."

And Mendoza had to listen. There was nothing a Spaniard could say.

Sources

THE bulk of the English documents are contained in: *State Papers relating to the Defeat of the Spanish Armada,* Vols. I and II, edited by Professor John Knox Laughton (Navy Records Society, MDCCCXCIV).

The bulk of the Spanish documents (in English translation) are contained in: *Calendar of Letters and State Papers relating to English Affairs preserved in, or originally belonging to, the Archives of Simancas,* Vol. IV, Elizabeth, 1587-1603, edited by Major Martin S. Hume (H.M.S.O., 1899).

But both these works contain documents from the other side: English reports sent to Spain by Spanish agents, and Spanish documents taken from captured ships by the English; the interrogations of Spanish prisoners and deserters are, naturally, in the English records, as well as letters written by some of them when in England.

The bulk of the Spanish documents (in Spanish) are contained in: *La Armada Invencible,* edited by Captain de Navio C. Fernandez Duro, and *La Armada Invencible: Documentos Procedentes del Archive General de Simancas, 1587-1589,* edited by Enrique Herrera Oria (Valladolid, 1929).

Some additional Spanish documents, printed by Oria, are available in English translation in: *The Spanish Armada,* edited by G. P. B. Naish (Navy Records Society), which also contains Ubaldino's *Commentary,* published 15 April, 1589.

Captain Cuellar's original narrative is No. 7, Folio 58, in the Salazar collection, Acadamy of History, Madrid. There are two English translations: *Captain Cuellar's Adventures in Connacht and Ulster,* edited by Hugh Allingham (Elliot Stock, London, 1897), and *A Letter written by Captain Cuellar to His Majesty King Philip II,* translated by Henry Dwight Sedgwick, Jn. (Elkin Mathews, London, and George H. Richmond & Co., New York, 1896).

Pedro Estrade's narrative, in English translation, is from the Calthorpe MSS, edited by M. Oppenheim (Navy Records Society

XXIII); the narrative of Fray Bernado de Gongora, in Spanish, is Appendix C to J. P. Lyell's *A Commentary* (Bodleian Library, Oxford and Harvard).

The *Naval Tracts of Sir William Monson*, edited by M. Oppenheim (Navy Records Society, 1902) give much useful background by an officer who fought the Armada.

Diving operations on the Irish wrecks are reported in *Calendar of State Papers, Carew*, 1589-1600 (H.M.S.O.). The wrecks generally are usefully documented in two articles: " The Wrecks of the Spanish Armada on the Coast of Ireland," by W. Spotswood Green, Chief Inspector of Irish Fisheries, in *The Geographical Journal*, May, 1906; and "Armada Losses on the Irish Coast," by Caoimhín ó Danachair, in *The Irish Sword*, Journal of the Military History Society of Ireland, Vol. II, No. 9, 1956. A translation of Marcos de Aramburu's narrative (from Duro), together with an account of Recalde and the Blasket sinkings, are contained in an article "Armada Ships on the Kerry Coast," by W. S. Green, in *Proceedings of the Royal Irish Academy*, Vol. XXVII, 1909. The saga of Don Alonso de Leyva is dealt with in an article in *London Diver*, December, 1961, by Roger Jefferis, who is planning an expedition to some of the Armada wrecks. The most reliable short account of the Tobermory Galleon is an article, " The Tobermory Story," by R. Larn, in *Triton*, the journal of the British Sub-Aqua Club, March-April, 1961. *Vasa, the King's Ship*, by Bengt Ohrelius (Cassell, 1962) and *The Raising of the Vasa*, by Roy Saunders (Oldbourne, 1962) should not be neglected by any student of ship construction, as this post-Armada galleon is, at the moment, the best evidence we have.

I must express my gratitude to the Central Library, Portsmouth, for research facilities afforded in their extensive Naval Collection, and to Mr. L. Sargeant, of Hayling Island, for some translations from the Spanish.

Index

287

10